Across Wide Fields

HARCOURT BRACE JOVANOVICH, PUBLISHERS

Orlando   San Diego   Chicago   Dallas

Across Wide Fields

ODYSSEY An HBJ Literature Program
Second Edition

Sam Leaton Sebesta

Consultants

Elaine M. Aoki	Myra Cohn Livingston
Willard E. Bill	Daphne P. Muse
Sonya Blackman	Sandra McCandless Simons
Sylvia Engdahl	Barre Toelken

Acknowledgments

For permission to reprint copyrighted material, grateful acknowledgment is made to the following sources:

Atheneum Publishers: "Mingled Yarns" from *One Winter Night in August and Other Nonsense Jingles* by X. J. Kennedy (A Margaret K. McElderry Book). Copyright © 1975, 1977, 1978, 1979 by X. J. Kennedy.

The Bobbs-Merrill Company, Inc. and Faber and Faber Limited: "My Sister Jane" from *Meet My Folks* by Ted Hughes. Copyright © 1961, 1973 by The Bobbs-Merrill Company, Inc.

Corona Publishing Company, San Antonio, TX: From *The Boy in the Alamo* (Titled: "Colonel Travis Draws the Line") by Margaret Cousins.

Curtis Brown, Ltd.: "Old Joe Clarke" by Ruth Crawford Seeger from *American Folk Songs for Children*. Copyright 1948 by Ruth Crawford Seeger; renewed © 1976 by Michael Seeger.

Dial Books for Young Readers, a division of E. P. Dutton, Inc.: From *Benjy in Business* (Titled: "It Pays to Advertise") by Jean Van Leeuwen. Copyright © 1982 by Jean Van Leeuwen.

Dodd, Mead & Company, Inc.: Text adapted from *An Eskimo Birthday* by Tom D. Robinson. Copyright © 1975 by Tom Robinson. "There was an old man with a beard" from *The Complete Nonsense Book* by Edward Lear.

Doubleday & Company, Inc.: Four illustrations from *The Erie Canal* by Peter Spier. Copyright © 1970 by Peter Spier.

E. P. Dutton, Inc.: "Puzzle" from *Street Poems* by Robert Froman. Copyright © 1971 by Robert Froman. "The Case of the Missing Roller Skates" from *Encyclopedia Brown, Boy Detective* by Donald J. Sobol. Copyright © 1963 by Donald J. Sobol.

Eakin Press, P. O. Box 23066, Austin, TX 78755: Adapted from *Spindletop* by Sibyl Hancock, illustrated by Patty L. Rucker. Copyright © 1980, 1984 by Sibyl Hancock and Patty L. Rucker.

Farrar, Straus & Giroux, Inc.: "Frog" from *Small Poems* by Valerie Worth. Copyright © 1972 by Valerie Worth. "At Night May I Roam" from *In the Trail of the Wind*, edited by John Bierhorst. Copyright © 1971 by John Bierhorst.

Follett Publishing Company, a division of Follett Corporation: *The Great Minu* by Beth P. Wilson. Text copyright © 1974 by Beth P. Wilson. This story is based on "The Honourable Minu," originally published in *West African Folk Tales* by George Harrap & Company Ltd., London, England.

Harcourt Brace Jovanovich, Inc.: "Arithmetic" by Carl Sandburg from *The Complete Poems of Carl Sandburg*. Copyright 1950 by Carl Sandburg. Slightly abridged excerpt from "The Ghost in the Attic" in *The Moffats* by Eleanor Estes. Copyright 1941, 1969 by Eleanor Estes. "The Princess on the Pea" by Hans Christian Andersen, slightly adapted from *It's Perfectly True and Other Stories*, translated by Paul Leyssac. Copyright 1938 by Paul Leyssac; renewed 1966 by Mary Rehan. "When My Canary" from *Cricket Songs: Japanese Haiku*, translated by Harry Behn. © 1964 by Harry Behn.

Harper & Row, Publishers, Inc.: From pp. 16–23 and illustrations from pp. 20, 21 and a portion of the jacket from *Charlotte's Web* by E. B. White, illustrated by Garth Williams. Copyright 1952, 1980 by E. B. White. Illustrations copyright renewed 1980 by Garth Williams. From *Little House on the Prairie* by Laura Ingalls Wilder. Text copyright 1935 by Laura Ingalls Wilder; renewed 1963 by Roger L. MacBride. Adapted text from pp. 7, 28, 38, 39, 49, 60, 61, 62 in *Kickle Snifters and Other Fearsome Critters* by Alvin Schwartz (J. B. Lippincott Co.). Text copyright © 1976 by Alvin Schwartz. "What Night Would It Be?" from *You Read to Me, I'll Read to You* by John Ciardi (J. B. Lippincott Co.). Copyright © 1962 by John Ciardi.

Houghton Mifflin Company: "Paddington Goes to the Hospital" from *Paddington on Stage* by Michael Bond and Alfred Bradley. © 1974 by Alfred Bradley and Michael Bond.

Alfred A. Knopf, Inc.: "Hope" from *Selected Poems of Langston Hughes*. Copyright 1942 by Alfred A. Knopf, Inc.; renewed 1970 by Arna Bontemps and George Houston Bass. "Dreams" from *The Dreamkeeper and Other Poems* by Langston Hughes. Copyright 1932 by Alfred A. Knopf, Inc.; renewed 1960 by Langston Hughes.

League of United Latin American Citizens: "The Other Pioneers" by Roberto Félix Salazar from *Lulac News*, July, 1939.

Ruth Lechlitner and POETRY: "Kansas Boy" by Ruth Lechlitner. Copyright 1931 by The Modern Poetry Association. Originally appeared in *Poetry*, November 1931.

Little, Brown and Company: "Concrete Cat" by Dorthi Charles from page 196 of *An Introduction to Poetry*, Fourth Edition, edited by X. J. Kennedy. Copyright © 1971, 1978 by X. J. Kennedy. From "The Texas Cowboy" by Arbie Moore in *American Folk Poetry An Anthology* by Duncan Emrich. First published in *Texas and Southwestern Lore*, 1927.

Little, Brown and Company in association with the Atlantic Monthly Press and the Canadian Publishers, McClelland and Steward Limited, Toronto: From *Owls in the Family* (Titled: "Wol to the Rescue") by Farley Mowat. Copyright © 1961 by Farley Mowat Ltd.

Lothrop, Lee & Shepard Company, a division of William Morrow & Co.: Adaptation of *The Carp in the Bathtub* by Barbara Cohen. Copyright © 1972 by Barbara Cohen.

Macmillan Publishing Co., Inc.: "Some People" from *Poems* by Rachel Field. Copyright 1924, 1930 by Macmillan Publishing Co., Inc.

McGraw-Hill Book Company: From *Miss Pickerell Goes on a Dig* (Retitled: "Digging Into the Past") by Ellen MacGregor and Dora Pantell. Copyright © 1966 by McGraw-Hill, Inc.

Eve Merriam: From "Metaphor" in *It Doesn't Always Have to Rhyme* by Eve Merriam. Copyright © 1964 by Eve Merriam. Published by Atheneum Publishers.

William Morrow & Company: From pp. 142–161, verbatim, in *Ramona the Brave* (Retitled: "Spunky Ramona") by Beverly Cleary. Copyright © 1975 by Beverly Cleary.

Calvin O'John, former student at the Institute of American Indian Arts, Santa Fe, New Mexico, a Bureau of Indian Affairs School: "Problems" by Calvin O'John from *The Whispering Wind*, edited by T. D. Allen. Copyright © 1972. Published by Doubleday & Company, Inc.

Parents' Magazine Press: Adaptation of *Mexicali Soup* by Kathryn Hitte and William D. Hayes. Text copyright © 1970 by Kathryn Hitte and William D. Hayes. Adapted from *The Crane Maiden* by Miyoko Matsutani. Text copyright © 1968 by Parents' Magazine Press. Adaptation of *Sound of Sunshine, Sound of Rain* by Florence Parry Heide. Text copyright © 1970 by Florence Parry Heide. Illustration copyright © 1970 by Kenneth Longtemps.

Prentice-Hall, Inc., Englewood Cliffs, NJ: Adapted from "The Monkey and the Crocodile" in *Jataka Tales*, retold by Ellen C. Babbitt. © 1912; renewed 1940.

G. P. Putnam's Sons: The Legend of the Bluebonnet by Tomie dePaola. Text and illustrations copyright © 1983 by Tomie dePaola.

Random House, Inc.: Text of "The Lion and the Mouse" from *Aesop's Fables*, retold by Anne Terry White. Copyright © 1964 by Anne Terry White.

Louise H. Sclove: "What the Gray Cat Sings" from *I Sing the Pioneer* by Arthur Guiterman. Copyright 1926 by E. P. Dutton and Co., Inc.; renewed copyright 1954 by Mrs. Vida Lindo Guiterman.

Charles Scribner's Sons: Adapted from the text of *Guess Who My Favorite Person Is* by Byrd Baylor. Copyright © 1977 by Byrd Baylor.

Simon & Schuster, Inc.: From *C D B!* by William Steig. Copyright © 1968 by William Steig.

Texas Folklore Society: From "The Texas Cowboy," contributed by Arbie Moore in *Texas and Southwestern Lore*, 1927.

Viking Penguin Inc.: "Buying a Puppy" from *Merlin & the Snake's Egg* by Leslie Norris. Copyright © 1978 by Leslie Norris. From *The Midnight Fox* (Titled: "The Black Fox") by Betsy Byars. Copyright © 1968 by Betsy Byars. All rights reserved.

Jerry Vogel Music Company, Inc.: "The Erie Canal" (text and melody line) also known as "Low Bridge, Everybody Down" or "Fifteen Years on the Erie Canal." Copyright 1912; renewed 1940. Copyright assigned to Jerry Vogel Music Co., Inc., 58 West 45th Street, New York, NY 10036. Reproduction prohibited.

Frederick Warne & Co., Inc.: "The Jumblies" by Edward Lear. From *Half a Kingdom* by Ann McGovern. Copyright © 1977 by Ann McGovern.

Art Acknowledgments

Chuck Bowden: 161, 219, 285, 325 (adapted from photographs from the following sources: 161, courtesy Harper & Row Publishers, Inc.; 219, courtesy UPI; 285, courtesy William Morrow and Company, Inc.; 325, courtesy Houghton Mifflin Company); Sybil Hancock, © Eakin Press: 489; Sharon Harker: 79, 103, 106–107 top, 108–109 top, 133, 160, 193, 267, 326–327 top, 326 bottom, 328–329 top, 328 top right, 329 bottom, 353, 413–414 top, 415 top, 416; Ron Himler: 411; Tony Kenyon: 324, 327 bottom, 328 top left, 328 bottom; Christa Kieffer: 413 bottom; Robert Masheris: 420, 444, 448–461 (adapted from photographs from the following sources: Daughters of the Republic of Texas; Texas State Library; Eugene C. Barker Texas History Center, University of Texas, Austin); Sarn Suvityasiri: 205, 266; Ed Taber: 106–107 bottom, 108–109 bottom, 383; John S. Walter: 74.

Cover: Tom Leonard.

Maps: Joanna Adamska Koperska.

Unit Openers: Mila Lazeravich, 1–6.
Phil Kantz, 7.

Photo Acknowledgments

HBJ PHOTO by Arthur Tress: 75.

RESEARCH CREDITS: Bruce Coleman, Inc., © Tom Brakefield: 73; Bruce Coleman, Inc., David deVries: 72 left; Bruce Coleman, Inc., Giorgio Gualco/U.P.: 72 right; Photo Researchers, Inc., © Dr. Georg Gerster: 76; Animals, Animals, Robert C. Fields: 249 right; Animals, Animals, Leonard Lee Rue: 249 left; Photo Researchers, Inc., © Tom Branch: 435 right; Photo Researchers, Inc., © Harold Hoffman: 435 left; Sullivan Association from *Texas Highways Magazine:* 491; Grant Heilman: 492; Photo Researchers, Inc., © Michael Murphy: 493 bottom; Rapho Div./Photo Researchers, Inc., © Sam C. Pierson, Jr.: 493 top; Photo Researchers, Inc., © Tom McHugh: 494 top right; © Earth Scenes, J. C. Stevenson: 494 top left; Michael D. Sullivan: 494 center; PhotoCorp Services, © Leo Touchet: 494 bottom left and right, 496.

Contents

5 What a Character! *269*

6 To Live with Animals 355

7 Tales of Texas *419*

1 Problems and Puzzles

The Case of the Missing Roller Skates

A story by Donald J. Sobol

Illustrated by Bert Dodson

Mr. Brown may be the Chief of Police of Idaville, but it is his son Leroy who puts the clues together and provides the solutions to many police cases. His success in solving his father's cases leads Leroy, also known as Encyclopedia Brown, to form his own detective agency with Sally Kimball as his partner. Then one day Encyclopedia finds that he himself is the victim of a crime.

Between nine and nine-thirty on Tuesday morning Sally Kimball's roller skates disappeared from the waiting room in Dr. Vivian Wilson's office.

And where was Encyclopedia Brown, boy detective? He was not ten feet away from the scene of the crime. He was sitting in a chair, with his eyes shut and his mouth wide open!

15

In a way, he had an excuse.

Dr. Wilson was pulling one of Encyclopedia's teeth.

"There!" said Dr. Wilson. He said it cheerfully, as if he were handing Encyclopedia an ice cream cone instead of a tooth.

"Ugh!" said Encyclopedia.

Dr. Wilson said, "All right. Hop down from the chair."

Encyclopedia hopped down and put the tooth in his pocket. He was going to give it to Charlie Stewart, who collected teeth and kept them in a flowered cookie jar.

Encyclopedia went into the waiting room. The chair on which he had left Sally's roller skates was empty!

He looked behind the chair. He dropped to his knees and looked under the chair.

"The skates—they're gone!" he exclaimed.

"Are you sure you brought them with you?" asked Dr. Wilson.

"I'm sure," answered Encyclopedia. "They were broken. I fixed them last night for my partner, Sally Kimball. I was going to take them over to her house on my way home from your office."

Dr. Wilson shook his head sadly. "I'm afraid you will never get them back."

But Dr. Wilson knew nothing about detective work. Encyclopedia liked the dentist, though he felt that Vivian was a better first name for a woman than a man.

"I'll find the skates," said the boy detective. He spoke with certainty. But he felt no such thing. What he felt was the blow to his pride; it hurt worse than his jaw. Imagine a detective being robbed!

In the corridor outside Dr. Wilson's office, Encyclopedia leaned against the wall. He closed his eyes and did some deep thinking.

Dr. Wilson's office was on the ground floor of the new Medical Building. The building had three floors and fifteen offices. All the offices were used by doctors or dentists.

What if the thief had followed him into the building in order to steal the skates? Then the case was closed. "I could spend the rest of my life looking through closets, school lockers, and garages all over Idaville," Encyclopedia thought.

But suppose the thief had simply come into the building to see a doctor. Suppose, on his way in, he had noticed a boy carrying a pair of roller skates. Well, that was something else!

Encyclopedia reasoned further. "The thief could be a grown-up, a boy, or a girl."

He ruled out a grown-up. First, because it was unlikely that a grown-up would steal an old pair of small skates. Second, because a grown-up would be too hard to catch. Too many men and women went in and out of the Medical Building every hour.

"I'll have to act on the idea that the thief is a boy or a girl," he decided. "It's a long chance, but the only one I have."

He opened his eyes. The case called for plain, old-fashioned police leg work!

Encyclopedia began on the ground floor. He asked the same question in every office: "Were any boys or girls here to see the doctor this morning?"

The answer was the same in every office: "No."

Things looked hopeless. But on the top floor he finally got a lead. The nurse in room 301 told him a boy named Billy Haggerty had been there this morning to have a sprained wrist treated.

Encyclopedia asked in the last two offices—just to be sure. Neither doctor had treated children that morning.

Billy Haggerty became suspect number one!

Encyclopedia got Billy Haggerty's address from the nurse in room 301. He hurried back to Dr. Wilson's office to use the telephone. He called Sally. He told her to meet him in front of the Haggerty's house in half an hour.

"We may have some rough going ahead of us," he warned.

But Billy Haggerty turned out to be only an inch taller than Encyclopedia, and shorter than Sally.

Billy drew himself up to his full height at Encyclopedia's first question: "Were you in Dr. Vivian Wilson's office this morning?"

"Naw," snapped Billy. "I don't know any Dr. Wilson."

"You didn't ask anyone about Dr. Wilson?" put in Sally.

"I never heard of him before you spoke his name," said Billy.

"Then you went straight to your own doctor on the third floor?" said Encyclopedia.

"Yeah. Dr Stanton in room 301. What's it to you?"

"Dr. Wilson's office is down the hall from both the stairs and the elevator," said Encylopedia thoughtfully. "You wouldn't pass his office going up or coming down."

"I don't know where his office is, and I don't care," said Billy. "It's none of your business where I was."

"We just want to be sure you weren't in Dr. Vivian Wilson's office this morning. That's all," said Sally.

"Well, I wasn't. I had a sprained wrist, not a toothache. So why should I go near his office?" demanded Billy. "I don't like snoopers. What are you after?"

"A pair of roller skates," said Encyclopedia.
"Do you mind returning them? You've given
yourself away."

WHAT GAVE BILLY AWAY?

Solution to
"The Case of the Missing Roller Skates"

Billy Haggerty said that he had never heard of Dr. Vivian Wilson and that he didn't know where his office was. But he knew too much about him.

He knew that Dr. Vivian Wilson was (1) a man, not a woman; and (2) a dentist, not a doctor.

When he was tripped by his fibs, Billy returned the roller skates to Sally.

Questions

1. Billy made two statements that showed he might be fibbing. What were they?

2. When did Encyclopedia first discover that he had a *problem?*

3. What did Encyclopedia do in the office building to try to *solve* the problem?

4. Why did the author put the *solution* after the story, not within it?

5. In this story, a *suspect* is a person who
   a. is the wrongdoer.
   b. might be the wrongdoer.
   c. is innocent, but is accused of being the wrongdoer.

6. Encyclopedia Brown has special skills. You'll find a clue to one of those skills in his name. What is that skill? Tell two other skills that Encyclopedia uses in his work.

Activity Write an Advertisement

If Encyclopedia Brown had not found Sally's roller skates, he might have put an advertisement in a newspaper, offering a reward for their return. Write an advertisement for Encyclopedia. In your advertisement, tell what the skates looked like, and where and when they were last seen.

Where R U?

Letter puzzles written
and illustrated by William Steig

I M N D L-F-8-R.

(I am in the elevator.)

D D-R S N D I-V.

(The deer is in the ivy.)

D C-L S N D C.

(The seal is in the sea.)

Puzzle

A poem by Robert Froman

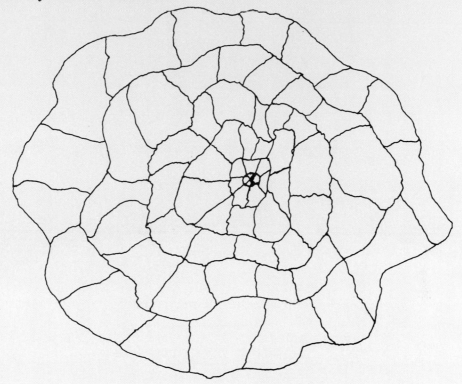

Map of a city with streets meeting at center?

Net to catch people jumping from a burning building?

Spider's web?

Burner on an electric stove?

Fingerprint?

No.

Frozen puddle after a hit by a rock.

Concrete Cat

A poem by Dorthi Charles

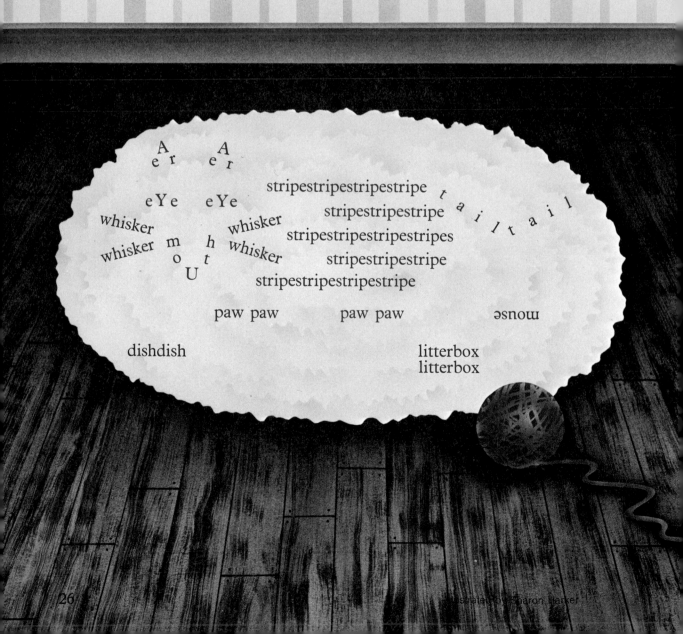

Mingled Yarns

A poem by X. J. Kennedy

What stories are mixed together?

1) Whose cherry tree did young George chop?
    It was Pinocchio's.
    And every time George told a lie
    He grew an inch of nose.

2) Jack be nimble,
    Jack be quick,
    Jack jump over
    the beanstalk stick!

3) Aladdin had a little lamp,
    It smelled all keroseny.
    And everywhere Aladdin took
    His lamp jam-packed with genii.

    He took his lamp to school one day,
    Which made the teacher blubber
    And all the children laughed to see
    Young Al the old lamp-rubber.

Illustrated by Marie-Louise Gay

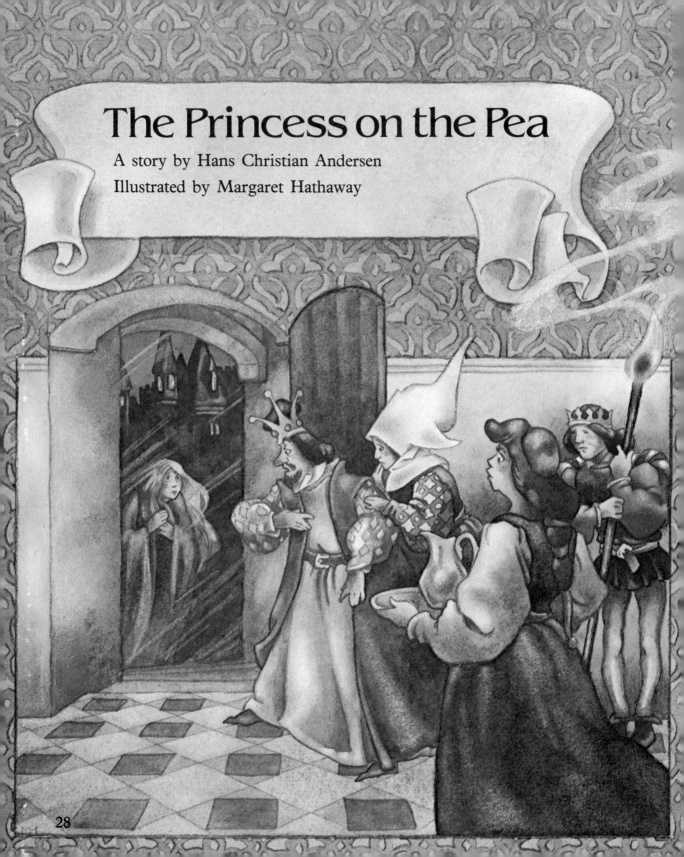

The Princess on the Pea

A story by Hans Christian Andersen

Illustrated by Margaret Hathaway

Once upon a time there was a Prince; he wanted to get himself a Princess, but she must be a *real* Princess. So he traveled all over the world to find one, but in every case something was the matter. There were any number of Princesses, but he could never quite make out whether they were real or not—there always seemed to be a catch somewhere. So he came back home and was very unhappy, for he did so want to find a true Princess.

One evening a terrible storm came on; lightning flashed, thunder rolled, and the rain poured down in torrents—it was simply awful! Suddenly there was a knock at the city gate, and the old King went out to answer it.

It was a Princess standing outside, but what a sight the rain and bad weather had made of her! The water streamed down her hair and down her clothes, it ran in at the toes of her shoes and out at the heels, and yet she said she was a real Princess.

"It won't take us long to find that out," thought
the old Queen, but she did not say anything. She
went into the bedchamber, took off all the bed-
clothes, and placed one pea on the bottom boards of
the bed. Then she took twenty mattresses and put
them on top of the pea, and after that she put twenty
feather beds stuffed with eiderdown on top of the
mattresses.

That's where the Princess was to spend the night.

In the morning they asked her how she had slept.

"Oh, dreadfully badly!" said the Princess. "I hardly slept a wink all night. Whatever could have been in the bed? I was lying on something so hard that I'm black and blue all over. It was simply awful!"

So of course they could see that she was a real Princess, since she had felt the pea right through the twenty mattresses and the twenty feather beds. No one but a real Princess could have such a tender skin as that.

So the Prince took her for his wife, because now he knew that he had got hold of a real Princess.

And the pea was put on view in the museum, where it is still to be seen—unless somebody has taken it.

Arithmetic

A poem by Carl Sandburg

Arithmetic is where numbers fly like pigeons in
    and out of your head.
Arithmetic tells you how many you lose or win if
    you know how many you had before you lost or
    won.
Arithmetic is seven eleven all good children go to
    heaven—or five six bundle of sticks.
Arithmetic is numbers you squeeze from your head
    to your hand to your pencil to your paper till
    you get the answer.
Arithmetic is where the answer is right and
    everything is nice and you can look out of
    the window and see the blue sky—or the answer
    is wrong and you have to start all over and
    try again and see how it comes out this time.

If you take a number and double it and double it
  again and then double it a few more times, the
  number gets bigger and bigger and goes higher
  and higher and only arithmetic can tell you
  what the number is when you decide to quit
  doubling.

Arithmetic is where you have to multiply—and you
  carry the multiplication table in your head
  and hope you won't lose it.

If you have two animal crackers, one good and one
  bad, and you eat one and a striped zebra with
  streaks all over him eats the other, how many
  animal crackers will you have if somebody
  offers you five six seven and you say No no no
  and you say Nay nay nay and you say Nix nix
  nix?

If you ask your mother for one fried egg for
  breakfast and she gives you two fried eggs
  and you eat both of them, who is better in
  arithmetic you or your mother?

Illustrated by Sharon Harker

IT PAYS TO ADVERTISE

From the story *Benjy in Business* by Jean Van Leeuwen
Illustrated by Ted Carr

*More than anything else, nine-year-old Benjy
wanted a Clyde Johnson catcher's mitt. But how was
he going to get it?*

*Benjy's parents suggest that he work for the
money, so Benjy goes into business for the summer.
His first job—taking care of his baby sister—is too
tiring, and Benjy doesn't feel he has the strength to
take care of her long enough to earn the money he
needs. His second business venture—washing cars—is
a failure. Not only do Benjy and his friend Jason not
get much business, but it rains the entire afternoon.
Discouraged, Benjy sits down to the table with his
mother to find a solution. He just has to have that
catcher's mitt!*

"Hot chocolate?" said his mother. "In the middle
of summer?"

Benjy watched the water roll from his hair down
his face to his shirt and then drip from his shorts
onto the kitchen floor. "Please?" he said.

"Well, all right," said his mother. "But get out of these clothes quickly before we have to bail out the kitchen."

When Benjy got back, she was just pouring the hot chocolate into his mug. "One marshmallow or two?" she asked.

"Two," said Benjy.

"Silly question," said his mother, smiling. She sat down across from him at the table. "Well, how did the car-wash business work out?"

"Terrible," said Benjy.

"That bad?" said his mother.

Benjy nodded. It was peaceful sitting in the kitchen drinking hot chocolate with the rain pouring down outside. And with just his mother for a change. Usually his sister was there, too, banging on her tray with her shoe or babbling away in her strange language. It was past time for her to be up from her nap—she must have overslept. Benjy told his mother about sitting by the mailbox for hours while all the cars went by without stopping, and keeping on adding things to his sign, and how when he finally got his first customer, it started to rain.

"That was bad luck about the rain," said his mother.

"It was bad luck about the whole day," said Benjy.

"What do you think went wrong?" asked his mother.

Benjy shrugged. "I guess no one wanted their car washed."

"Well," said his mother, "not enough people, anyway. Remember what your father said? You have to have something to sell that people want to buy." She looked out the window thoughtfully. "One other thing you might keep in mind if you want to be a businessman. People can't buy your service unless they know about it. You have to advertise."

"You mean like on TV and in the newspaper?" said Benjy.

"Not quite like that," said his mother. "But if you just have a sign on the mailbox, only people who happen to pass your mailbox will see it."

"I could make more signs," said Benjy. "And put them up on other roads, like they do for garage sales."

"That's what I mean," said his mother. "Then you can attract customers who don't live on our street."

"I could even put a sign on Route One Seventy-one," said Benjy.

"Well, maybe not there," said his mother. "Cars on the highway are usually going too fast to stop. Anyway, that's a suggestion if you decide to go into business again. It pays to advertise."

"Right," said Benjy.

Benjy didn't go into business again the next day. He thought he needed some time off. Besides, it was still raining.

He fished around under his bed and in his closet and a few other places and found all his baseball cards. Using two shoeboxes, he separated them into

this year's and last year's. Then he sorted this year's cards into piles according to teams and put rubber bands around them. That took most of the day. After that he copied Clyde Johnson's picture from last year's card, colored it with his colored pencils, and put it up on his bulletin board.

Looking at the picture made him think about the mitt again. He had to get it, and soon. Otherwise his

baseball career would never take off. But he still
needed $20.43. How was he ever going to get it?

The next morning Benjy went over to see Jason.
He was bound to have some ideas. Not that all of his
ideas were terrific, but he always had a lot of them.

"I've got it!" said Jason when he and Benjy were
hanging by their knees from the climbing bars of
Jason's swing set. "A worm farm!"

"A *worm* farm?" They were looking at the world upside down, with the worms on top. Something must have gotten jumbled inside Jason's brain.

"I'm not kidding," said Jason. "I read about it in a book. This kid digs up his backyard and makes pits and raises worms to sell. And he makes a fortune."

Benjy could just see his mother's face if he told her he was going to have a worm farm. He could also see his father's face if he told him he was going to dig pits in the backyard. This wasn't one of Jason's better ideas.

"It'll never fly," Benjy told him.

Jason let go with his hands and swung so his hair just brushed the ground.

"How about this?" he said, smiling upside down. "We open a gym in my basement, and we charge people to join. Like a health club. And they get to use my brother's barbells and his punching bag and all that stuff."

Too much blood must be rushing to Jason's head.

"Use your brother's stuff?" said Benjy. "Your brother won't even let *you* use his stuff."

"Oh, yeah," said Jason. "I forgot."

Maybe he'd do better right side up. Benjy did a quick skin-the-cat and went to sit in the shade.

Jason flopped down next to him. "Sure is hot," he said.

"The thing of it is," said Benjy, "that you have to have something to sell that people want to buy."

"Right," said Jason.

"If you were a customer, what would you like to buy?" asked Benjy.

"Right now," said Jason, "I'd like to buy a drink."

Benjy looked at him. Jason had done it again. He'd always known he could count on him for ideas.

"That's it," said Benjy.

"It is?" said Jason.

"Sure," said Benjy. "We can sell lemonade."

"Now, that is a good idea," said Jason.

41

They made six signs on big pieces of cardboard,
all with red arrows saying LEMONADE THIS WAY, and
put them up on nearby corners. The seventh sign
said LEMONADE HERE—15¢ A CUP. They stuck that
one on the mailbox. Benjy's mother gave them a
pitcher of lemonade and a stack of paper cups. She
let them use an old card table for a lemonade stand,
and Benjy got two folding chairs from the garage.

He sat down in one—just as Charlie Fryhoffer
drove by without even looking.

"Oh, no," groaned Benjy. "This better not be like
last time."

But it wasn't. In the first ten minutes three cars
stopped. One was Mrs. Bolton with her two little
kids and their two friends. She bought five cups. A
man from Adams Air Conditioning bought two cups.
And another woman in a station wagon with three
kids bought four cups. "I saw your sign over on
Laurel Lane," she said. "A cup of lemonade hits the
spot on a day like this."

As she drove away Jason stuck out his hand. "Congratulations, old pal," he said. "You're going to rake in a fortune.

Benjy grinned. "Same to you. It was your idea."

Money was jingling in his pocket. And the pitcher of lemonade was nearly empty. Already.

Benjy went to the house to get more.

"Already?" said his mother. "Business must be good."

"I'm going to rake in a fortune," he told her.

"In that case," said his mother, "you can pay me back for the lemonade. That's how it's done in business, you know. You have to invest money to make money."

"No problem," said Benjy. "I'll pay you when we close up the stand."

The second pitcher went fast too. And the third. Just about everyone on Benjy's street stopped at the lemonade stand. Mrs. Parkinson and a friend of hers and Mrs. Rosedale and Alex Crowley's mother and sister. And the mailman and the man who came to read the electric meters. And a lot of people Benjy had never seen before.

"Those signs are really working," said Jason.

"It pays to advertise," said Benjy.

His pockets were overflowing with money now. He needed a cash register. When he went to get the fourth pitcher of lemonade, he brought back one of his baseball-card shoeboxes. He dumped all the money into it.

"Wow!" said Jason. "It looks like you get your mitt tomorrow."

"Maybe," said Benjy.

He started counting it. But he'd only gotten to $2.50 when another car stopped, its brakes screeching.

Jason nudged him. "Look who finally decided to give us a break."

Benjy looked up. It was Charlie Fryhoffer.

"You guys got the right idea," he said, whipping out a comb and working over his hair. It was so long, Benjy didn't know how he could see where he was driving. He handed Charlie a cup of lemonade and Charlie drank it in one gulp and held out the cup for a refill. Then he tossed Benjy two quarters. "Keep the change," he said. And he took off down the road, his car clanking like a lawn mower.

44

"One of these days," said Jason, "his engine's going to fall out right in the middle of the road."

"If he doesn't drive into a tree first," said Benjy.

After Charlie Fryhoffer things quieted down a little. It was getting late in the afternoon and it wasn't as hot. Mrs. Bolton stopped again, but only to ask how they were doing. A man in a tan delivery van stopped and bought one cup. And then no one.

"Want to call it a day?" Jason asked.

"Not yet," said Benjy. "I've got to sell this last pitcher. I'm paying my mother for it."

"How about having a catch while we're waiting?" Jason suggested.

That sounded good to Benjy. He was tired of sitting in the folding chair. His legs felt like they were falling asleep.

Benjy got his mitt and a tennis ball. He let Jason use the old catcher's mitt that used to belong to his father. They took turns pitching a few.

Jason was wild. He walked two batters and then made a wild pitch.

But Benjy struck out the side. His fastball zipped right down the middle, and his change-up got the outside corner of the plate. Even his curve ball seemed to be curving a little.

"Nice throwing," said Jason.

"Thanks," said Benjy. There was a possibility that he might be a pitcher when he grew up instead of an outfielder. If he could just learn to throw a slider.

Then they gave each other high fly balls.

It was the last of the ninth and the Yankees were ahead, 1–0, on a homer by Clyde Johnson. But the Red Sox were threatening. They had two men on and two out and their cleanup hitter, Jim Barker, stepping up to the plate.

He swung on the first pitch. And it was a long fly ball out to deep centerfield. Clyde Johnson was racing back. Could he get there in time? He was all the way back, up against the centerfield wall. He leaped high in the air.

And he missed. Benjy tripped on a tree root and fell flat on his back. He heard a strange *clunk*. And then he heard Jason laughing.

Benjy looked up. There was the yellow tennis ball, in the pitcher of lemonade.

"Nice catch," said Jason.

"Nice throw," said Benjy. He picked himself up. "Well," he said, "we may as well call it a day."

Jason took the signs down and Benjy put everything away inside. Then they went up to Benjy's room to count the money in the shoebox. It came to $7.30.

"Looks like you don't get your mitt tomorrow," said Jason.

"No," said Benjy. "But at least I'm starting to get someplace."

He handed Jason a dollar.

"What's that for?" asked Jason.

"For helping," said Benjy. "A businessman has to pay his employees, you know."

He went downstairs to find his mother.

"How much do I owe you for the lemonade?" he asked.

"Well, it was fifty-nine cents a can and you used four cans," she said. "But I'll throw in the first one free. That comes to—let's see—a dollar seventy-seven."

Benjy counted out the money.

"Thanks," said his mother.

"Thanks for the free can," said Benjy.

He went back upstairs and counted what was left in the shoebox. Now it came to $4.53. Benjy stuffed it all into his monkey bank. Then he got his piece of paper and did some subtraction. Twenty dollars and forty-three cents minus $4.53 was $15.90. He still had $15.90 to go.

Benjy sighed. "Making money sure is tough work," he said to Jason.

Jason was looking through Benjy's baseball cards. "Yeah," he said. "Spending it is a lot easier." Then he looked up. "You know what you've got to do, Benjy? Start thinking big. Forget about stuff like lemonade, fifteen cents a cup. You need to go for big money."

Benjy nodded. That's what he needed, all right. Big money. "But what kind of business can a kid go into to make big money?" he asked.

"I don't know yet," said Jason. "But don't worry, I'll think of something. Hey, Benjy, want to trade your Jose Lopez? I'll give you two all-stars."

"No way," said Benjy.

Questions

1. On the first page of the story, you find out that Benjy is all wet. What sentence later on tells you how Benjy got wet?

2. Why is Benjy so eager to make money?

3. Benjy's mother charged him for the lemonade. Should she have also charged him for making the lemonade? Tell why or why not.

4. Choose a word to complete each sentence.
   a. If Benjy's mother *bails out* a boat, she should use _____.
   b. If someone *bails out* a friend in debt, he or she could use _____.
   c. If a pilot *bails out* of a plane, he or she should use _____.

      a parachute   a bucket   money

Activity   Make a New Sign

Besides the lemonade, Benjy has decided to sell three healthful juices. Jason will bake three dozen oatmeal cookies to sell, too. For a small extra charge, Benjy and Jason will act out the most exciting play of this year's World Series.

All of these activities call for a new sign for their stand to advertise their new business. Hurry! Hurry! Read all about it. Design the sign for Benjy and Jason's new business.

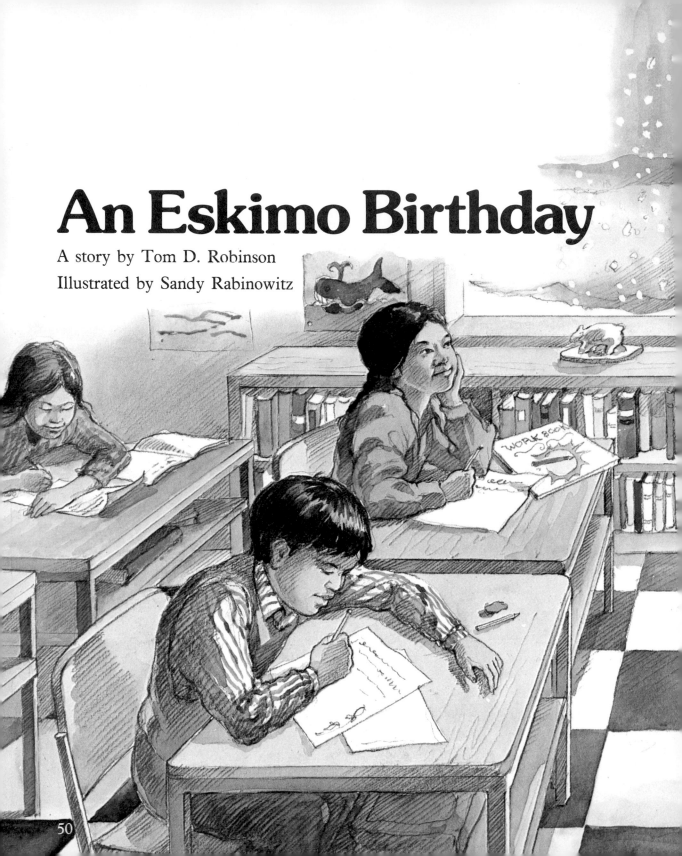

An Eskimo Birthday

A story by Tom D. Robinson

Illustrated by Sandy Rabinowitz

The Eskimo people live in a climate where it is below the freezing point for most of the year. Danger and death have been part of the Eskimos' daily life. Now that there are snow machines as well as dog teams, houses instead of igloos, electric lights, and stores, Eskimo life has changed. Still, many of the old people keep to the old ways while the young take on the new.

The strong wind that had brought the storm shook the windows of the little school with each gust. Often even the lights from the closest houses winked, then disappeared as swirls of snow were thrown against the side of the building.

Eeka kept looking, first at the storm, then at the clock above the blackboard. The hands seemed to be held back by giant weights. Only two-thirty—another whole hour to go! Oh, and it was such a special day! "My birthday," she muttered to herself, as she hit her desk softly with her clenched fist.

Eeka had so hoped everything would go perfectly. It had been calm when her father had gone out to check his traps early in the morning. Her mother was home cooking a big meal for the party that night, and then there was the beautiful new parka her mother had sewn, complete but for the fur ruff and trimming.

The trapping season had been a poor one, but there was always the chance that this time, especially this time, her father would have luck and find some fox in his traps so the parka could be finished. Now the storm that had completely covered the village with snow took that slim chance away. Eeka sighed and stared out at the darkness caused by the storm and lack of winter sun.

Just then, the door to the classroom opened. The principal came in and whispered something to Eeka's teacher, and when he left, she quietly asked the children to listen.

"Because the storm seems to be getting worse, we're dismissing school early. Many of your parents are out in the hall, waiting to take you home. If your parents are not there, please be careful when you leave. And," she added, "you fifth graders make sure and take home any little ones who live close to you."

Eeka gave a squeal of delight. She threw her books into her desk and went running to the door.

"Eeka! Eeka!" called her teacher. "Slow down before you run over somebody."

Eeka slowed to a quick walk, while one of the other students explained, "It's her birthday and her mother is cooking for her. That's why she's in a hurry."

The teacher was smiling. "Well, happy birthday, Eeka, but save some energy for the walk home! I'd like to see you in one piece for your party."

Out in the corridor, Eeka found her first-grade cousin waiting for her by the coat hooks. Eeka slipped her old parka over her head, pulled the hood up tight around her face, and thrust her hands into her mittens.

Between the wind and her slippery mukluks, it took all of Eeka's strength to get the school door open. Once outside, the girls were blown sideways several feet by a strong gust before they could regain their balance.

When they were headed in the right direction, they both put their heads down and away from the wind that raged against their sides. Eeka looked up only to check that she was going the right way. Each time, the stinging blasts of snow made her forehead ache with cold.

Neither girl spoke. They would have had to shout to have been heard above the wind, and walking up and down the quickly forming drifts didn't leave much breath for talking. Once in a while, Eeka caught the glimmer of a light from one of the houses. Between that and having walked this way hundreds of times before, she was able to keep on a fairly straight line home.

Eeka's cousin lived right next door to her, so, when they got near their houses, Eeka just let go of the little girl's hand, and she slid down the small drift between the two buildings, stopping with a bump against the storm porch of her house. Her cousin disappeared inside her door.

Eeka looked for her father's snow machine, but it wasn't there. She stood looking past her house in the direction she knew her father had gone, and wondered how he could ever find his way home in this weather.

Pulling a hand out of one of her mittens, she placed it over her nose to warm it up. With the other hand, she pushed the door open and entered the storm porch.

Inside the long, narrow building, Eeka carefully brushed all the fine snow from her parka and pants. The light from the single, bare bulb on the ceiling made scary shadows out of all her father's hunting gear that hung on the walls. Close by the inside door was a box which housed a female dog curled around her four new puppies. Eeka knelt down and let the mother lick her hand. It was a bad time for the pups to be born, these cold months, but her father wanted to build his team back up. His snow machine was old and a new one just cost too much. Eeka gave each puppy a pat.

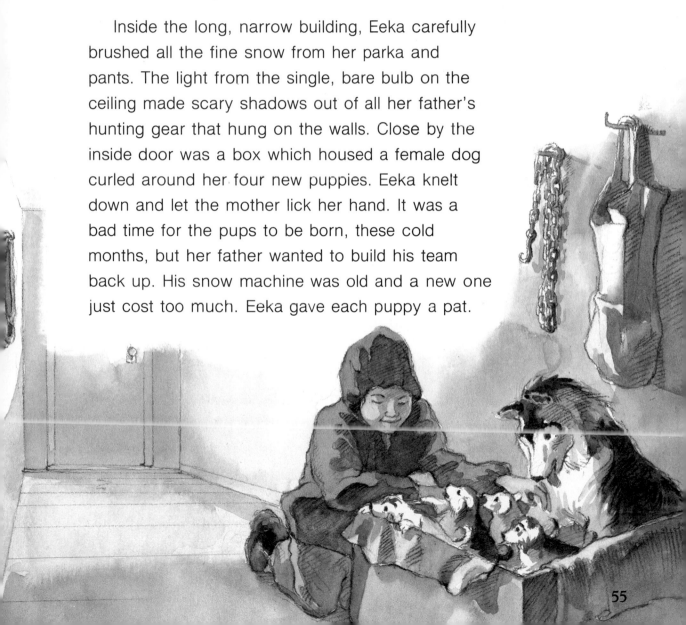

Eeka was greeted by the smell of freshly baked pies and cakes as she entered the house, and a loud screech from her little brother. On seeing her, he threw his bottle over the side of the crib and held out his arms to be picked up. Eeka's mother was bustling about the stove. Bending down for a hug, she said, "Happy birthday, little one."

Eeka walked into the only other room of the house, the bedroom she shared with her mother and father. She put her parka on her bed. On her parents' bed lay the new parka her mother had sewn, a beautiful, dark blue velveteen. There was no telling now when the parka would be done. It seemed enough just to hope her father would make it home all right.

Eeka heard her brother screech again; so she turned with a sigh and went back into the main room to pick him up. Her grandfather was sitting on the edge of his bed in the corner next to the oil stove. He was slowly stripping bits of baleen to use in making the shiny, black baskets he sold at the store. They were small, but they brought a good price when sold at the right time to the right people.

He raised his head and looked at Eeka, his white hair making his wrinkled, brown face seem even darker. Then he looked at the clock.

"Did they let you out early because it's your birthday?" he asked with a smile. His voice was almost a whisper. "Schools sure have changed."

Eeka laughed as she sat down and began to
bounce her brother on her knees. The warmth was
beginning to return to her cheeks. "Not because
of my birthday, Apah. Because of the storm."

"I remember coming home from Sunday school
once, when I was very little," her grandfather
began slowly. He had put his knife down and was
looking toward the window. "It was away from
town—you know the place—up toward the little
lagoon. Anyway, it was stormy like this, and we
were trying to follow the row of whale bones back
to the village. Somehow we got lost and wandered,
it seemed like for hours."

Eeka had heard most of her grandfather's stories, including this one, many times before, but they seemed to get better and better. When other old people came by to visit, they would talk with Grandfather about the way things were in the past. They usually spoke in Eskimo, so Eeka would sit close to her mother who would tell her everything that was being said.

"At first it was fun and then we got scared," Grandfather went on. "We stopped, and some of us started to cry while some of us started to pray. Suddenly, the clouds began to lift toward the south and the wind slowed down. We hadn't noticed the wind when we left the church, or we could have used it as a guide. We were way over on the north beach, almost out on the sea ice. People were looking all over for us. We never knew if it was our praying or our parents' shouting that drove the storm away."

"Well," laughed Eeka's mother, "I'm glad I don't have to worry about Eeka like Grandmother had to worry about you! She would take notice of the wind direction when going out in a storm."

Grandfather chuckled. "I guess children these days are a lot smarter in some things than we were. But," he added, "I'm not sure school gives them all the answers." His eyes were shining.

"It's Eeka's father I'm worried about," Eeka's mother said softly, as she began to dress the baby. A little frown crossed her face as she spoke. "We'd better hurry, Eeka, if we're going to get those things at the store for tonight. And bring the five-gallon can and the little sled so we can get some stove oil." She slipped the baby up under the back of her parka where he would ride safe and warm. Eeka put on her parka and went out to tie the can onto the sled.

The wind was at their backs as they walked to the store. Now and then, an extra strong gust would push them ahead, making them run for a few steps until they regained their balance. The light from a snow machine, or the outline of another figure, would appear close by them, then dissolve back into the snow and darkness. It wasn't as cold walking with the wind, but still Eeka and her mother were happy to see the lights of the new store and the warmth it offered.

Everyone greeted them when they got inside, most people calling out happy birthday to Eeka and kidding her about getting old. Eeka's mother took the baby out from inside her parka. She placed him in the shopping cart, which Eeka began pushing, following her mother up and down the aisles.

As they moved down the back row of the
store, past the hardware, snow machine parts, and
rifles, Eeka and her mother came to the corner
where the furs hung. Eeka stared at the five fox
skins, all of them small and stained yellow with the
oil of the seals the foxes had feasted on. Her
mother walked over and looked at each one.

"They're too expensive, Eeka, and not nearly
good enough for your parka. There were two
others, big and pure white, but they were even
more money. Perhaps your father will bring some
home from his traps."

"It is probably too stormy for him to find his
traps," offered Eeka. "I'll just be glad for him to
get home."

As they walked up to the cash register, Eeka was again teased about its being her "special" day. She blushed and turned away, but she couldn't hide her smile.

The men sitting on kegs and piles of rope near the check-out counter asked Eeka's mother many questions in Eskimo about Eeka's father—when he had left, the direction he had gone, how much gas he had with him, if he had a stove and a tent. Eeka wished at that moment that she'd listened more closely to her grandfather. He had tried to get her to speak Eskimo when she was younger, but she never seemed to have the time. And now, as the men spoke to each other in quiet tones, Eeka understood only that they were discussing a search party.

It seemed impossible to Eeka that in this great, white country one small man, also dressed in white, could be found in such a storm. How she wished he had never gone—and for her!

"Don't worry, little Eeka," her favorite uncle said, putting his big arm around her shoulders. "If your father's not back soon, we will go out and get him. We won't let him miss your birthday party." He smiled down at her, and Eeka began to feel much better.

The walk home was horrible! The wind that had pushed them over to the store now blew directly in their faces, some gusts making them stop completely. Both Eeka and her mother put their heads down, not daring to look up. Her mother pulled the sled, heavy with the stove oil and the fish. Eeka carried the rest of the things in a sack clutched tightly to her chest so it wouldn't blow away. Many times they turned their backs to the wind, resting and warming their noses and cheeks with a bare hand.

Whenever they did glance up to get their directions, the snow flew in their faces and made it almost impossible to see. As Eeka had done when coming home from school, they used drifts, oil drums, dog stakes, and the brief flicker of the light from a house to guide them.

Finally, when Eeka thought she was as cold as she could get, she saw the familiar shape of her house just ahead. And there, outside the little house, was her father—unloading caribou from his sled. He was home safe! Eeka nearly fell over a drift as she ran ahead to greet him.

Eeka's father had many things to do before he could finally come inside and warm up. First, he carried in a large piece of meat and placed it by the stove to thaw out so it could be used in caribou soup that evening. Then he and Grand-father had to unload the sled and cover the snow

machine. Finally, there was the oil to put in the drum alongside the house, and the four older dogs to be fed. Only then was he able to come in and get the hot cup of coffee that would start the wonderful heat flowing back into his body.

All this time, Eeka helped her mother unpack their groceries, anxiously waiting for a chance to see if her father had trapped a fox. When everything was put away, she crowded near him, but she couldn't bring herself to ask.

Then Eeka's father spoke to her.

"All my traps were covered by the snow, Eeka," her father said. "There was a bit of fur in one trap where a fox had been, but I think a wolverine beat me to him. Maybe he thinks he's found somebody who will feed him and he will return to the trap. The next thing he'll know, he will be a pair of new mittens for you, as punishment for having taken your fox." Eeka tried to smile, but it was hard not to look disappointed.

"Eeka," called her mother, "come and feed your brother. There is much to do before the party and it is almost time for people to come." Eeka was glad to be busy rather than have time to think about something that couldn't be helped. In fact, she was so busy that she was surprised when the door opened and the first of the guests walked in.

By the time all the people had arrived, the last cake had been iced and the caribou soup was done. Eeka and her mother laid a cloth out on the floor and put the food and dishes on it. People could help themselves, and eat either sitting on the floor or on one of the benches at the table.

When Eeka's mother called her to come open her presents, the girls began teasing about what they had brought. Eeka didn't like the idea of standing up in front of all the other people, but she was anxious to see what she had gotten.

Everyone had brought something, either an envelope with a card and money in it, or a present wrapped in a paper sack with a birthday message written across the outside. Eeka's mother insisted that she read every one before she opened it. Some were serious and some, like the message from her uncle, made people laugh until tears ran down their faces.

There were more things than Eeka had ever hoped to get—clothes from the store, a game, a deck of playing cards, a scarf knit by an aunt, a beautiful pair of caribou mukluks from her grandmother, and almost ten dollars from the envelopes.

Eeka was gladly just about to give up her place as the center of attention, when one of the women walked out of the bedroom and held the new parka up to Eeka.

"Here," she said, "put it on so everyone can
see the fine present your mother has made for you."

Eeka stared at the parka. Without a ruff or trim
it looked anything but nice. It was so lifeless!
Why? thought Eeka. Everything was going so well.
I hate that ugly thing! I hate it! But she blindly
shoved her hands into the sleeves and stood
there, head down, while everyone commented on
what a fine parka it was.

Suddenly, she could stand it no longer. Eeka turned to rush from the room, to take the parka off and hide the tears she knew would come if she had to hear another word.

She almost knocked her grandfather down as she spun around. He had left his place on the bed and had silently made his way to her side. He was holding a sack in his hand, which he gave to Eeka.

"Here," he said quietly. "They aren't very good, but it was all the store would give me for one of my little baskets."

All was silent as Eeka opened the sack and looked inside. Slowly, unable to believe her eyes, she pulled out two of the most beautiful white fox skins she had ever seen. They must have been the ones her mother had spoken of at the store!

Immediately, everyone began talking about what fine skins they were—surely the best taken that year! They were passed from hand to hand, so much so that Eeka feared all the fur would be rubbed off. The women discussed how best to cut them to get the most trim and biggest ruff, while the men talked about their whiteness and who had trapped them.

Grandfather sat on the edge of his bed, holding a cup of tea and looking at the floor. The only sign that he heard the remarks about the skins

was his smile—a smile that showed how proud
he was.

And after being asked time and time again to
tell how he had gotten the skins into the house
without Eeka knowing, he related the story, quietly
in Eskimo. He told how he had gone to the store
the day before the party and how he had carefully
hidden the lovely, full furs under his bed so no
one would learn of his secret.

The rest of the evening was a blur to Eeka. She remembered holding the fox skins and rubbing the soft fur against her cheek.

On her way to bed, she stopped by where Grandfather lay. He seemed to be asleep, but Eeka knelt down beside him and whispered, ''Thank you, Apah. Thank you very much.'' The old man put out a hand and touched Eeka gently on her head. He was smiling, his eyes closed, when she left him.

The last sound she heard, before drifting off to sleep, was her mother humming an old, old song as she swiftly cut up the skins and sewed them onto the new parka.

Questions

1. When trying to solve their problems, which characters in the story *might* have said the following:
    a. "I'll buy two white fox skins."
    b. "I'll keep busy so I won't be sad about something I won't receive."
    c. "If your father doesn't come back soon, we'll go and get him."

2. A story's *setting*—the time and place where the story happens—can cause problems. Tell two problems caused by this story's setting.

3. Find the words the author used to make the setting exciting.
    a. The wind _____ the windows. (page 51)
    b. The lights from the houses _____ in the swirls of snow. (page 51)

4. How does the author show you that Eeka's life is happy even though the setting is often cold and dangerous?

Activity   Make a Village Map

Make a map to show the village in the story. Draw pictures to show the school, Eeka's house, and the store. Label the places on your map.

CONNECTIONS

Meeting Nature's Challenges

People all around the world live in different *environments,* or surroundings, that affect their lives. Some people live in hot, dry deserts. Some people live in cold, snowy mountains. Some people live near hot, wet jungles. Some people live near cool, dry forests. In many environments, the weather changes with the seasons: warm in the summer, cold in the winter.

People have learned to *adapt,* or learn a way of life that suits their different environments. People can adapt to their environments with the houses they build, with the clothes they wear, and by the ways they live their day-to-day lives.

Here are two very different environments. Notice how the people in those environments have adapted.

The Frozen North

This is northern Alaska, a land of challenge. Northern Alaska is near the Arctic Circle and the North Pole. Life here is not easy. Winters are eight or nine months long. They are dark and bitterly cold. In the winter, the sun shines only an hour or two each day, and temperatures drop to about −60°F.

Temperatures rise above freezing (32°F) for only two or three months of the year. These two or three summer months are cool, even though the sun almost never sets. During these months, the top one or two feet of soil may thaw. Then mosses, shrubs, weeds, and wildflowers grow. The ground underneath, however, stays frozen all year round and cannot be plowed for farming.

Eskimos, or *Inuit* (IN·oo·it) as they call themselves, have lived in this harsh environment for thousands of years. They can live here because they have found ways to meet the problems of life in the Arctic.

Look at the Eskimo winter house on page 74. It has thick earth walls that keep in warm air and keep

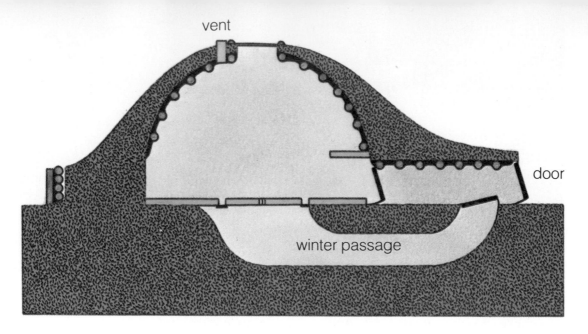

vent

door

winter passage

out cold air. The house has an opening, or *vent*, in the ceiling. The door is lower than the floor of the house and is separated from the house by a long, underground tunnel.

The Eskimos heat their houses with oil lamps. Two or three lamps can heat a house to 80° or 90°F. The door stays open, even in the coldest weather. Cold air collects in the underground tunnel. However, cold air is heavier than warm air, so the cold air in the tunnel cannot flow into the warm air in the house unless the Eskimos open the vent in the ceiling.

Once the vent in the ceiling is opened, the warm air in the room rises and flows outside. This leaves room for the cold air from the tunnel to come in and cool the house.

When the house has been cooled as much as the Eskimos want, they close the vent. The warm air settles back down into the house, stopping the cold air from the tunnel.

Eskimos also have learned to adapt their clothing to the weather. In winter they wear *two* suits made from the skins of the *caribou* (KAIR·ih·boo), the great deer that roam the Arctic. Eskimos wear the inner suit with the fur next to the body and the outer suit with the fur facing out. Body heat is trapped next to the body and between the two suits. Eskimo boots are sewn from caribou skins, too. The boots are so watertight that they can be blown up like balloons!

By adapting their homes and their clothing, Eskimos can live and thrive in one of nature's most challenging environments.

The Hot, Dry Desert

Far from Alaska lies the land of North Africa. The North African environment is quite different from northern Alaska, yet its climate is just as harsh. North Africa contains the world's largest desert—the *Sahara* (suh·HAR·uh), which is more than three million square miles in size.

The Sahara has mountains, rocky plateaus (pla· TOHZ), treeless plains, and sandy wasteland. The Sahara has less than eight inches of rain every year. Temperatures during the day are very hot, as high as 110°F. However, the desert sand does not hold the heat. When the sun sets, the desert becomes cool.

The problems faced by the North Africans living in the hot desert are different from those of the Eskimos living in the cold Arctic. Yet the desert people have adapted to their environment in ways much like the Arctic people have adapted to theirs.

Like the Eskimos, the people of the Sahara build houses with thick walls. In the desert, thick walls help keep heat *out* during the hot days and *in* during the cold nights. Mostly, though, their homes protect the North Africans from the scorching heat.

Desert people paint their homes white to reflect the sun's rays. They build houses close together to shade one another, and they plant trees for even more shade. Under their homes, they dig cool cellars in which they often stay during the hottest times of the year.

Desert people also use their clothing for protection from the heat. People of the Sahara wrap themselves up much like the Eskimos. However, the Eskimos wrap themselves up to stay warm, while the desert people wrap themselves up to stay cool. The desert people's robes, turbans, and veils keep the sun and wind from reaching their bodies. Because of the harsh desert heat and dryness, desert people must also protect themselves from *dehydration* (DEE·hy· DRAY·shuhn), or loss of water from the body. They must always be near water or carry it with them when they travel.

Nature's Challenge

The hot Sahara and the cold Arctic are only two of the many environments in which the people of the Earth live and make homes. Yet as different as one environment is from the other, people have found ways to adapt. A difficult environment is nature's challenge—to be met and overcome.

Questions

1. Why can people live in places as different as the frozen north and the blazing desert?

2. What special problems does nature give to people who live in the frozen north? to people who live on a blazing desert?

3. In what kind of an environment do you live? How have you adapted to your environment?

Activities

1. **Locate Places on a Map**
    Look at a map or globe. Find these places:
    a. two countries as far north as Alaska
    b. the Sahara desert in North Africa
    c. the Alps mountains in Europe
    Talk about what kind of an environment each place may have. Then talk about ways that people may have adapted to these environments. Read an encyclopedia to learn if you are right.

2. **Plan a New Environment**
    Imagine that you have landed on a distant planet. Draw a picture of the new environment.
    Now write about how you will adapt to your environment. Think about what kind of clothes you will wear; where you will find food, water and shelter; and how you will travel around.

Problems

A poem by Calvin O'John

The end of the day is near.
Gather up your problems
for this day.
Keep some,
Throw some away.

Photograph by Grant Heilman

BOOKSHELF

A Game of Catch by Helen Cresswell. Macmillan, 1977. During a game of tag in an empty castle gallery, Kate and Hugh hear children's laughter. Kate suspects it came from one of the paintings, but none of her friends or family believe her.

Peter Pitseolak's Escape from Death by Peter Pitseolak. Delacorte Press, 1978. Peter, an Eskimo and an artist, tells his story of the great danger he and his son faced while stranded on a sheet of ice one night.

Sprout and the Magician by Jenifer Wayne. McGraw-Hill, 1977. The rabbit belonging to Tilly, Sprout's sister, disappears. A magician is Sprout's number one suspect.

Encyclopedia Brown Sets the Pace by Donald Sobol. Four Winds Press, 1982. This junior detective and his assistant Sally have their hands full looking for a stolen painting and exposing a "fixed" race.

The Frog Band and the Onion Seller by Jim Smith. Little, Brown, 1976. Dressed as an onion seller, Detective Le Flic, master of disguises, travels to England to find a hidden treasure.

2 When the Moon Shines

The Great Minu

A West African folk tale retold by Beth P. Wilson

Illustrated by Lyle Miller

Since ancient times storytelling has been important throughout the great continent of Africa. Long ago, people in villages would gather together in the evenings and tell stories. Often they would sit in a circle around an open fire. Sometimes one person would begin a story only to have others continue it until the story's end. The tales were both entertaining and clever, often with animals playing tricks on other animals or on people. Usually the wrongdoer was punished in some way.

Some storytellers journeyed from village to village, weaving a magic spell with tales of the tricky hare or the clever spider, and learning new stories as they moved along. Often the listeners would clap their hands, beat on drums, or dance during or after the storytelling.

Today African children are just as excited about telling and listening to folk tales as were their parents and grandparents before them. In West African villages, families often gather in the early evening after a meal of foo-foo (cooked yam balls dipped in vegetable-beef stew). Soon someone in the group, usually a grandmother, begins a story. Frequently the story is The Great Minu, which has long been a favorite of young and old.

Across the ocean and far away, a poor African farmer prepared to make a journey to the big city of Accra. He walked around his small farm, taking note of the yams and corn growing in the garden. Then he fed his chickens and goats, latched his thatched-roof hut, and took off down the narrow, dusty road.

The farmer hummed happily to himself as the morning sun came into view. How exciting to be going to the big city! Nothing much happened in his tiny village, but since Accra was the largest city in Ghana, he would find much excitement there.

After walking for some time, he stopped to rest under a tulip tree. He leaned against the tree trunk and breathed in the morning air. Birds swooped and soared in the sunshine, but no man, woman, or child traveled the dusty road in either direction.

Soon he jumped to his feet and started down the road again. As he reached the first village along the way, he saw a woman on her knees, washing clothes in a stream of water. "Good day!" he called to the woman. "I'm on my way to the big city—I'm on my way to Accra!" The woman just smiled and went on washing her clothes.

Farther down the road he saw some men and boys making iron. They were too busy to look up when he passed, but he called out just the same. "Good day! I'm on my way to the big city—I'm on my way to Accra!" The men and boys stopped for a moment and nodded. Then they went on working as if he hadn't spoken.

Soon he saw a grandmother telling stories to her little grandchildren. The traveler loved a story and was tempted to stop. But he knew he must be on his way. He waved his hand high and called out, "Good day! I'm on my way to the big city—I'm on my way to Accra!" The children turned to look, and the grandmother smiled and waved. Then she went on telling her story.

The traveler trudged along until he felt tired and hungry. Finding a cool spot, he sat down by the side of the road and opened his lunch bag. He ate a piece of chicken and a big red banana. Then he took a short nap under a cocoa tree.

As soon as the traveler woke up, he started off again because he still had quite a long way to go. At last he approached some farms on the outskirts of Accra. The first thing he noticed was a great herd of cows. He wondered who could own such a herd. Seeing a man with them, he asked, "To whom do these cows belong?"

The man did not know the language of the traveler. So he shrugged his shoulders and said, "Minu," meaning, "I do not understand."

The traveler thought Minu must be a person, and so he exclaimed, "Mr. Minu must be very rich!"

Entering the city, the traveler saw some large new buildings in the town square. He wondered who might own the fine buildings. But the man he asked could not understand his question, so he answered, "Minu."

"Good heavens!" cried the traveler. "What a rich fellow Mr. Minu must be to own all those cows and all these buildings, too!"

Soon he came to a great hotel surrounded by beautiful grounds and mahogany trees. A group of fashionably dressed ladies came down the front steps of the hotel. The traveler stepped up to them and asked who might be the owner of such a grand hotel.

The ladies smiled and said softly, "Minu."

"How wealthy Mr. Minu is!" exclaimed the astonished traveler.

He wandered from one neighborhood to another. Seeing a large house with many columns and porches, he stopped in surprise. "These homes in Accra are so grand—not a bit like the huts of my village," he said.

Just then a servant came out. The traveler stepped up hurriedly and asked, "Please tell me who owns this fine house."

The young woman humped her shoulders. "Minu," she mumbled.

"How foolish of me to ask," the traveler said. "The Great Minu, of course." He stood for a moment, admiring the house and garden. Then he went on.

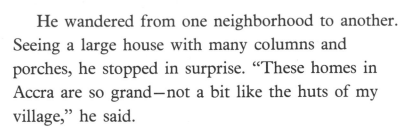

Finally he came to the harbor, where he saw men loading bananas, cocoa beans, and mahogany onto a huge ship. The blue sky above, the foamy green ocean below, and the sailors rushing about on board ship made quite a sight. Surprised at the great cargo, the traveler inquired of a bystander, "To whom does this fine vessel belong?"

"Minu," replied the puzzled man, who couldn't understand a word the traveler said.

"To the Great Minu also?" the traveler asked. "He is the richest man I ever heard of!"

Just as the traveler was setting out for home, he
saw men carrying a coffin down the main street of
Accra. A long procession of people, all dressed in
black, followed the men. People on the sidelines
shook their heads slowly. Sad faces looked up now
and then. When the traveler asked one of the
mourners the name of the dead person, he received
the usual reply, "Minu."

"Mr. Minu is dead?" wailed the traveler. "Poor
Mr. Minu! So he had to leave all his wealth—his
herd of cows, his buildings, his grand hotel, and his
fine ship—and die just like a poor person. Well, well,
in the future I'll be content to live a simple life, to
breathe the fresh air on my little farm, and to help
the poor people in my little village."

The long dusty road back didn't seem as long as
it had before. When the farmer arrived home, he
unlatched the door of his hut and looked around
inside. Then he climbed into his own snug bed and
dreamed of the good *foo-foo* he would eat the next day.

Questions

1. If you tell this story to an audience, you must be sure that they know the meaning of a certain word. What is the word? Why must your audience know it?

2. Do you think that the farmer would have enjoyed his trip to the city if he had understood what people where saying? Tell why or why not.

3. If the farmer told his neighbors about his exciting trip to the city, what would he describe as the lesson he learned?

4. Choose a word to complete each sentence.
   a. *Foo-foo* is a cooked (meat, vegetable).
   b. A thatched (door, roof) keeps out the rain.
   c. Men loaded the vessel in the (harbor, garden).

Activity   Make a Story Plan

Suppose you are getting ready to tell the story "The Great Minu." Here is a plan to help you remember the first part of the story.

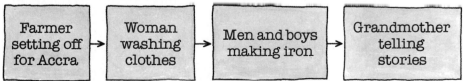

Finish this plan for the rest of the story. List, in order, the people or events the farmer saw.

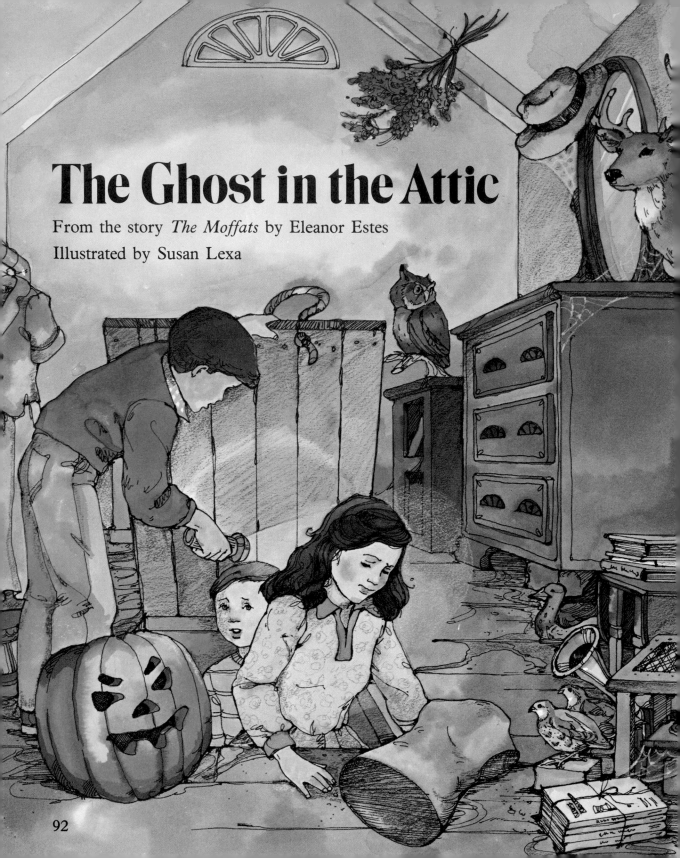

The Ghost in the Attic

From the story *The Moffats* by Eleanor Estes

Illustrated by Susan Lexa

It's Halloween and the Moffat children have told Peter Frost that a ghost is in their attic. Since Peter Frost has played mean tricks on each of them, all of the Moffats want to scare him. Even Catherine-the-cat helps when she gets tangled in the rope attached to the ghost the Moffats have created. As they march to the attic with sheets, a carved pumpkin head, a scooter, and their mother's dressmaking form (Madame-the-bust), Joe, Sylvie, Jane, and Rufus don't realize how frightening their ghost will be.

Slowly the procession made its way out of the Grape Room, into the hall, up the stairs to the second floor. Joe led the way with his pocket flashlight. From the hall upstairs, a stepladder led to the attic which did not have a regular door but a hatch which Joe had to push up with his shoulders. It fell open with a groan and the strange musty smell of the attic greeted them. Joe set the head on the floor and flashed the light down the stepladder so the others could see to climb up.

Sylvie hoisted Madame up before her and climbed in. Then Rufus handed up his scooter and hoisted himself in. As Jane was making her way up, Catherine-the-cat leaped past her and disappeared into the dark recesses of the attic. Jane bit her tongue but managed to keep from screaming. That cat! She was always doing unexpected things behind you.

The four Moffats stood around the entrance, the nearest point to the kitchen, to safety. Joe's tiny flashlight scarcely penetrated the darkness of the attic. But they knew what was up here all right without seeing. Dr. Witty had had many different hobbies. Collecting and stuffing wild animals and birds was one of them. He stored these in the attic in the yellow house. In one corner was a stuffed owl. In another, a stuffed wildcat. And all around were a great many little stuffed partridges and quail. The four children shivered, partly from cold, partly from excitement.

"Oh, let's hurry and get out of this place," said Jane.

They placed the scooter in the corner by the owl. Then they put Madame on the scooter, put the pumpkin head with its ominous, gaping mouth on her headless neck, and draped the sheets about her.

They tied one end of the rope to the scooter and made a loop in the other end in order to be able to pull the ghost around easily. The end of the rope with the loop they placed near the hatchway.

"All right," said Sylvie. "Now let's see how she looks."

They went to the head of the ladder. Joe flashed his light on Madame—Madame-the-bust no longer, or Mrs. Shoemaker or Miss Nippon either, but Madame-the-ghost!

"Phew!" he whistled.

"Boy, oh, boy!" said Rufus.

"Oh," shivered Jane, "come on."

As fast as they could, they pushed the hatch back in place and hurried helter-skelter to the kitchen where they warmed their hands over the kitchen fire.

"Boy, oh, boy!" said Rufus again, "what a ghost!"

Then they all put on the most fearful masks that Sylvie had made for them. And just in the nick of time too, for here was Peter Frost stamping on the back porch.

"Hey there, Moffats," he said witheringly.
"Where's your old ghost then?"

Oh, his arrogance was insufferable.

"Don't worry," said Sylvie, "you'll see her all
right. But you must be quiet."

"Haw-haw," jeered Peter Frost. But he stopped
short, for out of the night came a long-drawn howl, a
howl of reproach.

Sylvie, Joe, Jane, and Rufus had the same
thought. Catherine-the-cat! They had forgotten her
up there with the ghost. But Peter Frost! Why, he
knew nothing of that of course, and although he was
inclined to toss the matter lightly aside, still he
blanched visibly when again from some mysterious
dark recess of the house came the same wild howl.

The four Moffats knew when to be silent and they were silent now. So was Peter Frost. So was the whole house. It was so silent it began to speak with a thousand voices. When Mama's rocking-chair creaked, Peter Frost looked at it as though he expected to see the ghost sitting right in it. Somewhere a shutter came unfastened and banged against the house. The clock in the sitting-room ticked slowly, painfully, as though it had a lump in its throat, then stopped altogether. Even the Moffats began to feel scared, particularly Rufus. He began to think this whole business on a par with G–R–I–N–D your bones in "Jack and the Beanstalk."

Peter Frost swallowed his breath with a great gulp and said in a voice a trifle less jeering, "Well, what're we waitin' for? I want to see yer old ghost."

"Very well, then," said the four Moffats in solemn voices. "Follow us."

Again they left the warm safety of the kitchen, mounted the inky black stairs to the second floor, each one holding to the belt of the one in front. When they reached the stepladder, they paused a moment to count heads.

"Aw, you don't think I'm gonna skin out without seeing your silly old ghost, do yer?" asked Peter Frost. However, blustering though his words were, there could be no doubt that his hand, the one that held onto Joe's belt, was shaking and shaking.

"Now we go up the stepladder," said Joe in a hoarse whisper. "I'll push open the hatch."

Cautiously the five mounted the stepladder. It seemed to lead to a never-ending pit of darkness.

"Why don't you light your flash?" asked Peter Frost, doing his best to sound carefree and easy.

"And scare away the ghost, I suppose," snorted Joe. "You know, a ghost isn't comin' out where there's a light and all this many people. That is, unless there's a certain one around it happens to be interested in."

Another howl interrupted Joe's words. This sounded so close to them now that the four Moffats were afraid Peter Frost would recognize the voice of Catherine-the-cat. But he didn't. He began to shake and shake more violently than ever, making the stepladder they were standing on shiver and creak.

Joe pushed the trap door up with his shoulders. It fell open with a groan just as it had done before. They all climbed in and stood on the attic floor. Except for a pale glow from the light below, the attic was in the thickest blackness. For a moment they stood there in silence. Then suddenly Joe gave a swift flash into the corner of the attic. It fell for a second on the stuffed wildcat.

Peter Frost started but said not a word.

Then swiftly Joe flashed the light in the other corner. The stuffed owl stared at them broodingly.

But Peter Frost said nothing.

And then Joe flashed his light on Madame-the-ghost, herself. There she was, lurking in the corner, her orange head gaping horribly. All the children gasped, but still Peter Frost said nothing. All of a sudden, without any warning whatsoever, Madame-the-ghost started careening madly toward them. And dragging heavy chains behind her too, from the sound.

Jane called out in a shrill voice:

"Peter Frost! Peter Frost!

E-e-e-e-e-e-e-e-e-e!"

Joe flashed his light on and off rapidly. Madame-the-ghost dashed wildly round and round the attic. The same howl rent the air! The shutters banged. Then Peter Frost let out a roar of terror. That THING was after HIM. He tore around the attic room, roaring like a bull. And the ghost, dragging its horrible chains, tore after him.

"Let me go," he bellowed. But he couldn't find the hatch. Around the attic and around the attic he stumbled, kicking over stuffed partridges and quail. Finally he tripped over the wildcat and sprawled on the floor. Joe flashed his light on them for a second and when Peter Frost saw that he was sitting on the wildcat, he let out another piercing yell and leaped to his feet. He had seen now where the hatch was and he meant to escape before that ghost could catch up with him. Again he tripped and was down once more, this time with the ghost right on top of him. She would smother him with those ghastly robes of hers.

"She's got me! She's got me!" he roared.

Frantically he shook himself free of the ghost, and in wild leaps he made again for the hatch.

But now Rufus and Jane too had stood all they could of this nerve-racking business. They both began howling with fright and screaming, "Mama, Mama!" What with Peter Frost's yelling, Catherine-the-cat's yowling, the screams of Rufus and Jane, Sylvie herself began laughing hysterically and the place sounded like bedlam. To make matters worse, the battery of Joe's flashlight gave out, so there was no way of turning on the light and showing everyone there was no real ghost.

No, the ghost was real enough to Peter Frost, and as he finally reached the hatch and clattered down the stairs he thought he could still feel its cold breath on his neck and cheeks. The four Moffats followed after him, half tumbling, half sliding, until they reached the kitchen. Peter Frost tore out the back door with a bang and left the four of them there in the kitchen, breathless and sobbing and laughing all at once.

Questions

1. Why did the Moffats want to scare Peter Frost?

2. Why did the Moffats choose the attic as the place to scare Peter?

3. Should the Moffats tell Peter what really happened? Why or why not?

4. Match each group of words with the sentence that gives the meaning: **ominous and gaping, howl of reproach, insufferable arrogance.**
   a. "You can't scare me—ever!"
   b. "Then I saw the monster's wide-open jaws!"
   c. "Shame on you for forgetting me."

Activity   Describe the Strange Sounds

In the story, the Moffats' house "began to speak with a thousand voices" on Halloween night. Reread page 97 and make a list of the "voices" heard in the house. Then add other sounds you might hear in or around a house when it is dark. Use your list to help write a paragraph describing the sounds, or voices, in a strange dark house. Imagine that the house is speaking and you are listening.

What Night Would It Be?

A poem by John Ciardi

If the moon shines
On the black pines
And an owl flies
And a ghost cries
And the hairs rise
On the back
  on the back
    on the back of your neck—

If you look quick
At the moon-slick
On the black air
And what goes there
Rides a broom-stick
And if things pick
At the back
  at the back
    at the back of your neck—

Would you know then
By the small men
With the lit grins
And with no chins,
By the owl's *hoo*,
And the ghost's *boo*,
By the Tom Cat,
And the Black Bat,
On the night air,
And the thing there,
By the thing,
   by the thing,
      by the dark thing there

(Yes, you do,
   yes, you do
      know the thing I mean)

That it's now,
   that it's now,
      that it's—Halloween!

Illustrated by Sharron O'Neil

Facts About Fiction

In the picture, each person is giving the answer *fiction*. That's because all three stories are made up. All such imaginary stories are fiction. Now if you asked what *kind* of fiction each person is reading, you would get three different answers. The first person would say *realistic fiction.* The second person would say *a folk tale.* The third person would answer *a fantasy.* Each story is an example of a different kind of fiction.

Although there are many kinds of fiction, the following chart tells you about these three.

Three Kinds of Fiction

Realistic Fiction
The story usually takes place in the present.
The story is imaginary but could probably happen.
The main characters may remind you of people
you know.
The story has an author.

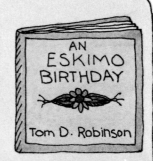

Folk Tale
Ordinary people often have their wishes granted.
Most of the characters act only one way—always
good, always bad, silly, clever.
Some magic may happen—witches may cast spells
or people may receive magic objects.
People made up the folk tale long ago.
The words *retold by* and the storyteller's name
may appear with the tale.

Fantasy
Magical things happen—people fly or animals and
toys talk.
The story has an author.

Here are six fiction books you might find in the library. Read the title and the description of each story. On a sheet of paper, write *realistic fiction, folk tale,* or *fantasy* to tell what kind of fiction is in each book.

1

Charlie is having a terrible time in first grade. He is very curious and is always getting into trouble. He never seems to behave well enough to have the honor of carrying the flag.

2

A poor young man, called the Fool of the World, finds a flying ship and meets seven people with magic powers. When the Fool must perform several difficult tasks to please the Czar, his new friends help him.

3

Pearl, a pig, meets a talking bone. They like each other immediately and start home together. On the way, a fox catches Pearl for his dinner, and the talking bone must try to save her.

4
The Chinese Story Teller
Retold by
Pearl S. Buck

A dog and a cat are friends until a thief steals their master's good-luck ring. The two friends set off together to find it, but they return as enemies. (This story explains why dogs don't like cats.)

5
HALF MAGIC
EDWARD EAGER

Jane finds a magic coin that can grant any wish. She and her brother and sisters wish for exciting adventures that take them to other countries and even through time!

6
THE HUNDRED PENNY BOX
Sharon Bell Mathis

Aunt Dew keeps one hundred pennies in an old wooden box—one penny for every year of her life. With these pennies, she tells Michael about her life—one event for each penny.

Think of a favorite fiction story. Write the story's title, the author's name, and what *kind* of fiction it is. Be prepared to tell your classmates why you think your story is realistic fiction, a folk tale, or a fantasy.

The Crane Maiden

A Japanese folk tale retold by Miyoko Matsutani

English version by Alvin Tresselt

Illustrated by Masami Miyamoto

Long years ago, at the edge of a small mountain village in the snow country of Japan, there lived an old man and his wife. They had little in this world that they could call their own. But they were happy in their life together.

Now one winter morning the old man set out for the village with a bundle of firewood fastened to his back. It was bitter cold. He knew he would have little trouble selling the wood. Then with the money, he would buy some food so that he and his wife could have a good supper.

As the old man trudged through the falling snow, he was suddenly aware of a fluttering sound, and a pitiful cry of *Koh, koh*. Turning from the path to investigate, he came upon a great crane frantically trying to free herself from a trap.

The old man's heart was touched with pity for the magnificent bird. While he tried to soothe the crane with tender words, his hands released the cruel spring of the trap. At once the crane flew up, joyfully calling *Koh, koh*, and disappeared into the snowy sky.

With a lighter step the old man went on through the snow. And when he had sold his wood, he returned once more to his humble house. While his old wife busied herself with preparing supper, he told her about rescuing the crane.

"That was a good deed," she said. "Surely the gods will one day reward you for your kind heart."

As she spoke these words, there came a tapping on the door. The old wife hurried to see who was there. Upon opening the door, she saw a beautiful young girl standing in the swirling snow. Her delicate face glowed like a peach beginning to ripen in the summer sun. And her dark eyes sparkled in the dancing firelight.

"Forgive my knocking at your door," she said in a soft voice, "but I have lost my way in the snow. May I share the warmth of your fire tonight?" Then bowing low before the two old people, she said, "My name is Tsuru (SOO•roo)."

"Oh, you poor child!" cried the old wife. "Come in at once before you freeze in the bitter cold." They sat the girl down close to the hearth. Then the old wife piled more wood on the flames so that the girl would soon be warm.

The old couple shared their simple supper of hot porridge with Tsuru-san, all the time feasting their eyes on her great beauty. Then they gave her their bed with its warm quilts to sleep on, while they spent the night huddled on a pile of straw.

In the morning when they awoke, the old man and his wife were surprised to see a good fire already burning on the hearth. The water jar was filled with fresh clear water, the floors had been swept, and all the rooms were clean and tidy.

Tsuru-san, the sleeves of her kimono neatly tied back with a red cord, was busily stirring a pot over the fire. "Good morning," she said, bowing to the old couple. "If you will wash your hands we may eat breakfast, for the porridge is cooked and ready."

"In our old age we have a daughter!" said the old man, laughing.

"It is the gods smiling on us for your good deed of yesterday," replied his wife happily.

The snow and bitter cold continued for many days. And so Tsuru-san stayed in the shelter of the old couple's home. As she had neither mother nor father, it was at last decided that she would remain as a daughter to these people.

The children of the neighborhood were soon attracted to the house as Tsuru-san was such a delight to be with. The house rang with happy laughter. The hearts of the old man and his wife were filled with joy at the sound.

115

And so the days of early winter passed. Soon it was time for the great New Year celebration. The old man spoke to his wife, saying, "Tsuru-san has been such a delight to us. If only I could give her a gift of a new kimono."

"Or if I could make her a rice cake for the New Year," his wife added.

But, alas, the winter had been hard. The old man had not been able to cut wood to sell. There was no money to buy even rice, much less a kimono.

Now Tsuru-san had heard them talking. It saddened her that these good people should be so poor. Coming before them she bowed low and said, "Dear parents, I know there has been no wood to sell. But perhaps I can help you and repay your great kindness to me. There is an old loom in the back room. I will weave cloth on it for you to sell in the village. Only you must promise that no one shall look at me while I am weaving."

The old man and his wife thought this was an odd request, but they quickly agreed. Tsuru-san locked herself in the room. Soon the old man and

his wife heard the sound of

> *Tin kola, kola, pon, pon,*
> *Tin kola, kola, pon, pon*

as the shuttle sped back and forth and the fabric grew in length.

For three days this continued. Tsuru-san stopped for neither food nor rest. Then at last the door opened and she stepped out, holding in her hands a bolt of cloth such as the old man and his wife had never seen in all their lives. They gasped at its beauty and marveled at its softness.

"Dear father," said the girl, "take this cloth into the village and sell it. It will be but small payment for the happy home you have given me."

Without wasting a moment, the old man hurried into the center of the village. When people saw the beautiful cloth he was carrying, a crowd soon gathered.

"I will pay ten gold pieces for your cloth," said one man.

"No, no!" cried another. "Sell it to me for twenty gold pieces!"

Each person who saw the cloth offered more money than the one before, until the old man finally sold the cloth for one hundred pieces of gold.

Stopping only long enough to buy rice for rice cakes, a kimono for Tsuru-san, and a few treats for New Year's Day, the man hurried home with his pockets jingling. "Tomorrow, tomorrow is the New Year's Day," he sang. "The New Year is the happy time, eating rice cakes whiter than snow."

Then such a hustle and bustle there was, as the old man and his wife prepared for the feast. As the old man pounded the rice, his wife made it into fine white cakes. And on New Year's Day all the children came in for a great party with their friend Tsuru-san.

Still the cold days of winter followed one after the other. At last one day Tsuru-san said to the old couple, "It is time for me to weave another bolt of cloth for you so that you will have money to live until the spring returns. But remember what I told you. No one is to look at me while I am working."

Again they promised. And the girl once more locked herself in the room and began weaving.

> *Tin kola, kola, pon, pon,*
> *Tin kola, pon, pon*

went the loom.

One day passed, and then the second. Still the sound of the loom filled the house. By now, the neighbors had grown curious.

"Is Tsuru-san weaving again?" asked one.

"Ah, soon you will have more gold pieces to hide under the floor," said another with a smile and a wink.

"The loom makes such an interesting sound," remarked the first one. "I would love to see what Tsuru-san is doing."

"We have promised not to watch her while she works," said the old man.

"What an odd request," cried one of the people. "I would not make such a promise to *my* daughter, you can believe me. What harm could there be in taking one look?"

Now in truth, the old woman had been most curious about Tsuru-san's weaving. Encouraged by her neighbor's remarks, she stepped up to a crack in the door.

"Stop, stop, old woman!" cried her husband when he saw what was happening. But it was too late. His wife had already peeked through the crack.

What a sight it was that met her eye! There, sitting at the loom, was a great white crane, pulling feathers from her body and weaving them into cloth.

The old woman stepped back. Before she could tell what she had seen, the door opened. Out stepped Tsuru-san, thin and pale, holding in her hands a half-finished bolt of cloth.

"Dear parents," she said in a weak voice, "I am the crane you rescued from the trap. I wanted to repay your kindness by weaving you another bolt of cloth." Then her eyes filled with tears. "But now that you have seen me in my true form I can no longer stay with you."

With this she kissed the man and his wife tenderly, and walked out of the house. Instantly she became a crane once more and, with a great whish of her wings, flew up into the sky. Slowly she circled overhead. Then with a single cry of *Koh* as if to say good-bye, the crane maiden was gone forever.

Questions

1. The main characters in this story are kind to one another. List three kind things the characters did for one another.

2. Match the characters with the lessons they learned.

   Crane Maiden   old man   old woman
   a. "Do not break a promise."
   b. "A good deed will be rewarded."
   c. "Be kind to someone who is kind to you."

3. Draw or write what *bolt* means in each sentence.
   a. The Crane Maiden wove a *bolt* of cloth.
   b. The barn was struck by a *bolt* of lightning.
   c. The old woman *bolted* the door at night.
   d. The carpenter put a *bolt* through the wood.

4. Someone said, "I don't think the Crane Maiden should have gone away. She should have given the old couple one more chance." Do you agree? Why or why not?

Activity   Write Questions and Answers

Suppose you were able to ask Tsuru-san three questions. Write the three questions that you would most like to ask her. Then be Tsuru-san and answer them.

When my canary

A haiku by Shiki

Translated by Harry Behn

When my canary
flew away, that was the end
of spring in my house.

Illustrated by Carlos Marchiori

What the Gray Cat Sings

A poem by Arthur Guiterman

The Cat was once a weaver,
  A weaver, a weaver,
An old and withered weaver
  Who labored late and long;
And while she made the shuttle hum
And wove the weft and clipped the thrum,
Beside the loom with droning drum
  She sang the weaving song:
    "Pr-rrum, pr-rrum,
Thr-ree thr-reads in the thr-rum,
    Pr-rrum!"

The Cat's no more a weaver,
  A weaver, a weaver,
An old and wrinkled weaver,
  For though she did no wrong,
A witch hath changed the shape of her
That dwindled down and clothed in fur
Beside the hearth with droning purr
  She thrums her weaving song:
    "Pr-rrum, pr-rrum,
Thr-ree thr-reads in the thr-rum,
    Pr-rrum!"

Illustrated by Marie-Louise Gay

Animals as Symbols

To the Japanese, the crane is special. Artists paint it. Poets write poems about it. Many people honor it in their folk tales. The crane is a *symbol* (SIM·buhl), or something that stands for something else. In Japan, the crane stands for good fortune or good luck. The crane brought luck to the old people in the Japanese tale "The Crane Maiden."

Symbols of Early Peoples

Using birds or animals as symbols is not a new idea. People did this long before there were towns or cities or nations. The early people lived close to nature. They knew and admired the animals and the way these animals seemed able to trick their enemies. Large family groups, called *clans,* often took an animal as their symbol. They carved their animal symbol over their doorways or on poles outside their houses.

When warriors of a clan went to battle, they placed a carving of their symbol on top of a pole. If the warriors got separated during a battle, they looked for their symbol and were able to find their leader.

Illustrated by Robert Masheris

Symbols of Ancient Nations

More than 5,000 years ago, soldiers in ancient Egypt used the falcon as their symbol. The falcon stood for the Egyptian king, or *pharaoh* (FAIR·oh). The people believed that the pharaoh really was a falcon in a human form.

In ancient Greece, cities had symbols. Soldiers from the city of Athens used an owl as their symbol. Soldiers from the city of Corinth fought under the symbol of a winged horse. The Roman army used the eagle as its symbol.

Symbols in the New World

Long before Europeans came to America, the American Indians were organized into clans, tribes, and even nations. The Iroquois Indians had eight clans. Each had an animal or bird as its symbol. The clans took the names of their symbols: Wolf, Deer, Bear, Beaver, Turtle, Snipe (a bird of the marshes), Heron, and Hawk. The clan's symbol was carved or painted above the doorway of every Iroquois house.

Members of the same clan thought of themselves as brothers and sisters. If a man of a Wolf clan visited a distant Iroquois village, he would go at once to a house with a wolf over the door. There he was sure to be welcomed as a brother, even though he was a total stranger.

About a thousand years ago, Vikings landed in
North America. It is possible that the first true flag
to fly over America had a raven on it. (A raven is
like a crow, but larger.) The raven was a symbol of
the Vikings. Their symbol was known as "Raven,
Terror of the Land."

In the 1700s, when America was being settled, many symbols were suggested for the new nation: a bucking horse, a beaver, a codfish, a deer, a wild turkey, and a pine tree. At that time, the symbol most widely used in America was the rattlesnake. In 1776, at the time of the American Revolution, rattlesnake flags were flown over many battlefields where Americans were fighting for independence from England. The words on the flag were a warning to England. (The word *tread* means "step.")

The American bald eagle was finally chosen as the symbol of America. On July 4, 1776, the day the Declaration of Independence was signed, Congress appointed three men to design a national seal, or symbol. Those men were Benjamin Franklin, John Adams, and Thomas Jefferson. It took them years to decide on what would be the best symbol for their new nation. Others joined with them to help. Benjamin Franklin was in France in 1782, when the final decision was made: the American bald eagle would be the national bird and symbol. Franklin was disappointed. He had wanted the wild turkey to be our national bird.

Here is the seal of the United States of America. At its center is the dignified and powerful American eagle. When Americans see this eagle, they know that it stands for, or *symbolizes*, America and its people.

Questions

1. What is a symbol?

2. Why did early peoples use symbols?

3. How did early peoples use animals as symbols?

4. What bird or animal would you choose for your symbol? Why?

Activities

1. **Find Out About More Symbols**
   These animals are often used as symbols. Match each animal with the meaning of the symbol. Use a dictionary or an encyclopedia to help you.

a. dove	bad luck
b. fox	courage
c. beaver	evil
d. snake	busyness
e. black cat	cleverness
f. lion	peace

2. **Find Out About Your State**
   What is your state bird and your state flower? What does your state flag look like? Look in an encyclopedia or a book about the states. Find out why your state's bird and flower were chosen. If you like, draw a picture of your state's bird, flower, or flag.

BOOKSHELF

The Ghost on Saturday Night by Sid Fleischman. Little, Brown, 1974. Opie guides a mean-looking stranger through the thick fog. His reward is two tickets to a ghost-raising. Opie doesn't know he has front-row seats to a bank robbery, too.

The Trouble with Jenny's Ear by Oliver Butterworth. Little, Brown, 1960. When Jenny hears thoughts before they are spoken, she begins to wonder what is wrong with her.

The Heavenly Zoo retold by Alison Lurie. Farrar, Straus & Giroux, 1979. A collection of tales from all over the world to explain the shapes people see in the star groups called the *constellations.*

A-Haunting We Will Go; Ghostly Stories and Poems collected by Lee Bennett Hopkins. Albert Whitman, 1977. Some of these ghost stories and poems will make you laugh. Some will make you shiver.

The Shrinking of Treehorn by Florence Parry Heide. Holiday House, 1971. Treehorn sees that shelves are getting higher and his clothes are getting looser. Can he really be shrinking?

3 Across the Land and Sea

Building the Erie Canal

An article

In the 1800s Americans were trying to solve the problems of transportation to the west. One solution was to build a long canal across New York State to Lake Erie.

The Erie Canal was begun in 1817. Thousands of immigrants, using shovels and pickaxes, had to dig the canal through a wilderness of swamps and forests.

Completed in 1825, the Erie Canal was 4 feet deep and 363 miles long. Horses, mules, and oxen were used to pull the boats and rafts that carried people, food, goods, and animals back and forth. A fast speed was eighty miles in twenty-four hours. Whenever a low bridge was approached, the cry went out, "Low bridge, everybody down!"

After eight years of work, the Erie Canal finally provided a route through the Appalachian Mountains and opened up the way west.

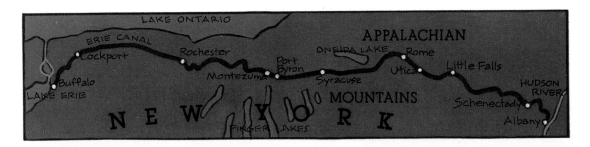

Illustrated by Dennis Ziemienski

The Erie Canal

A folk song

Illustrated by Peter Spier

| Dm | Dm | Gm | A7 | Dm | Dm |

1. I've got a mule, her name is Sal, Fif - teen miles on the
2. We better get on our way, old gal, Fif - teen miles on the

| Dm | Dm | Dm | Dm | Gm | A7 |

E - rie Ca - nal. She's a good old work - er and a good old pal,
E - rie Ca - nal. 'Cause you bet your life I'd nev - er part with Sal,

| Dm | Dm | Dm | Dm | F | F | F | C7 |

Fif - teen miles on the E - rie Ca - nal. We've hauled some barg - es in our day,
Fif - teen miles on the E - rie Ca - nal. Git up there, mule, here comes a lock,

| Dm | Dm | Dm | A7 | Dm | Dm |

Filled with lum - ber, coal, and hay, And we know ev - 'ry
We'll make Rome 'bout six o' - clock, Just one more trip and

| Gm | A7 | Dm | Dm | A7 | Dm C7 |

inch of the way From Al - ba - ny to Buf - fa - lo.
back we'll go Right back home to Buf - fa - lo.

Refrain

| F | F | F | C7 | F | F | F C7 | F |

Low bridge, ev - 'ry - bod - y down! Low bridge, for we're go - ing through a town, And you'll

| F | C7 | F | C7 |

al - ways know your neigh - bor, You'll al - ways know your pal, If you

| F | C7 | F | C7 | F |

ev - er nav - i - gat - ed on the E - rie Ca - nal.

137

I've got a mule, her name is Sal,
Fifteen miles on the Erie Canal.
She's a good old worker and a good old pal,
Fifteen miles on the Erie Canal.

We've hauled some barges in our day,
Filled with lumber, coal, and hay,
And we know ev'ry inch of the way
From Albany to Buffalo.

Low bridge, ev'rybody down!
Low bridge, for we're going through a town,

And you'll always know your neighbor,
You'll always know your pal,
If you ever navigated on the Erie Canal.

Crossing the Creek

From the story *Little House on the Prairie*
by Laura Ingalls Wilder
Illustrated by Michel Allaire

Before leaving Wisconsin, the Ingalls family said farewell to their home, their friends, and most of their possessions. They were moving in a covered wagon to the prairie land of Kansas. Besides Pa and Ma Ingalls, there were three girls in the family—Mary, Laura, and Baby Carrie. There were no roads across the prairie, and days passed without the family seeing another person. At night the wolves howled. Laura and Mary were often frightened, but they felt safe when Ma, Pa, or Jack, their bulldog, was near.

In this part of their story, the Ingalls family comes to one of the many creeks they will have to cross on their journey west.

Laura was surprised because she did not see the creek. But the bottom lands were wide. Down here, below the prairie, there were gentle hills and open sunny places. The air was still and hot. Under the wagon wheels the ground was soft. In the sunny open spaces the grass grew thin, and door had cropped it short.

For a while the high, bare cliffs of red earth stood up behind the wagon. But they were almost hidden behind hills and trees when Pet and Patty stopped to drink from the creek.

The rushing sound of the water filled the still air. All along the creek banks the trees hung over it and made it dark with shadows. In the middle it ran swiftly, sparkling silver and blue.

"This creek's pretty high," Pa said. "But I guess we can make it all right. You can see this is a ford, by the old wheel ruts. What do you say, Caroline?"

"Whatever you say, Charles," Ma answered.

Pet and Patty lifted their wet noses. They pricked their ears forward, looking at the creek; then they pricked them backward to hear what Pa would say. They sighed and laid their soft noses together to whisper to each other. A little way upstream, Jack was lapping the water with his red tongue.

"I'll tie down the wagon-cover," Pa said. He climbed down from the seat, unrolled the canvas sides and tied them firmly to the wagon box. Then he pulled the rope at the back, so that the canvas puckered together in the middle, leaving only a tiny round hole, too small to see through.

Mary huddled down on the bed. She did not like fords; she was afraid of the rushing water. But Laura was excited; she liked the splashing. Pa climbed to the seat, saying, "They may have to swim, out there in the middle. But we'll make it all right, Caroline."

Laura thought of Jack and said, "I wish Jack could ride in the wagon, Pa."

Pa did not answer. He gathered the reins tightly in his hands. Ma said, "Jack can swim, Laura. He will be all right."

The wagon went forward softly in mud. Water
began to splash against the wheels. The splashing
grew louder. The wagon shook as the noisy water
struck at it. Then all at once the wagon lifted and
balanced and swayed. It was a lovely feeling.

The noise stopped, and Ma said, sharply, "Lie
down, girls!"

Quick as a flash, Mary and Laura dropped flat on
the bed. When Ma spoke like that, they did as they
were told. Ma's arm pulled a smothering blanket over
them, heads and all.

"Be still, just as you are. Don't move!" she said.

Mary did not move; she was trembling and still. But
Laura could not help wriggling a little bit. She did so
want to see what was happening. She could feel the

wagon swaying and turning; the splashing was noisy again, and again it died away. Then Pa's voice frightened Laura. It said, "Take them, Caroline!"

The wagon lurched; there was a sudden heavy splash beside it. Laura sat straight up and clawed the blanket from her head.

Pa was gone. Ma sat alone, holding tight to the reins with both hands. Mary hid her face in the blanket again, but Laura rose up farther. She couldn't see the creek bank. She couldn't see anything in front of the wagon but water rushing at it. And in the water, three heads; Pet's head and Patty's head and Pa's small, wet head. Pa's fist in the water was holding tight to Pet's bridle.

Laura could faintly hear Pa's voice through the rushing of the water. It sounded calm and cheerful, but she couldn't hear what he said. He was talking to the horses. Ma's face was white and scared.

"Lie down, Laura," Ma said.

Laura lay down. She felt cold and sick. Her eyes were shut tight, but she could still see the terrible water and Pa's brown beard drowning in it.

For a long, long time the wagon swayed and swung, and Mary cried without making a sound, and Laura's stomach felt sicker and sicker. Then the front wheels struck and grated, and Pa shouted. The whole wagon jerked and jolted and tipped backward, but the wheels were turning on the ground. Laura was up again, holding to the seat; she saw Pet's and Patty's

scrambling wet backs climbing a steep bank, and Pa running beside them, shouting, "Hi, Patty! Hi, Pet! Get up! Get up! Whoopsy-daisy! Good girls!"

At the top of the bank they stood still, panting and dripping. And the wagon stood still, safely out of that creek.

Pa stood panting and dripping, too, and Ma said, "Oh, Charles!"

"There, there, Caroline," said Pa. "We're all safe, thanks to a good tight wagon-box well fastened to the running-gear. I never saw a creek rise so fast in my life. Pet and Patty are good swimmers, but I guess they wouldn't have made it if I hadn't helped them."

If Pa had not known what to do, or if Ma had been too frightened to drive, or if Laura and Mary had been naughty and bothered her, then they would all have been lost. The river would have rolled them over and over and carried them away and drowned them, and nobody would ever have known what became of them. For weeks, perhaps, no other person would come along that road.

"Well," said Pa, "all's well that ends well," and Ma said, "Charles, you're wet to the skin."

Before Pa could answer, Laura cried, "Oh, where's Jack?"

They had forgotten Jack. They had left him on the other side of that dreadful water and now they could not see him anywhere. He must have tried to swim after them, but they could not see him struggling in the water now.

Laura swallowed hard, to keep from crying. She knew it was shameful to cry, but there was crying inside her. All the long way from Wisconsin poor Jack had followed them so patiently and faithfully, and now they had left him to drown. He was so tired, and they might have taken him into the wagon. He had stood on the bank and seen the wagon going away from him, as if they didn't care for him at all. And he would never know how much they wanted him.

Pa said he wouldn't have done such a thing to Jack, not for a million dollars. If he'd known how that creek would rise when they were in midstream, he would never have let Jack try to swim it. "But that can't be helped now," he said.

He went far up and down the creek bank, looking for Jack, calling him and whistling for him.

It was no use. Jack was gone.

At last there was nothing to do but to go on. Pet and Patty were rested. Pa's clothes had dried on him while he searched for Jack. He took the reins again, and drove uphill, out of the river bottoms.

Laura looked back all the way. She knew she wouldn't see Jack again, but she wanted to. She didn't see anything but low curves of land coming between the wagon and the creek, and beyond the creek those strange cliffs of red earth rose up again.

Then other bluffs just like them stood up in front of the wagon. Faint wheel tracks went into a crack between those earthen walls. Pet and Patty climbed till the crack became a small grassy valley. And the valley widened out to the High Prairie once more.

No road, not even the faintest trace of wheels or of a rider's passing, could be seen anywhere. That prairie looked as if no human eye had ever seen it before. Only the tall wild grass covered the endless empty land and a great empty sky arched over it. Far away the sun's edge touched the rim of the earth. The sun was enormous and it was throbbing and pulsing with light. All around the sky's edge ran a pale pink glow, and above the pink was yellow, and above that blue. Above the blue the sky was no color at all. Purple shadows were gathering over the land, and the wind was mourning.

Pa stopped the mustangs. He and Ma got out of the wagon to make camp, and Mary and Laura climbed down to the ground, too.

"Oh, Ma," Laura begged, "Jack has gone to heaven, hasn't he? He was such a good dog, can't he go to heaven?"

Ma did not know what to answer, but Pa said: "Yes, Laura, he can. God that doesn't forget the sparrows won't leave a good dog like Jack out in the cold."

Laura felt only a little better. She was not happy. Pa did not whistle about his work as usual, and after a while he said, "And what we'll do in a wild country without a good watchdog I don't know."

Camp on the High Prairie

Pa made camp as usual. First, he unhitched and unharnessed Pet and Patty, and he put them on their picket-lines. Picket-lines were long ropes fastened to iron pegs driven into the ground. The pegs were called picket-pins. When horses were on picket-lines they could eat all the grass that the long ropes would let them reach. But when Pet and Patty were put on them, the first thing they did was to lie down and roll back and forth and over. They rolled till the feeling of the harness was all gone from their backs.

While Pet and Patty were rolling, Pa pulled all the grass from a large, round space of ground. There was old, dead grass at the roots of the green grass, and Pa would take no chance of setting the prairie on fire. If fire once started in that dry under-grass, it would sweep that whole country bare and black. Pa said, "Best be on the safe side, it saves trouble in the end."

When the space was clear of grass, Pa laid a handful of dry grass in its center. From the creek bottoms he brought an armful of twigs and dead wood. He laid small twigs and larger twigs and then the wood on the handful of dry grass, and he lighted the grass. The fire crackled merrily inside the ring of bare ground that it couldn't get out of.

Then Pa brought water from the creek, while Mary and Laura helped Ma get supper. Ma measured coffee beans into the coffee-mill and Mary ground them. Laura filled the coffee-pot with the water Pa brought, and Ma set the pot in the coals. She set the iron bake-oven in the coals, too.

While it heated, she mixed cornmeal and salt with water and patted it into little cakes. She greased the bake-oven with a pork-rind, laid the cornmeal cakes in it, and put on its iron cover. Then Pa raked more coals over the cover, while Ma sliced fat salt pork. She fried the slices in the iron spider. The spider had short legs to stand on in the coals, and that was why it was called a spider. If it had had no legs, it would have been only a frying pan.

The coffee boiled, the cakes baked, the meat fried, and they all smelled so good that Laura grew hungrier and hungrier.

Pa set the wagon-seat near the fire. He and Ma sat on it. Mary and Laura sat on the wagon tongue. Each of them had a tin plate, and a steel knife and a steel fork with white bone handles. Ma had a tin cup and Pa had a tin cup, and Baby Carrie had a little one all her own, but Mary and Laura had to share their tin cup. They drank water. They could not drink coffee until they grew up.

While they were eating supper the purple shadows closed around the camp fire. The vast prairie was dark and still. Only the wind moved stealthily through the grass, and the large, low stars hung glittering from the great sky.

The camp fire was cozy in the big, chill darkness. The slices of pork were crisp and fat, the corncakes were good. In the dark beyond the wagon, Pet and Patty were eating, too. They bit off bites of grass with sharply crunching sounds.

"We'll camp here a day or two," said Pa. "Maybe
we'll stay here. There's good land, timber in the
bottoms, plenty of game—everything a man could
want. What do you say, Caroline?"

"We might go farther and fare worse," Ma replied.

"Anyway, I'll look around tomorrow," Pa said. "I'll
take my gun and get us some good fresh meat."

He lighted his pipe with a hot coal, and stretched
out his legs comfortably. The warm, brown smell of
tobacco smoke mixed with the warmth of the fire. Mary
yawned, and slid off the wagon tongue to sit on the
grass. Laura yawned, too. Ma quickly washed the tin
plates, the tin cups, the knives and forks. She washed
the bake-oven and the spider, and rinsed the dish-cloth.

For an instant she was still, listening to the long,
wailing howl from the dark prairie. They all knew what
it was. But that sound always ran cold up Laura's
backbone and crinkled over the back of her head.

Ma shook the dish-cloth, and then she walked into the dark and spread the cloth on the tall grass to dry. When she came back Pa said: "Wolves. Half a mile away, I'd judge. Well, where there's deer there will be wolves. I wish——"

He didn't say what he wished, but Laura knew. He wished Jack were there. When wolves howled in the Big Woods, Laura had always known that Jack would not let them hurt her. A lump swelled hard in her throat and her nose smarted. She winked fast and did not cry. That wolf, or perhaps another wolf, howled again.

"Bedtime for little girls!" Ma said, cheerfully. Mary got up and turned around so that Ma could unbutton her. But Laura jumped up and stood still. She saw something. Deep in the dark beyond the firelight, two green lights were shining near the ground. They were eyes.

Cold ran up Laura's backbone, her scalp crinkled, her hair stood up. The green lights moved; one winked out, then the other winked out, then both shone steadily, coming nearer. Very rapidly they were coming nearer.

"Look, Pa, look!" Laura said. "A wolf!"

Pa did not seem to move quickly, but he did. In an instant he took his gun out of the wagon and was ready to fire at those green eyes. The eyes stopped coming. They were still in the dark, looking at him.

"It can't be a wolf. Unless it's a mad wolf," Pa said. Ma lifted Mary into the wagon. "And it's not that," said Pa. "Listen to the horses." Pet and Patty were still biting off bits of grass.

"A lynx?" said Ma.

"Or a coyote?" Pa picked up a stick of wood; he shouted, and threw it. The green eyes went close to the ground, as if the animal crouched to spring. Pa held the gun ready. The creature did not move.

"Don't, Charles," Ma said. But Pa slowly walked toward those eyes. And slowly along the ground the eyes crawled toward him. Laura could see the animal in the edge of the dark. It was a tawny animal and brindled. Then Pa shouted and Laura screamed.

The next thing she knew she was trying to hug a jumping, panting, wriggling Jack, who lapped her face and hands with his warm wet tongue. She couldn't hold him. He leaped and wriggled from her to Pa to Ma and back to her again.

"Well, I'm beat!" Pa said.

"So am I," said Ma. "But did you have to wake the baby?" She rocked Carrie in her arms, hushing her.

Jack was perfectly well. But soon he lay down close to Laura and sighed a long sigh. His eyes were red with tiredness, and all the under part of him was caked with mud. Ma gave him a cornmeal cake and he licked it and wagged politely, but he could not eat. He was too tired.

"No telling how long he kept swimming," Pa said. "Nor how far he was carried downstream before he landed." And when at last he reached them, Laura called him a wolf, and Pa threatened to shoot him.

But Jack knew they didn't mean it. Laura asked
him, "You knew we didn't mean it, didn't you, Jack?"
Jack wagged his stump of a tail; he knew.

Questions

1. The author used colors to help you see the scene at the creek. What colors did she use to describe the following:
   a. The water in the creek was _____ and _____.
   b. The cliffs beyond the creek were _____.
   c. The shadows on the land were _____.
   d. The sky was _____, _____, and _____.

2. What was one way that Laura showed she was brave?

3. Imagine that you are Jack. Tell what happened to you from the time you watched the Ingalls family start across the creek until the time you found them again.

4. What do you think Pa would do differently if the family had to cross another creek? Give reasons for your answer.

Activity   Retell an Event

In this story, the Ingalls family tried to be cheerful, brave, and kind even when they were in danger. Think about how the family acted in those ways. Then think of another story in which the characters showed those traits. Write the title of the story and the author's name. Tell about one event in the story when the characters face a challenge the same way the Ingalls family did.

About LAURA INGALLS WILDER

Laura Ingalls Wilder's books make the past come alive for readers of today. Her books begin with the Ingalls family living in a cabin in Wisconsin in the 1860s. They follow Laura and her family across the prairie by covered wagon to Kansas, Minnesota, and the Dakotas. All these adventures are seen through the eyes of the young Laura Ingalls as she grows up on the frontier.

Laura Ingalls Wilder did not begin writing her books until she was more than sixty years old. Her daughter Rose encouraged her to write about her early life. Every day Mrs. Wilder recalled her past and wrote about it in pencil on orange-colored tablets. Mrs. Wilder's first book was *The Little House in the Big Woods.* By the time she died at the age of ninety, she had written eight more.

More Books by Laura Ingalls Wilder

On the Banks of Plum Creek
By the Shores of Silver Lake
Little Town on the Prairie

CONNECTIONS

From Sea to Shining Sea

The new land of the United States seemed a land of promise to many people. People came from many places, across great oceans, north from Mexico, and south from Canada, to settle in the new country. Still other people moved from one part of the United States to another. This is the land these people traveled in their search for land or riches or a new home.

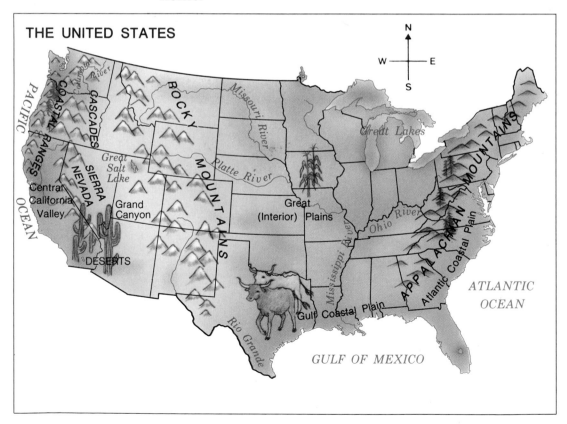

THE UNITED STATES

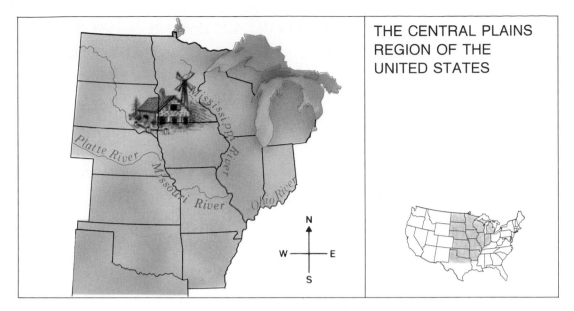

The Central Plains

Many thousands of people came to settle in the
huge middle part of the United States called the
Central Plains. This area had been explored and
claimed by the French and Spanish during the 1500s
and 1600s. Two hundred years later, all of this land
was part of the United States.

The pioneers who came to this section wanted the
land for farming and ranching. Some of the richest
farm and grazing land in the world lies in the
Central Plains of the United States.

The Plains are watered by one of the world's
largest river systems: the Mississippi River and its
tributaries (TRIB·yoo·tehr·eez), or branch rivers. The
Mississippi begins high up in northern Minnesota
and flows all the way down to the Gulf of Mexico.
In an old folk song, people sang, "Mighty Mississippi, roll along."

The Mississippi did roll along. It carried the earliest French and Spanish explorers. It carried water to farms and ranches all over the Central Plains. It carried boats full of goods from United States factories as well as goods from Europe. People moving north or south, east or west, used the Mississippi and its tributaries to carry their belongings.

Many of the people who crossed the Mississippi settled in the Central Plains. Others moved on. Moving east or moving west, settlers found they had to cross mountains: the Appalachians (AP·uh·LAY·shunz) in the east and the Rockies in the west.

The Mountains

The **Appalachian Highlands** stand between the Central Plains and the East Coast of the United States. The Appalachian Highlands are made up of mountains, steep forested valleys, and low, level lands. Some of the valleys and lowlands have·rich farmlands. Other parts of the Appalachian Highlands are rich in coal and petroleum. Some settlers to this area became farmers. Others became miners.

The **Rocky Mountains** stand between the Central Plains and the West Coast of the United States. These mountains are very different from the Appalachian Highlands. The Rocky Mountains, jagged and snow-capped, are among the world's highest mountains.

People who crossed the Rockies told of danger and hardships. Many others died crossing the mountains. They died from the cold, from exhaustion, and

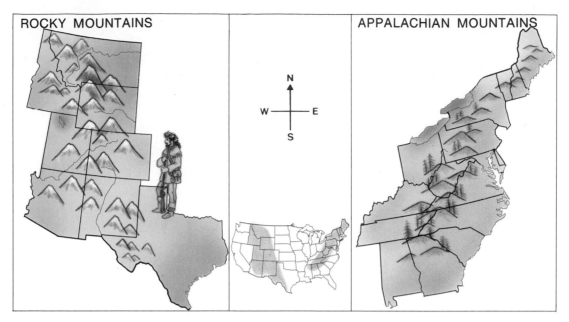

ROCKY MOUNTAINS

APPALACHIAN MOUNTAINS

from hunger. Yet people had to cross the Rockies going west. There was no way around the mountains. The Rocky Mountains stretch all the way from northern New Mexico through Canada and into Alaska.

The Deserts

Many people crossed the desert regions of the United States in their search for land or riches. The desert regions lie west of the Rocky Mountains. The land in this area is very dry and hot with few plants. The **Great Basin** is the largest desert, 200,000 square miles of barren land in California, Idaho, Nevada, Oregon, Utah, and Wyoming.

The **Painted Desert** in Arizona, the **Mojave** (moh·HAH·vee) **Desert** in California, and the **Sonoran** (saw·NAW·rahn) **Desert** in New Mexico

165

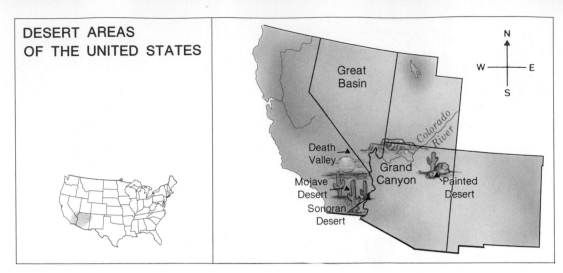

DESERT AREAS OF THE UNITED STATES

are other desert regions that people may have crossed on their journeys from Mexico or parts of the United States. Just as some people were not prepared for the ruggedness of the Rockies, so others were not prepared for the harshness of the deserts. Many died from the heat or from thirst.

The Coasts

Some of the earliest people to come to the United States sailed from Europe across the Atlantic Ocean. The English and French settled along the Atlantic Coast. The Spanish settled in what is now Florida and along the coast of the Gulf of Mexico. The Spanish then moved across the desert regions to settle in what is now New Mexico, Arizona, and California.

People who came to the Atlantic Coast found flat lands that run along the Atlantic Sea Coast and the Gulf of Mexico. Along the Atlantic Coast, the plains are called the **Atlantic Coastal Plains.**

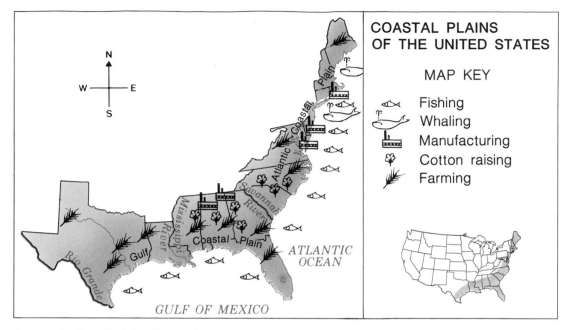

MAP KEY

Fishing
Whaling
Manufacturing
Cotton raising
Farming

Around the Gulf of Mexico, the plains are called the
Gulf Coastal Plains.

English colonists who first came to the upper
Atlantic Coastal Plains started small farms. The
land was not very good for farming, however. The
Atlantic Coast had many good *harbors,* places where
ships can dock safely. Later colonists turned to
fishing, whaling, and shipping.

Many rivers cross the Atlantic Coastal Plains. The
rushing waters from the rivers provided power for
manufacturing, which started to grow in the middle
of the 1880s.

Colonists from France and England settled the
lower Atlantic Coastal Plains. The climate there and
across the Gulf Coastal Plains ranges from warm to
hot, ideal for growing cotton. Great cotton planta-
tions were built where the coastal plain widens in
Virginia.

167

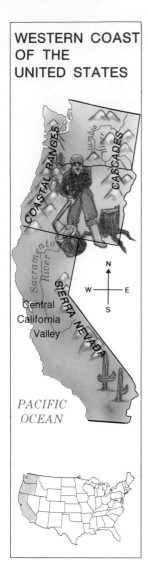

WESTERN COAST OF THE UNITED STATES

The same Mississippi River that waters the Central Plains flows through the Gulf Coastal Plains. Another important river in this region is the Rio Grande (REE·oh GRANDE), or Big River, as it was named by the Spanish settlers. The Rio Grande is the boundary between the United States and Mexico.

The far western coast of the United States looks out over the Pacific Ocean. Mountain ranges lie along the edge of the coast and plunge to the sea. Beyond these mountains lie the Central Valley of California and two more mountain ranges, the Sierra Nevada and the Cascade Mountains.

The Central Valley of California has very rich farmland that is good for growing fruits and vegetables. During the 1840s and 1850s, the discovery of gold led many people to California. It was the rich farmland, however, that made many stay and trade their miners' picks and axes for plows and hoes.

The Sierra Nevada range and the Cascade range extend almost the length of the Pacific Coast from Canada to Mexico. The Cascade Mountains are heavily forested. Settlers to the area now called Washington and Oregon turned to logging. These loggers supplied much of the United States with lumber for homes, furniture, and paper goods.

From east to west, north to south, across mountains and rivers and deserts, people pioneered and settled and built in the United States. By the end of the 1800s, people from all over the world had become Americans living in a proud, young nation that stretched "from sea to shining sea."

Questions

1. Look at the map on page 162. Find your state. In what region do you live? What is the land like in your region?

2. If you were a pioneer moving west, where would you choose to stop and build your home? Why?

Activities

1. **Plan a Trip**

   Suppose you were a pioneer traveling from the East Coast of the United States to the West Coast. You want to travel across the middle of the United States in a straight line. List the land regions you will travel through as you go. Then make a list of supplies you will need to make your trip. Use the map on page 162 to help you.

2. **Be a Settler**

   Look back over this selection and decide where you would like to settle and build a home. Then tell about or draw the kind of house you would build; how you would get food and water; what kinds of clothing you would need; and what problems you might face. If you need more information about pioneers, look in books about the history of the West or in an encyclopedia.

Kansas Boy

A poem by Ruth Lechlitner

This Kansas boy who never saw the sea
Walks through the young corn rippling at his knee
As sailors walk; and when the grain grows higher
Watches the dark waves leap with greener fire
Than ever oceans hold. He follows ships,
Tasting the bitter spray upon his lips,
For in his blood up-stirs the salty ghost
Of one who sailed a storm-bound English coast.
Across wide fields he hears the sea winds crying,
Shouts at the crows—and dreams of white gulls flying.

The Jumblies

From the poem

by Edward Lear

They went to sea in a sieve, they did;
   In a sieve they went to sea:
In spite of all their friends could say,
On a winter's morn, on a stormy day,
   In a sieve they went to sea.
And when the sieve turned round and round,
And every one cried, "You'll all be drowned!"
They called aloud, "Our sieve ain't big;
But we don't care a button, we don't care a fig:
   In a sieve we'll go to sea!"
     Far and few, far and few,
       Are the lands where the Jumblies live:
       Their heads are green, and their hands are blue;
        And they went to sea in a sieve.

They sailed away in a sieve, they did,
    In a sieve they sailed so fast,
With only a beautiful pea-green veil
Tied with a ribbon, by way of a sail,
    To a small tobacco-pipe mast.
And every one said who saw them go,
"Oh! won't they be soon upset, you know?
For the sky is dark, and the voyage is long;
And, happen what may, it's extremely wrong
    In a sieve to sail so fast."
        Far and few, far and few,
            Are the lands where the Jumblies live:
            Their heads are green, and their hands are blue;
            And they went to sea in a sieve.

Illustrated by Jane Teiko Oka

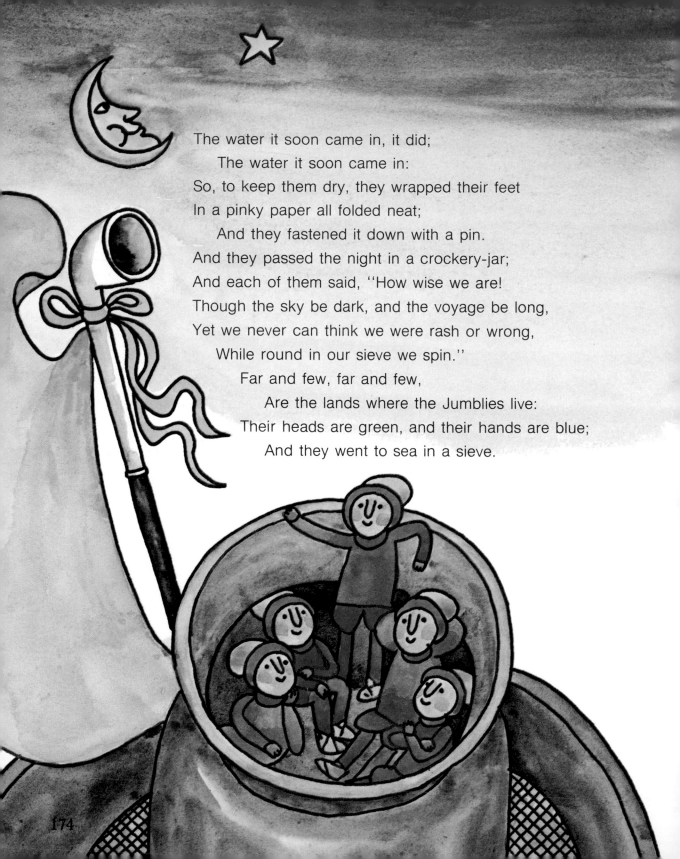

The water it soon came in, it did;
   The water it soon came in:
So, to keep them dry, they wrapped their feet
In a pinky paper all folded neat;
   And they fastened it down with a pin.
And they passed the night in a crockery-jar;
And each of them said, "How wise we are!
Though the sky be dark, and the voyage be long,
Yet we never can think we were rash or wrong,
   While round in our sieve we spin."
      Far and few, far and few,
         Are the lands where the Jumblies live:
         Their heads are green, and their hands are blue;
            And they went to sea in a sieve.

And in twenty years they all came back,—
    In twenty years or more;
And every one said, "How tall they've grown!"
For they've been to the Lakes, and the Torrible Zone,
    And the hills of the Chankly Bore."
And they drank their health, and gave them a feast
Of dumplings made of beautiful yeast;
And every one said, "If we only live,
We, too, will go to sea in a sieve,
    To the hills of the Chankly Bore."
        Far and few, far and few,
            Are the lands where the Jumblies live:
            Their heads are green, and their hands are blue;
                And they went to sea in a sieve.

Half a Kingdom

An Icelandic folk tale retold by Ann McGovern
Illustrated by Jane Teiko Oka

When you wake up in the morning, you never can tell what might happen to you during the day.

One fine morning, Prince Lini woke up in his castle on the hill. He didn't have the slightest idea what was going to happen to him that day.

He rode into the forest with his friends. Suddenly, from nowhere, a thick cold fog blew into the woods. The cloud of fog covered the prince from head to toe. A minute later the fog drifted away and was gone. Gone, too, was Prince Lini.

His friends searched for him all that day and all that night. And in the morning they rode to the castle to tell the king the strange story of the fog that rolled in from the sky and took away his son.

Now the king loved his son more than anything, even more than the riches of his kingdom, which he loved very much. He sent for his strongest men and his wisest men. "Whoever finds Prince Lini," he said, "and brings him back to me, will win half of my kingdom."

The strongest men (and those not so strong) searched far and wide. The wisest men (and those not so wise) searched wide and far. All over the kingdom people heard the news that the prince had disappeared in a cloud of fog. Anyone who had ever wanted half a kingdom set out to search for the prince.

One fine morning, Signy, a poor peasant girl, woke up in her cottage at the edge of the forest. She didn't have the slightest idea what was going to happen to her that day.

But she had heard about the missing prince and about the king's reward of half the kingdom. She knew that the strongest and the wisest men had looked far and wide.

I'll look near and narrow, she thought.

Signy knew the secret places of the forest better than anyone else. She put on a pair of sturdy shoes for walking and took along some food. And she set out to search for Prince Lini.

All that day she looked. She saw nothing but tree shapes in the snow. All that day she called. She heard nothing but the song of the icy wind.

The sun began to set and the sky turned rosy. Soon it would be dark. Signy walked through a narrow place between the rocks to her favorite warm cave and peered inside. There, stretched out on a golden bed, was Prince Lini, fast asleep.

She ran into the cave and tried to wake him. But he slept on, in a deep, deep sleep.

All of a sudden she heard a clattering, a chattering. She ran to hide in the darkest corner of the cave.

Two troll girls—a tall troll and a shorter troll—entered the cave. "Fee, Foo, Fum, Firl. I smell the flesh of a human girl," sang the short troll.

"No," said the tall troll, "it's only Prince Lini."

Then the trolls whistled. Signy listened carefully to the notes of the whistle. Two swans flew into the cave. The short troll said:

Sing O sing O swans of mine,
Sing Prince Lini awake.

The swans sang. Prince Lini stirred, rubbed his eyes, and sat up.

"Now," said the short troll, "for the ninety-seventh time, will you marry one of us?"

"Never," said the prince. "Never, never, never."

"You'll be sorry," the tall troll said. Then she commanded the swans:

> *Sing O sing O swans of mine,*
> *Sing Prince Lini asleep.*

The swans sang and Prince Lini fell fast asleep again. The swans flew out of the cave.

From her hiding place, Signy could see and hear everything. The next morning the trolls left the cave with a clattering and a chattering. Signy crept from her hiding place. She remembered how the trolls whistled, and she whistled the same notes.

The swans flew into the cave. Signy said:

> *Sing O sing O swans of mine,*
> *Sing Prince Lini awake.*

The swans sang.

Prince Lini stirred, rubbed his eyes, sat up, and rubbed his eyes again. "Troll!" he said. "What has happened to you? You look very different."

"I'm not a troll," said Signy, "and nothing has happened to me except that I found you. I'm Signy."

"I'm very pleased to meet you," said the prince.

The prince told Signy how the trolls had cast a spell upon him with their magic fog and how they were holding him a prisoner until he agreed to marry one of them.

Then Signy told the prince how sad the king was, and how he had even offered half the kingdom to anyone who found his son and brought him home.

"No one has found me yet except you," said the prince. "But I don't know whether I *want* to be found. It's nice and warm in this cave. It's nice to have the trolls asking me to marry them every day."

Signy gave the prince a funny look.

"That wasn't true," said the prince. "The real reason is that I don't want to go home. It makes me sad to see how the kingdom is run. And the king will listen to no one. The rich are too rich and hardly work. The poor are too poor and work too hard."

"Yes," said Signy sadly.

The prince looked at Signy and began to laugh. He jumped up and down on the golden bed, laughing and laughing.

"What's so funny about being poor?" Signy asked.

"That's just it!" cried the prince. "You won't be poor if you get half the kingdom and you can share it with everyone! Please, Signy, take me back to the king and take half the kingdom. Please!"

"First things first," said Signy. "The first thing is to get you out of here."

"Why can't we run away right now while I'm awake?" said the prince.

"No," said Signy. "The trolls would surely send down their magic fog before we got out of the woods. They would make me a prisoner, too, along with you. You must find out from the trolls where they go and what they do during the day. It's the only way."

The prince agreed.

The sun began to set and the sky turned rosy. Then Signy whistled. The swans flew into the cave and sang Prince Lini asleep.

Again Signy hid in the dark corner. Soon the trolls came in with a clattering, a chattering. They woke Prince Lini in their usual way. And in their usual way they asked him their usual question.

"Now," said the tall troll, "for the ninety-eighth time, will you marry one of us?"

The prince pretended to think about it. "Tell me," he said, "where do you go and what do you do during the day?"

"We go to the big oak tree in the middle of the forest," the tall troll said.

"And we take out our giant golden egg," the short troll said.

"And we toss it back and forth, and back and forth," the tall troll said.

"What happens if you drop it?" Prince Lini asked.

"Oh, we never drop it," the short troll said. "If we drop it and it breaks, we would disappear forever."

"Enough of this chatter," said the tall troll. "Now for the ninety-ninth time, will you marry one of us?"

"Never, never, never, never, NEVER!" said the prince.

"Oh," said the tall troll, shaking with rage. "Tomorrow you will see how sorry you will be!"

"The end is near for you," said the short troll.

The trolls whistled. The swans sang and Prince Lini slept.

The next morning when the trolls left the cave, Signy whistled for the swans. The swans sang and Prince Lini awoke.

"You were wonderful," Signy said. "Now we will go to the middle of the forest to the big oak tree. You must do exactly what I tell you." And she whispered her plan to the prince.

They left the cave and walked to the middle of the forest. There they saw the two trolls under the big oak tree. The trolls were throwing the giant golden egg to and fro, to and fro.

Signy whispered to the prince, "Be careful. Your life is in danger."

Prince Lini picked up a stone. He aimed carefully and threw it. The stone hit the giant golden egg. It fell to the ground, broken to bits.

Suddenly from nowhere a thick cold fog blew into the woods. The cloud of fog covered the two trolls. A minute later the fog drifted away and was gone. And gone, too, were the trolls. Gone forever, to the place where trolls live.

Signy and Prince Lini ran all the way to the palace. "Wait outside," Signy told the prince. "It's better if I see your father alone."

"Who are you?" the king asked when he saw Signy. "And what do you want?"

"I am Signy, a peasant girl," she said, "and I want half of your kingdom, for I found your son."

"Don't be silly," said the king. "How can a girl find my son when my strongest and my wisest men could not find him!"

"That's too bad for them," Signy said. "If what I say is true, will you keep your promise and give me half of your kingdom?"

"Go away," said the king. "It can't be true."

Signy ran to the door and flung it open. The king was beside himself with joy to see his lost

son. After the two hugged and cried tears of
happiness, Prince Lini told his father about the
trolls and the magic spell and how Signy found
him and freed him.

"Now will you give up half your kingdom?"
Signy asked the king.

"Oh, my precious kingdom!" the king sighed.

"What about your precious son and your
promise!" said the prince.

The king looked at Signy carefully. "A girl
like you found my son? A peasant girl—not even
a princess! But my precious son is right. And a
promise is a promise. I give you half my kingdom."

Prince Lini turned to Signy. "I love you," he said. "Will you marry me? I'll help you rule your half of the kingdom, if you like."

Signy said, "Let's play checkers while I think it over."

They played checkers and Signy thought it over. She thought it would be wonderful to marry Prince Lini. "We can share half the kingdom and share adventures, too, for the rest of our lives," she told him.

And that is exactly what they did, happily and forever after.

Questions

1. Who might have said the following:
   a. "We can't find Prince Lini."
   b. "Prince Lini won't marry either of us."
   c. "I don't want to share my kingdom."

2. Tell two problems Signy had to solve before she could return Prince Lini to the king.

3. Which word best describes the story? Give reasons for your answer.
   a. serious   b. fanciful   c. sad

4. Will Signy be a good queen? What did you learn about her in the story that makes you think the way you do?

5. Folk tales often describe settings and happenings that make you "see" exciting pictures in your mind. Which part of the story causes you to "see" the most exciting picture in your mind? Describe it.

Activity   Write the Beginning of a Story

"Half a Kingdom" has a bright, happy beginning. Read the first three paragraphs of the beginning again. Then write a lively beginning that might start a story about the further adventures of Signy and Lini.

At Night May I Roam

A Sioux chant

at night may I roam
against the winds may I roam
at night may I roam
when the owl is hooting
may I roam

at dawn may I roam
against the winds may I roam
at dawn may I roam
when the crow is calling
may I roam

Illustrated by Sarn Suvityasiri

BOOKSHELF

Pioneers on Early Waterways by Edith McCall. Children's Press, 1980. With a great deal of determination, early settlers made their way to the lands out West by raft, flatboat, barge, and even steamboat.

The Prairie Community by Kathleen Vyn. Julian Messner, 1978. Plant and animal life on the prairie changed when people began to live there. Read about what it was like before the settlers came.

Stowaway to the Mushroom Planet by Eleanor Cameron. Little, Brown, 1956. David and Chuck return to the small planet of Basidium. Unknown to them, a stowaway is on their ship.

Letters to Horseface: Wolfgang Amadeus Mozart's Journey to Italy 1769–1770 When He Was a Boy of Fourteen by F. N. Monjo. Viking Press, 1975. A young composer writes humorous letters to his sister, whom he calls Horseface.

Explorers in a New World by Edith McCall. Children's Press, 1980. Imagine yourself discovering a new area. Take a look at how some of the people felt who first explored our land.

4 When Paths Cross

The Lion and the Mouse

An Aesop fable retold by Anne Terry White
Illustrated by Masami Sam Daijogo

In the heat of the day a Lion lay asleep at the edge of a wood. He lay so still that a Mouse ran right across his nose without knowing it was a nose, and a Lion's at that.

Bang! The Lion clapped his paw to his face and felt something caught. It was furry. Lazily he opened his eyes. He lifted up one side of his huge paw just a little bit to see what was under it and was amused to find a Mouse.

"Spare me, Great King!" he heard the little creature squeak in its tiny voice. "I didn't mean to do it! Let me go, and someday I will repay you."

"That's very funny," said the Lion, and he laughed. "How can a little thing like you help me, the great King of Beasts?"

197

"I don't know," the Mouse replied, "but a little creature *can* sometimes help a big one."

"Well, you have made me laugh," the Lion said, "which is something I seldom do. And anyway, you would hardly make half a mouthful. So—" He raised his paw and let the Mouse go.

A few days later the Lion was caught in a hunter's net. The woods rang with his angry roaring and the little Mouse heard him.

"That is my kind Lion!" she cried. "He is in trouble!" As fast as she could, she ran toward the spot from which the roaring came, and there he was. The Lion was thrashing around so in the net that the Mouse didn't dare to come near for fear of being crushed.

"O King, be patient!" she cried. "I will gnaw through the ropes and set you free."

So the Lion lay still while the Mouse worked away with her sharp teeth. And in a short time he was able to creep out of the net.

"You see? I told you I would repay you," the Mouse said happily. "A little creature sometimes really can help a big one."

And the Lion had to admit it was true.

Little friends may prove to be great friends.

199

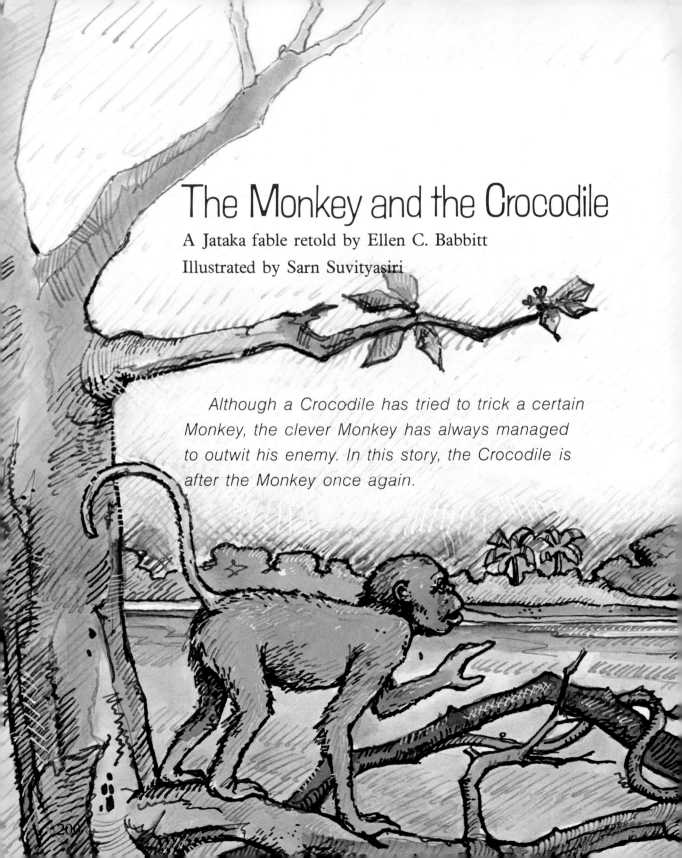

The Monkey and the Crocodile

A Jataka fable retold by Ellen C. Babbitt

Illustrated by Sarn Suvityasiri

Although a Crocodile has tried to trick a certain Monkey, the clever Monkey has always managed to outwit his enemy. In this story, the Crocodile is after the Monkey once again.

The Monkey lived in a great tree on a river-bank. The Monkey soon moved away from that tree. He wanted to get away from the Crocodile, so that he might live in peace.

But the Crocodile found him, far down the river, living in another tree.

In the middle of the river was an island covered with fruit trees. Halfway between the bank of the river and the island, a large rock rose out of the water. The Monkey could jump to the rock, and then to the island. The Crocodile watched the Monkey crossing from the bank of the river to the rock, and then to the island.

He thought to himself, "The Monkey will stay on the island all day, and I'll catch him on his way home at night."

The Monkey had a fine feast, while the Crocodile swam about, watching him all day.

Toward night the Crocodile crawled out of the water and lay on the rock, perfectly still.

When it grew dark among the trees, the Monkey started for home. He ran down to the river bank, and there he stopped.

"What is the matter with the rock?" the Monkey thought to himself. "I never saw it so high before. The Crocodile is lying on it!"

But he went to the edge of the water and called, "Hello, Rock!"

No answer.

Then he called again, "Hello, Rock!"

Three times the Monkey called, and then he said, "Why is it, Friend Rock, that you do not answer me tonight?"

"Oh," said the stupid Crocodile to himself. "The rock answers the Monkey at night. I'll have to answer for the rock this time."

So he answered: "Yes, Monkey! What is it?"

The Monkey laughed, and said, "Oh, it's you, Crocodile, is it?"

"Yes," said the Crocodile. "I am waiting here for you. I am going to eat you."

"You have caught me in a trap this time," said the Monkey. "There is no other way for me to go home. Open your mouth wide so I can jump right into it."

Now the Monkey well knew that, when Crocodiles open their mouths wide, they shut their eyes.

While the Crocodile lay on the rock with his mouth wide open and his eyes shut, the Monkey jumped.

But not into his mouth! Oh, no! He landed on the top of the Crocodile's head, and then sprang quickly to the bank. Up he whisked into his tree.

When the Crocodile saw the trick the Monkey had played on him, he said, "Monkey, you have great cunning. You know no fear. I'll let you alone after this."

"Thank you, Crocodile," said the Monkey. "But I shall be on the watch for you just the same."

Questions

1. "I was smart to lie on the rock, but I made a mistake." Who in the story might say that? What was his mistake?

2. Why didn't the Monkey trust the Crocodile at the end of the fable?

3. If the Monkey told this fable to his friends, which lesson might he give at the end?
   a. "Don't go near the water."
   b. "Jump now and ask questions later."
   c. "Look before you leap."

4. Why would a storyteller like to tell this story? Why would people like to hear it?

5. The Monkey said, "You have caught me in a trap." What does he mean?
   a. You have outwitted me.
   b. You have frightened me.
   c. You have put me in a cage.

Activity   Finish a Fable

One day the Monkey climbed a tree to get a coconut. Meanwhile, the Crocodile pretended to be a log beneath the tree. "This time," he said, "I won't say a word, and I'll keep my eyes open."

Finish the fable. End with a *moral,* or lesson.

From

Guess Who My Favorite Person Is

A story by Byrd Baylor

Illustrated by Christa Kieffer

I happened to be in an alfalfa field,
barefoot, sort of lying down
watching ladybugs climb yellow flowers
when I saw this little kid
who was also barefoot,
sort of lying down
watching ladybugs climb yellow flowers,
helping them up again when they fell off.

"Want to see my favorite one?"
she called to me.

So I went over to where she was.

She pointed to a bug.
To tell the truth,
I couldn't see much difference
between that one
and about a million others.

I was going back
to my own part of the field
when she said,
"Now choose *your* favorite one."

It wasn't easy because
I hadn't ever practiced choosing ladybugs
but finally I did.

She looked surprised.
"I can't believe you like that one.
I passed her up about two days ago . . .
but that's your business."

For a while we didn't talk at all.

I stretched out
and closed my eyes
and just let the alfalfa be taller
than I was.

But she said,
"What's your favorite thing—
sleeping or being awake?"

"Awake," I said.

"Then wake up and we can play
the tell-what-your-favorite-thing-is game."

"I think we are already playing it,"
I said.

She said,
"We are, and it's my turn.
My favorite turn is FIRST."

So I said, "Go ahead."

She said,
"Tell me your favorite color."

I said, "Blue."

But she said,
"See, you've already done it wrong.
In this game you can't just say it's blue.
You have to say what *kind* of blue."

So I said,
"All right. You know the blue
on a lizard's belly?
That sudden kind of blue
you see just for a second sometimes—
so blue that afterwards
you always think you made it up?"

"Sure," she said.
"I know that kind of blue."

Then she told me *hers*
and it was brown.
She said, "And the brown I like the best
is a dark reddish brown
that's good for mountains and for rocks.
You see it in steep cliffs a lot."

I said,
"I know that kind of brown."

Then we chose our favorite sounds.

She said hers was *bees*
but not just one or two.
She said it takes about a thousand bees
buzzing in all the fields around
to make the kind of loud bee sound
she likes.

For mine, I chose a bird I'd heard
one morning in the mountains in New Mexico
and never saw and never heard again
and couldn't even say why
I still remembered it.

She said it was all right
that I didn't know its name.

We must have named
a hundred favorite things
that afternoon.

Her favorite thing to taste
is snow and honey mixed . . .
a little more honey than snow.

Mine is bread just baked at home,
still warm.

Her favorite smell is the alfalfa
growing in this field.

Mine is *desert* rain—
not rain anywhere else.

Finally I said,
"What's your favorite time of day?"

And she said,
"Now, just about now
when I've been running in the field
and getting out of breath
and falling down
and watching ladybugs
and finding someone to play
the tell-what-your-favorite-thing-is game
and playing it and then maybe
walking back as far as the road together."

I was going to say
that sunrise is my favorite time of day

but when I thought about it
I wanted to choose *now* too.

I wasn't sure she'd let us both
choose the same thing
but she was nice about it.

She said, "We can.
That's my favorite way
to end the game."

By then it was getting late
so we walked back as far as the road
together.

Questions

1. In this story two girls talked about their favorite ladybugs and their favorite colors. What other favorite things did they describe?

2. Look at the pictures on pages 212 and 213. What favorite things from the story do these pictures show you? Which two senses (sight, hearing, touch, taste, smell) do they describe?

3. Why did one girl claim it was wrong to say that blue is someone's favorite color?

4. If *you* were describing your favorite color, what would you say?

5. Choose the correct word for each sentence.
   a. Ice cream is my favorite (desert, dessert).
   b. My cactus was found in the (desert, dessert).

Activity   Write Word Pictures

The two girls in this story used *word pictures* to describe their favorite things. A favorite color was described as "a dark reddish brown that's good for mountains and for rocks." The word pictures helped you see, hear, taste, touch, or smell each favorite thing.

Think of three of your favorite things. Write word pictures to describe them.

Some People

A poem by Rachel Field

Isn't it strange some people make
    You feel so tired inside,
Your thoughts begin to shrivel up
    Like leaves all brown and dried!

But when you're with some other ones,
    It's stranger still to find
Your thoughts as thick as fireflies
    All shiny in your mind!

Illustrated by Francis Livingston

Hope

A poem by Langston Hughes

Sometimes when I'm lonely,
Don't know why,
Keep thinkin' I won't be lonely
By and by.

Dreams

A poem by **Langston Hughes**

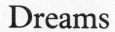

Hold fast to dreams
For if dreams die
Life is a broken-winged bird
That cannot fly.

Hold fast to dreams
For when dreams go
Life is a barren field
Frozen with snow.

Illustrated by Francis Livingston

About LANGSTON HUGHES

Langston Hughes, one of
America's great poets, came to
national attention almost by
accident. He was working as a
busboy in a hotel restaurant in
Washington, D.C. One night he
saw Vachel Lindsay, a famous
poet, eating in the restaurant.
Too shy to speak, Langston
Hughes instead dropped three
of his poems at Vachel Lindsay's
plate. That evening Mr. Lindsay
praised these poems and read
them to a large group of people.

The next morning newspaper reporters interviewed
Langston Hughes and took his picture in his busboy's
uniform. His poems appeared in the newspaper. Soon
he was publishing his work in books and newspapers.

In addition to poetry, Langston Hughes wrote
stories, plays, books, and operas. Much of his writing
is about his experiences as a member of the Black
community. His writing has helped others to understand and appreciate this experience.

Books of Poetry by Langston Hughes

The Dream Keeper
Selected Poems of Langston Hughes

The Escape

From the story *Charlotte's Web* by E. B. White

Illustrated by Garth Williams

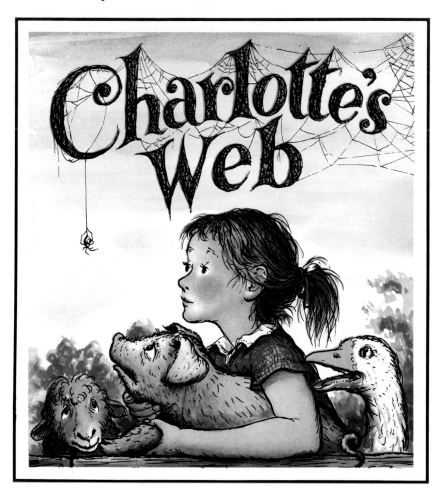

Ever since Wilbur, the runt of the pig litter, was given to Fern to raise, he has had constant love and care. He was fed from a bottle, played with, and allowed to follow Fern around like a puppy. The day came, though, when Wilbur had to be sold. Parting from Fern was made a little easier when her uncle Homer Zuckerman agreed to buy him. Wilbur would then be close by, and Fern could walk down the road to visit him in the Zuckerman barn.

One afternoon in June, when Wilbur was almost two months old, he wandered out into his small yard outside the barn. Fern had not arrived for her usual visit. Wilbur stood in the sun feeling lonely and bored.

"There's never anything to do around here," he thought. He walked slowly to his food trough and sniffed to see if anything had been overlooked at lunch. He found a small strip of potato skin and ate it. His back itched, so he leaned against the fence and rubbed against the boards. When he tired of this, he walked indoors, climbed to the top of the manure pile, and sat down. He didn't feel like going to sleep, he didn't feel like digging, he was tired of standing still, tired of lying down. "I'm less than two months old and I'm tired of living," he said. He walked out to the yard again.

"When I'm out here," he said, "there's no place to go but in. When I'm indoors, there's no place to go but out in the yard."

"That's where you're wrong, my friend, my friend," said a voice.

Wilbur looked through the fence and saw the goose standing there.

"You don't have to stay in that dirty-little dirty-little dirty-little yard," said the goose, who talked rather fast. "One of the boards is loose. Push on it, push-push-push on it, and come on out!"

"What?" said Wilbur. "Say it slower!"

"At-at-at, at the risk of repeating myself," said the goose, "I suggest that you come on out. It's wonderful out here."

"Did you say a board was loose?"

"That I did, that I did," said the goose.

Wilbur walked up to the fence and saw that the goose was right—one board was loose. He put his head down, shut his eyes, and pushed. The board gave way. In a minute he had squeezed through the fence and was standing in the long grass outside his yard. The goose chuckled.

"How does it feel to be free?" she asked.

"I like it," said Wilbur. "That is, I *guess* I like it." Actually, Wilbur felt queer to be outside his fence, with nothing between him and the big world.

"Where do you think I'd better go?"

"Anywhere you like, anywhere you like," said the goose. "Go down through the orchard, root up the sod! Go down through the garden, dig up the radishes! Root up everything! Eat grass! Look for corn! Look for oats! Run all over! Skip and dance, jump and prance! Go down through the orchard and stroll in the woods! The world is a wonderful place when you're young."

"I can see that," replied Wilbur. He gave a jump in the air, twirled, ran a few steps, stopped, looked all around, sniffed the smells of afternoon, and then set off walking down through the orchard. Pausing in the shade of an apple tree, he put his strong snout into the ground and began pushing, digging, and rooting. He felt very happy. He had plowed up quite a piece of ground before anyone noticed him. Mrs. Zuckerman was the first to see him. She saw him from the kitchen window, and she immediately shouted for the men.

"Ho-*mer*!" she cried. "Pig's out! Lurvy! Pig's out! Homer! Lurvy! Pig's out. He's down there under that apple tree."

"Now the trouble starts," thought Wilbur. "Now I'll catch it."

The goose heard the racket and she, too, started hollering. "Run-run-run downhill, make for the woods, the woods!" she shouted to Wilbur. "They'll never-never-never catch you in the woods."

The cocker spaniel heard the commotion and he ran out from the barn to join the chase. Mr. Zuckerman heard, and he came out of the machine shed where he was mending a tool. Lurvy, the hired man, heard the noise and came up from the asparagus patch where he was pulling weeds. Everybody walked toward Wilbur and Wilbur didn't know what to do. The woods seemed a long way off, and anyway, he had never been down there in the woods and wasn't sure he would like it.

"Get around behind him, Lurvy," said Mr. Zuckerman, "and drive him toward the barn! And take it easy—don't rush him! I'll go and get a bucket of slops."

The news of Wilbur's escape spread rapidly among the animals on the place. Whenever any creature broke loose on the Zuckerman's farm, the event was of great interest to the others. The goose shouted to the nearest cow that Wilbur was free, and soon all the cows knew. Then one of the cows told one of the sheep, and soon all the sheep knew. The lambs learned about it from their mothers. The horses, in their stalls in the barn, pricked up their ears when they heard the goose hollering; and soon the horses had caught on to what was happening. "Wilbur's out," they said. Every animal stirred and lifted its head and became excited to know that one of his friends had got free and was no longer penned up or tied fast.

Wilbur didn't know what to do or which way to run. It seemed as though everybody was after him. "If this is what it's like to be free," he thought, "I believe I'd rather be penned up in my own yard."

The cocker spaniel was sneaking up on him from one side, Lurvy the hired man was sneaking up on him from the other side. Mrs. Zuckerman stood ready to head him off if he started for the garden, and now Mr. Zuckerman was coming down toward him carrying a pail. "This is really awful," thought Wilbur. "Why doesn't Fern come?" He began to cry.

The goose took command and began to give orders.

"Don't just stand there, Wilbur! Dodge about, dodge about!" cried the goose. "Skip around, run toward me, slip in and out, in and out, in and out! Make for the woods! Twist and turn!"

The cocker spaniel sprang for Wilbur's hind leg. Wilbur jumped and ran. Lurvy reached out and grabbed. Mrs. Zuckerman screamed at Lurvy. The goose cheered for Wilbur. Wilbur dodged between Lurvy's legs. Lurvy missed Wilbur and grabbed the spaniel instead. "Nicely done, nicely done!" cried the goose. "Try it again, try it again!"

"Run downhill!" suggested the cows.

"Run toward me!" yelled the gander.

"Run uphill!" cried the sheep.

"Turn and twist!" honked the goose.

"Jump and dance!" said the rooster.

"Look out for Lurvy!" called the cows.

"Look out for Zuckerman!" yelled the gander.

"Watch out for the dog!" cried the sheep.

"Listen to me, listen to me!" screamed the goose.

Poor Wilbur was dazed and frightened by this hullabaloo. He didn't like being the center of all this fuss. He tried to follow the instructions his friends were giving him, but he couldn't run downhill and uphill at the same time, and he couldn't turn and twist when he was jumping and dancing, and he was crying so hard he could barely see anything that was happening. After all, Wilbur was a very young pig— not much more than a baby, really. He wished Fern were there to take him in her arms and comfort him. When he looked up and saw Mr. Zuckerman standing quite close to him, holding a pail of warm slops,

he felt relieved. He lifted his nose and sniffed. The smell was delicious—warm milk, potato skins, wheat middlings, Kellogg's Corn Flakes, and a popover left from the Zuckerman's breakfast.

"Come, pig!" said Mr. Zuckerman, tapping the pail. "Come pig!"

Wilbur took a step toward the pail.

"No-no-no!" said the goose. "It's the old pail trick, Wilbur. Don't fall for it, don't fall for it! He's trying to lure you back into captivity-ivity. He's appealing to your stomach."

Wilbur didn't care. The food smelled appetizing. He took another step toward the pail.

"Pig, pig!" said Mr. Zuckerman in a kind voice, and began walking slowly toward the barnyard, looking all about him innocently, as if he didn't know that a little white pig was following along behind him.

"You'll be sorry-sorry-sorry," called the goose.

Wilbur didn't care. He kept walking toward the pail of slops.

"You'll miss your freedom," honked the goose. "An hour of freedom is worth a barrel of slops."

Wilbur didn't care.

When Mr. Zuckerman reached the pigpen, he climbed over the fence and poured the slops into the trough. Then he pulled the loose board away from the fence, so that there was a wide hole for Wilbur to walk through.

"Reconsider, reconsider!" cried the goose.

Wilbur paid no attention. He stepped through the fence into his yard. He walked to the trough and took a long drink of slops, sucking in the milk hungrily and chewing the popover. It was good to be home again.

While Wilbur ate, Lurvy fetched a hammer and some 8-penny nails and nailed the board in place. Then he and Mr. Zuckerman leaned lazily on the fence and Mr. Zuckerman scratched Wilbur's back with a stick.

"He's quite a pig," said Lurvy.

Questions

1. Wilbur was bored at the beginning of the story. How did he feel when he escaped? How did he feel when he was discovered? How did he feel at the end of the story?

2. Did Wilbur fail in his escape? What might Wilbur say that he gained from his attempt to escape?

3. At the end of the story the goose said to Wilbur, "An hour of freedom is worth a barrel of slops." How might Wilbur have answered?

4. The goose said the same words over and over: "run-run-run" and "push-push-push" and "no-no-no." Why did the goose do that?

5. What words in the story are the *opposites* of these words?

          outdoors   captivity   contented

6. Wilbur acts the way a real pig would act, except for one thing. What is it? Do you think it helps make the story more fun to read? Tell why or why not.

Activity   Write a Letter to Wilbur

Write Wilbur a letter that will help him when he is bored. In your letter, suggest at least three things that Wilbur can do to end his boredom.

Sound of Sunshine, Sound of Rain

A story by Florence Parry Heide

Illustrated by Kenneth Longtemps

Morning Voices

It must be morning, for I hear the morning voices.

I have been dreaming of a sound that whispers *Follow me, Follow me,* but not in words. I follow the sound up and up until I feel I am floating in the air.

Now I am awake, and I listen to the voices.

My mother's voice is warm and soft as a pillow.

My sister's voice is little and sharp and high, like needles flying in the air.

I do not listen to the words but to the sound. Low, high, low, high, soft, hard, soft, hard, and then the sounds coming together at the same time and making a new sound. And with it all, the sharp sounds of my sister's heels putting holes in what I hear.

Then I hear the slamming of kitchen drawers and the banging of pans and there is no more talking.

My bed is in the living room. I reach out to feel whether my mother has laid my clothes on the chair beside my bed. They are there, and I feel the smoothness and the roughness of them.

I reach under the chair to find which shoes my mother has put there. They are my outside shoes, not my slippers, so today must be a warm day. Maybe I can go to the park.

I tap my good luck song on the wall beside my bed.

I put my feet on the floor and feel the cool wood and curl my toes against it. Then it is four steps to the table, then around the table, touching the chairs, and then seven steps to the window. I put my cheek against the window, and I can feel the warm sun. Now I am sure I can go to the park, if my sister has time to take me on her way to study.

I take my clothes into the bathroom, and I wash and dress there. Hot water, cold water, soapy water, plain water, loud water, still water. Then I make sure I have turned the faucets tight. I make sure I have buttoned all of my buttons the right way, or my sister will be cross, and maybe not have time to take me to the park.

I tap my good luck song against the door before I open it.

When I open the door, I hear the voices again. My sister's voice is like scissors cutting away at my mother's voice.

I sit at the table, and my mother gives me my breakfast. I breathe on the hot chocolate so I can feel it on my face coming back warm. I drink just a little at a time so I can keep holding the warm cup.

"Eat while it's hot," says my sister to me, loudly.

"Does he have to be so slow?" says my sister to my mother in her quiet voice. My sister thinks because I cannot see that maybe I cannot hear very well, and she talks loudly to me, and softly when she does not want me to hear, but I hear.

"You spilled," says my sister, loudly.

"I can't be late," she says in her quiet voice to my mother. "Everybody's always late but me, and I won't be late."

After breakfast I go over to the window again. When I put my cheek against the glass it is warmer than before, so today will be a good day. I tap my good luck song against the window.

My sister says she will take me to the park on her way to study. She gives me my jacket and tells me to wait for her outside on the steps.

I go down the outside steps. There are seven steps. Seven is my most magic number. Seven up, seven down, seven up, seven down. I go up and down, waiting for my sister.

My sister comes out. She takes my hand. She walks very fast, but I can still count the steps to the park, and I can still remember the turns. Someday I can go there by myself. I listen to the street noises and try to sort them out.

My sister's hand is not soft. I can feel her nails, little and sharp, like her voice, and I listen to her heels making holes in all the other sounds.

The park seems a long way off.

When we get to the park we go first to the bench. My sister waits to make sure I remember my way in the park. Fourteen steps to the bubbler. Around the bubbler, twenty steps to the curb.

I go back to the bench. I try to hurry so my sister won't have to wait long and be cross. Now seventeen steps to the phone booth, four benches on the way and I touch them all. Then I come back to my bench. My sister puts money in my pocket so I can telephone.

She talks to me and to herself.

"Filthy park," she says, and it is as if she were stepping on the words. "No grass. Trees in cages. Since when do benches and old newspapers make a park?" She pulls my jacket to straighten it.

Now she is gone and I have my morning in the sun.

I try each bench, but mine is still the best one.

I go to the bubbler and press my mouth against the water and feel it on my tongue, soft and warm. I put my finger on the place where the water comes out. I walk around and around the bubbler, and then I try to find my bench. It is one of my games. I have many games.

I walk over to the telephone booth, touching the four benches on the way. I stand inside the booth. I feel in my pocket to see if the money my sister gave me is still there. It is.

I practice dialing our number so I will be sure I have it right. Then I put my dime in and call. I let it ring two times and then I hang up and get my dime back. My sister says that way my mother will know I am all right.

I blow on the glass and it blows back to me. I tap my good luck song on it and go back to my bench.

I play one of my games. I listen to every sound and think if that sound would be able to do something to me, what it would do. Some sounds would scratch me, some would pinch me, some would push me. Some would carry me, some would crush me, and some would rock me.

A New Voice

I am sitting on my bench tapping my good luck song with my shoes when I hear the bells of an ice cream truck. I feel the money in my pocket. I have

the dime and I also have a bigger one. I know I have
enough for an ice cream bar.

I walk out to the curb, touching the cages around
the trees. I wait until the bells sound near, and I
wave.

The ice cream man stops. He is near enough for
me to touch his cart. I hold out my money.

Now I feel him seeing me, but he does not take
my money.

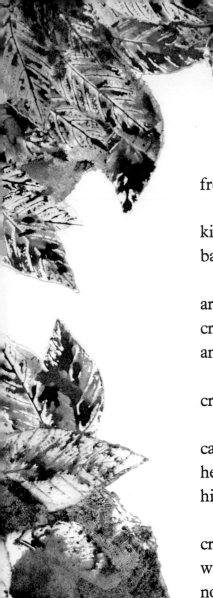

"Here," I say, but he does not take the money from me.

"Guess what?" he says, and his voice is soft and kind as fur. "Every tenth kid wins a free ice cream bar, and you're the lucky one today."

I can feel him getting off his cart and going around to open the place where he keeps his ice cream bars. I can feel him putting one near my hand and I take it. I start back to my bench.

"You gonna be okay by yourself now?" the ice cream man calls, so I know he is seeing me.

I sit on the bench. I listen for the sound of his cart starting up and his bells ringing, but I can only hear the other sounds, the regular ones. Then I hear him walking over to my bench.

I am sorry, because I only want to feel the ice cream and see how long I can make it last. I do not want anyone to sit with me, but he is sitting with me now. I am afraid I will spill and he will see me.

He starts to talk, and his voice is soft as a sweater. His name is Abram. He tells me about the park.

My sister says the trees are in cages because if they weren't in cages they wouldn't stay in such a terrible park. They'd just get up and go somewhere pretty.

Abram says the trees are in cages to keep them safe so they can grow up to be big and tall. "Like

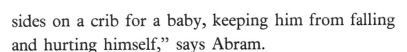

sides on a crib for a baby, keeping him from falling
and hurting himself," says Abram.

My sister says the park is ugly and dirty.

Abram says there are a few little bits of paper,
and a couple of cans and some bottles, but he says he
can squint up his eyes and all those things lying
around shine like flowers. Abram says you see what
you want to see.

My sister says the park is just for poor folks, and
that no one would ever come here if they had a
chance to go anywhere else.

Abram says the park is just for lucky people, like
him and me. He says the people who come to this
park can see things inside themselves, instead of just
what their eyes tell them.

After a while Abram goes away. He says he will
come back and look for me tomorrow. I hear his ice
cream bells go farther and farther away until I do
not hear them anymore.

While I am waiting for my sister to come for me,
I fall asleep on the bench. I have a good dream. I
dream that Abram lifts me so I can touch the leaves
of a tree. All of the leaves are songs, and they fall
around me and cover me. I am warm and soft under
the songs.

My sister shakes me awake. "You'll catch cold
lying here," she says.

The next day while I am sitting on my bench, I hear the ice cream bells and I walk out to the curb, touching the cages of the trees as I go. Abram gives me an ice cream bar and we walk together back to the bench. I do not have to touch the cages because I am with him.

After I finish my ice cream bar, Abram gives me some paper clips so I can feel them in my pocket. He shows me how I can twist them to make little shapes.

After he leaves, I feel them. There are seven paper clips.

That night I dream that someone is gathering in a big net everything in the world that makes a sound, and I am tumbled in the net with dogs and cars and whistles and busses. I try to get out of the net and my sister shakes me awake.

"Stop thrashing around," she says. "You're all tangled up in the blanket."

Something Special

The next day Abram brings me a balloon. I can feel it round and tight. It tugs at the string.

Abram says some balloons are filled with something special that makes them want to fly away, up to the sun, and this balloon is filled with that something special.

He says some people are filled with something special that makes them pull and tug, too, trying to get up and away from where they are.

241

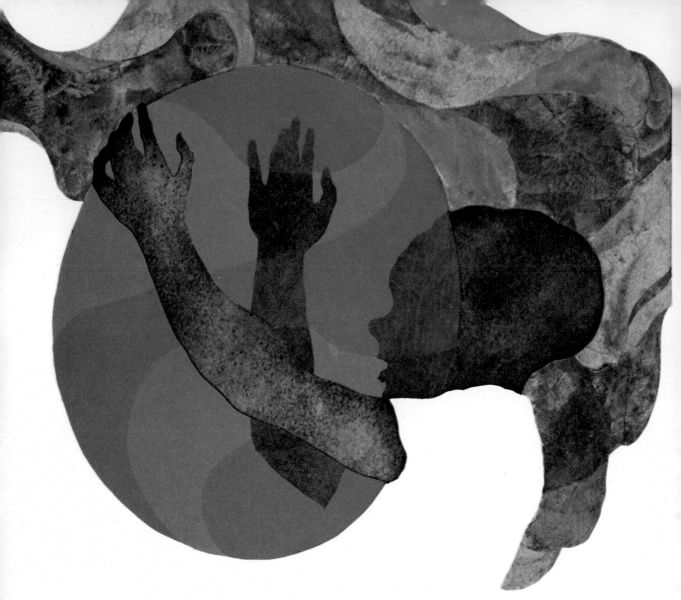

His voice is like a kitten curled on my shoulder.

He tells me my balloon is red, and then he tells me about colors.

He says colors are just like sounds. Some colors are loud, and some colors are soft, and some are big and some are little, and some are sharp and some are tender, just like sounds, just like music.

What is the best color, I wonder?

He says all colors are the same, as far as that goes. There isn't a best color, says Abram. There isn't a good color or a bad color.

Colors are just on the outside. They aren't important at all. They're just covers for things, like a blanket.

Color doesn't mean a thing, says Abram.

When my sister comes, she asks me where I got my balloon. I tell her about my friend. I hold on to the string of my balloon while we walk.

When we get home, I tie the string of my balloon to my chair.

I have a bad dream in the night. I dream that my ears are sucking in every sound in the world, so many sounds I cannot breathe. I am choking with the sounds that are pulled into me and I have to keep coughing the sounds away as they come in or I will smother.

"Here's some stuff for your cold," says my sister.

When I am awake again, I cannot tell if it is morning. I hear noises but they are not the morning noises. My sister has her quiet voice, and I do not hear the little hard sounds of her heels making holes in the morning.

She is wearing slippers. She tells my mother she is not going to go to study today.

There is no hurry about today. I reach for my balloon. The string lies on the chair, and I find the balloon on the floor, small and soft and limp. It does not float. It lies in my hand, tired and sad.

I lie there and listen to the sound of slippers on the kitchen floor.

I tap my good luck song against the wall over and over, but I hear the rain and know I will not go to the park today.

Tomorrow it will be a nice day. Tomorrow my sister will feel better, and I will go to the park and find Abram. He will make my balloon as good as new.

Now I walk over to the window and lean my head against it. The rain taps its song to me against the glass, and I tap back.

Questions

1. In this story, whose voice was like scissors cutting? Whose voice was like a kitten? Whose voice was like a pillow?

2. Abram said that you can see what you want to see. What did he mean?

3. What do you think happened to the boy on the day after the story ended?

4. The pictures do not show exactly how the boy's home looked, or how the park looked, or how the balloon looked. Why? How has the artist helped you feel as the boy felt by making the pictures as they are?

5. The boy in the story imagined that different sounds might scratch, pinch, push, crush, or rock him. He did not say what might cause each sound. For example, a tree branch *scratching* a moving car might cause a certain sound. Describe what you think might cause sounds that would pinch, push, crush, or rock.

Activity   Draw a Picture of the Park

Draw a picture of the park as Abram described it. Add things that you think Abram might see in the park, but that he did not talk about.

The Turkey or the Eagle?

I'm a true native of America.

When the United States first declared itself a free country, its leaders felt that the new nation needed a symbol. The leaders wanted a symbol that would stand for the ideals that their new country was fighting for. From July 1776 until June 1782, many ideas were suggested.

One idea was the Greek hero Hercules, who is thought to be very strong and brave. Another idea was Moses, who is said to have led the people of Israel out of Egypt and into the Promised Land. A third idea was Liberty and Justice drawn as strong women overcoming the English king, George.

The United States Congress did not like any of these ideas. Then, in 1782, a Philadelphian named William Barton drew a picture that showed a golden eagle as the symbol of the new country. Secretary of Congress Charles Thompson changed the golden eagle to the American bald eagle.

I'm a true native, too.

After making a few more changes to Mr. Barton's design, Secretary Thompson presented the design to Congress. Congress liked it. On June 20, 1782, the American bald eagle became the official symbol of the new United States of America.

Right away, many people disagreed with the choice of the bald eagle. These people thought that

246   Illustrated by Ed Parker

the American wild turkey would have been a more fitting choice. The argument between these two groups has continued to this very day. Read why each side believes its choice to be the right one. Then decide for yourself.

Wild Turkey

People who wanted the wild turkey pointed out that it was a true American. The bird had always been admired by the Indians. When colonists came to the eastern shores, the wild turkey quickly became a favorite. The colonists thought that it was one of the most beautiful birds in the New World. The wild turkey's bronze-green feathers were prized as decorations for the colonists' hats or blankets.

People also thought that the wild turkey was a proud bird. Its great size and weight seemed to give it a stately appearance. A full-grown wild turkey weighs between ten and thirty pounds. It is four feet long from the tip of its beak to its tail feathers and stands three feet tall. The bird's broad wings can open to a length of five feet from one wing tip to the other.

Wild turkeys are also known for their swiftness and sharp senses. Wild turkeys do not fly very often, but they *do* run—up to 20 miles an hour. They also have very sharp eyesight and hearing. Hunters say that a wild turkey can easily lead them into wild forest country and then get away.

Ben Franklin summed up the argument for the wild turkey by pointing out that it was not only a handsome and useful bird, but also a "respectable" one. The wild turkey gathers its own food supply of small nuts, seeds, and insects. The bald eagle has been known to take prey caught by another bird.

Bald Eagle

Many people agreed with the choice of the bald eagle as the symbol of the United States. They said that it, too, was a true American, for the bald eagle can be found only in North America. With its shining white head feathers and its deep brown wings, many people believe it to be a very handsome bird.

An American bald eagle stands three feet tall from beak tip to *talons,* or claws. Those same talons and hooked beak, along with the bird's large pale eyes, make the American bald eagle look fierce and brave. With outspread wings, the American bald eagle measures seven feet long and seems to fly effortlessly. Many people say that the bald eagle flies so high that it disappears from sight.

Those people who favor the eagle point out that it feeds mostly on fish and other small animals. They say that the eagle takes prey from other birds only when the food supplies are short. President Kennedy said this about the bald eagle, "The fierce beauty and proud independence of this great bird aptly symbolize the strength and freedom of America."

Questions

1. If you were voting for our national symbol, which would you choose, the turkey or the eagle? Why?

2. If you were choosing another animal to represent the United States, which animal would you choose? Why?

Activities

1. **Make a Poster**

    Design and draw a poster to support your candidate for the symbol of the United States. Your poster should contain a picture of your animal and a *slogan,* or catchy phrase, that will make people want to support your choice.

2. **Write a Summary**

    Write a one-paragraph summary of your argument for the bald eagle or the wild turkey. The summary should state the main reasons for your choice. Try to give at least three reasons in your paragraph.

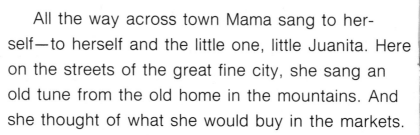

Mexicali Soup

A story by Kathryn Hitte and William D. Hayes
Illustrated by Bill and Judy Anderson

All the way across town Mama sang to herself—to herself and the little one, little Juanita. Here on the streets of the great fine city, she sang an old tune from the old home in the mountains. And she thought of what she would buy in the markets.

Only the best of everything. Potatoes and peppers—the best! Tomatoes and onions—the best! The best garlic. The best celery. And then, cooked all together, ah! The best soup in the world! Mama's Special Mexicali Soup. The soup that always made everyone say, "Mama makes the best soup in the world."

"Ah, sí!" Mama thought with a smile. "Yes! Our supper tonight will be a very special supper for my Rosie and Antonio and Juan and Manuel and Maria, and for the little one—and for Papa, too. A very special supper of my Mexicali Soup."

"Mama! Yoo-hoo, Mama!"

There was the fine new school building where Juan and Manuel and Maria went to school, and there was Maria with her new city friend, waving and calling.

"Wait a minute, Mama!" Maria came running to put her schoolbooks in the stroller with Juanita. "Mama, may I play a while at Marjorie's house? Please?"

"Very well," Mama said. "A while. But do not be late for supper, Maria. I am making my special soup tonight."

"Mmmm-mmm, Mexicali Soup!" Maria said. Then she looked thoughtful. Then she frowned. "But—Mama?"

"Yes, Maria?"

"Mama, there are such a lot of potatoes in your Mexicali Soup."

"Of course," Mama said, smiling.

"Marjorie doesn't eat potatoes. Her mother doesn't eat them. Her sister doesn't eat them. Potatoes are too fattening, Mama. They are too fattening for many people in the city. I think we should do what others do here. We are no longer in the mountains of the West, Mama, where everyone eats potatoes. We are in the city now. So would you—Mama, would you please leave out the potatoes?"

"No potatoes," Mama said thoughtfully. She looked at Maria's anxious face. She shrugged. "Well, there are plenty of good things in the Mexicali Soup without potatoes. I will add more of everything else. It will still make good soup."

Maria kissed Mama's cheek. "Of course it will, Mama. You make the best soup in the world."

Mama went on with Juanita to the markets, to the street of little markets, thinking aloud as she went. "Tomatoes, onions, celery. Red peppers, chili peppers, good and hot. And garlic. But no potatoes."

Mama went to Mr. Santini's little market for the best tomatoes and celery. She went to Mr. Vierra's little market for the best onions and garlic. "And the peppers," she said to Juanita. "We will buy the peppers from Antonio. Our own Antonio, at the market of Mr. Fernandez. Here is the place. Ah! What beautiful peppers!"

Antonio came hurrying out of the store to the little stand on the sidewalk. "Let me help you, Mama! I hope you want something very good for our supper tonight. I get very hungry working here," Antonio said.

"Ah, *sí!*" Mama said. "Yes, Antonio. For tonight—something special!" She reached for the hot red peppers strung above her head. "Mexicali Soup."

"Hey! That's great," Antonio exclaimed. Then he looked thoughtful. Then he frowned. "But— Mama—"

"Yes?" Mama said, putting some peppers on the scale.

"Well—Mama, you use a lot of hot peppers in your soup."

"Of course," Mama said, smiling.

"A lot," Antonio repeated. "Too many, Mama. People here don't do that. They don't cook that way. They don't eat the way we did in the mountains of the West. I know, Mama. I have worked here for weeks now, after school and Saturdays. And in all that time, Mama, I have not sold as many hot peppers to other ladies as you use in a week."

"*Mamacita*," Antonio said. "Please don't put hot peppers in the soup."

"No peppers," Mama said thoughtfully. She looked at Antonio's anxious face. "Well—" Mama shrugged. "There are plenty of good things in the soup without peppers. I will add more of something else. It will still make good soup."

Antonio took the peppers out of the scale and put them back on the stand. "Of course it will, Mama." He kissed her cheek. "Everyone knows you make the best soup in the world."

Mama went on with Juanita toward home. "Tomatoes, onions, garlic, celery," she said to herself. "Yes. I can still make a good soup with those." She hummed softly to herself as she crossed a

street blocked off from traffic, a street that was only for play.

"Hey, Mama! *Mamacita*!"

Juan and Manuel left the game of stickball in the play street. They raced each other to the spot where Mama stood.

"Oh, boy! Food!" said Juan when he saw the bags in the stroller. He opened one of the bags. "Tomatoes and celery—I know what that means."

"Me, too," said Manuel. He peeked into the other bag. "Onions and garlic. Mexicali Soup! Right, Mama?" Manuel rubbed his stomach and grinned. Then he looked thoughtful. Then he frowned. "But, Mama—listen, Mama."

"I am listening," Mama said.

"Well, I think we use an awful lot of onions," Manuel said. "They don't use so many onions in the lunchroom at school, or at the Boy's Club picnics. You know, Mama, they have different ways of doing things here, different from the ways of our town on the side of the mountain. I think we should try new ways. I think we shouldn't use so many onions. *Mamacita*, please make the Mexicali Soup without onions."

"Manuel is right!" Juan said. "My teacher said only today there is nothing that cannot be changed, and there is nothing so good that it cannot be made better, if we will only try. I think there may be better ways of making soup than our old way. Make the soup tonight without tomatoes, Mama!"

"No tomatoes?" Mama said. "And no onions? In Mexicali Soup?" Mama looked at the anxious faces of Juan and Manuel. Then she shrugged. She closed the two bags of groceries carefully. She pushed the stroller away from the play street. She shrugged again.

Voices came after her. Juan's voice said, "We will be hungry for your soup tonight, Mama!" Manuel's voice called, "*Mamacita*! You make the best soup in the world!"

In the big kitchen at home, Mama put the groceries on the table by the stove. She hummed a little soft tune that only Mama could hear. She stood looking at the groceries. No potatoes. No peppers. Tomatoes—Mama pushed the tomatoes aside. Onions—she pushed the onions aside.

Mama sat down and looked at what was left.

The front door clicked open and shut. Rosie came into the kitchen. Rosita, the young lady of the family.

"Hi, Mama. Oh, Mama—I hope I'm in time! I heard you were making—" Rosie stopped to catch her breath. She frowned at the groceries on the table. "All the way home I heard it. The boys and Maria—they all told me—and Mama! I want to ask you—please! No garlic."

Mama stopped humming.

Rosie turned up her nose and spread out her hands. "No garlic. Please. Listen, Mama. Last night, when my friend took me to dinner, I had such a fine soup! Delicious! The place was so elegant, Mama—so refined. So expensive. And no garlic at all in the soup!"

Rosie bent over and kissed Mama's cheek. "Just leave out the garlic, *Mamacita*. You make the best soup in the world."

A deep voice and many other voices called all at once, and the front door shut with a bang. "Mama! We are home, Mama!" Then all of them, Juan and Manuel and Antonio, with Maria pulling Papa by the hand—all of them came to stand in the kitchen doorway.

Papa reached for the baby, the little Juanita, and swung her onto his shoulders. "I have heard of something special," Papa said. "I have heard we are having Mexicali Soup tonight."

Mama said nothing. But Mama's eyes flashed fire. She waited.

"Your soup, Mama—" Papa said. "It is simply the best soup in the world!"

"Ah, *sí!* But you want me to leave out something?" Mama's voice rose high. "The celery,
perhaps? You want me to make my Mexicali Soup
without the celery?"

Papa raised his eyebrows. "Celery?" Papa
opened his hands wide and shrugged. "What is
celery? It is a little nothing! Put it in or leave it out,
Mamacita—it does not matter. The soup will be
just as—"

"Enough!" Mama said. "Out of my kitchen—all
of you!" Mama waved her arms wide in the air.
The fire in Mama's eyes flashed again. "I am
busy! I am busy getting your supper. I will call
you. Go."

"But, Mama," said Rosie, "we always help you
with—"

"No!" Mama said. "Out!"

Rosie and Juan and Manuel, Antonio and
Maria, and Papa with the baby, tiptoed away to
the living room.

There was only silence coming from the
kitchen. Then, the sound of a quiet humming.
Soon the humming mixed with the clatter of plates
and spoons, the good sounds of the table being
set for supper.

The humming turned into singing. Mama was
singing a happy song from the old home in the
mountains. Juan and Manuel, Antonio and Maria,
Rosie and Papa, looked at one another and smiled
and nodded. Mama was singing.

Then from the kitchen Mama's voice called to them. "The soup is finished. Your supper is ready. Come and eat now."

"Ah! That is what I like to hear," said Papa, jumping up with Juanita. "The soup is ready before I have even begun to smell it cooking."

"Mmm-mmm!" said Juan and Manuel, racing for the big kitchen table.

"Mmm-mmm!" said Maria and Antonio and Rosie when they saw the steaming bowls on the table. "Mama makes the best soup in the world."

But what was the matter?

"This doesn't look like Mexicali Soup," said Maria, staring at the bowl before her.

"It doesn't smell like Mexicali Soup," said Antonio, sniffing the steam that rose from his bowl.

"It doesn't taste like Mexicali Soup," said Juan and Manuel, sipping a sip from their spoons.

"This is not Mexicali Soup," said Rosie, setting her spoon down hard with a clang. "This is nothing but hot water!"

Everyone looked at Mama.

Mama smiled and hummed the old tune from the mountains.

"You have forgotten to bring the soup, *Mamacita*?" suggested Papa.

"No," Mama said, still smiling. "The soup is in your bowls. And it is just what you wanted. I made the soup the way my family asked me to make it.

"I left out the potatoes that Maria does not want. I left out the peppers that Antonio does not want. I left out the tomatoes that Juan does not want. I left out the onions that Manuel does not want. For Rosita, I left out the garlic. And for Papa, I left out the celery, the little nothing that does not matter.

"The *new* Mexicali Soup! It is so simple! So quick! So easy to make," Mama said. "You just leave everything out of it."

Questions

1. What are the two recipes for Mama's Special Mexicali Soup? Write the old recipe and the new recipe.

2. Tell what Mama was thinking when:
   a. Mama's eyes flashed fire.
   b. Mama smiled and hummed the old tune from the mountains.

3. What lesson do you think the family learned from Mama's new Mexicali Soup? Do you think it is a useful lesson? Tell why or why not.

4. Complete the sentences with words from the story.
   a. When Antonio was worried, his face was _____.
   b. When Rosita told about an expensive place to eat, she said it was _____ and _____.

Activity   Write a Cast of Characters

Cast of Characters

Mama
Juanita

If you were making *Mexicali Soup* into a play, you would need a *cast of characters,* which is a list of all the actors in the play. Finish the cast of characters started here. List all the characters in the order in which they appear in the story.

BOOKSHELF

The Great Bamboozlement by Jane Flory. Houghton Mifflin, 1982. Set in pioneer days, a family trades their Pennsylvania farm for a floating store and sets off down the Monongahela River only to find themselves in the middle of trouble.

A Dog on Barkham Street by Mary Stolz. Harper & Row, 1960. Edward has two problems—not having a dog and being hounded by Martin, the bully of Barkham Street. Martin's side of the story is told in another book, *The Bully of Barkham Street.*

Do You Have the Time, Lydia? by Evaline Ness. E. P. Dutton, 1971. Lydia starts many projects, but she never finishes what she begins. When her brother asks her to build a box car with him, Lydia never seems to have the time to help.

Sadako and the Thousand Paper Cranes by Eleanor Coerr. G. P. Putnam's, 1977. While in a hospital, Sadako begins to fold paper cranes. She hopes her wish for health will be granted if she can fold a thousand cranes.

Three Wishes by Lucille Clifton. Viking Press, 1976. When Zenobia finds a penny with her birth year on it, her friend Victor tells her she will be granted three wishes.

5 What a Character!

Spunky Ramona

From the story *Ramona the Brave* by Beverly Cleary
Illustrated by Jennie Williams

Ramona Geraldine Quimby is convinced nobody loves her. Even the family cat, Picky-picky, keeps away from her. Ramona likes being a little different though. She signs her last name with a special Q: ⌇, and she can draw better than anyone in her first grade class. Then one day a girl named Susan copies an owl Ramona is drawing, and the teacher, Mrs. Griggs, picks up Susan's owl to praise. Terribly angry, Ramona scrunches up Susan's owl. Later she has to apologize in front of the class. Ramona begins to hate school. If only her older sister Beezus felt the same way!

One afternoon Mrs. Griggs handed each member of Room One a long sealed envelope. "These are your progress reports for you to take home to your parents," she said.

Ramona made up her mind then and there that she was not going to show any progress report to her mother and father if she could get out of it. As soon as

she reached home, she hid her envelope at the bottom
of a drawer under her summer playclothes. Then she
got out paper and crayons and went to work on the
kitchen table. On each sheet of paper she drew in
black crayon a careful outline of an animal: a mouse
on one sheet, a bear on another, a turtle on a third.
Ramona loved to crayon and crayoning made her
troubles fade away. When she had filled ten pages with
outlines of animals, she found her father's stapler and
fastened the paper together to make a book. Ramona

could make an amazing number of things with paper, crayons, staples, and Scotch tape. Bee's wings to wear on her wrists, a crown to wear on her head, a paper catcher's mask to cover her face.

"What are you making?" asked her mother.

"A coloring book," said Ramona. "You won't buy me one."

"That's because the art teacher who talked to the P.T.A. said coloring books were not creative. She said children needed to be free and creative and draw their own pictures."

"I am," said Ramona. "I am drawing a coloring book. Howie has a coloring book, and I want one too."

"I guess Howie's mother missed that meeting." Mrs. Quimby picked up Ramona's coloring book and studied it. "Why, Ramona," she said, sounding pleased, "you must take after your father. You draw unusually well for a girl your age."

"I know." Ramona was not bragging. She was being honest. She knew her drawing was better than most of the baby work done in Room One. So was her printing. She went to work coloring her turtle green, her mouse brown. Filling in outlines was not very interesting, but it was soothing. Ramona was so busy that by dinnertime she had forgotten her hidden progress report.

Ramona forgot until Beezus laid her long white envelope on the table after the dessert of canned peaches and store macaroons. "Mr. Cardoza gave us our progress reports," she announced.

Mr. Quimby tore open the envelope and pulled out the yellow sheet of paper. "M-m-m. Very good, Beezus. I'm proud of you."

"What did he say?" Beezus asked. Ramona could tell that Beezus was eager to have the family hear the nice things Mr. Cardoza had to say about her.

"He said, 'Beatrice has shown marked improvement in math. She is willing and a conscientious pupil, who gets along well with her peers. She is a pleasure to have in the classroom.'"

"May I please be excused?" asked Ramona and did not wait for an answer.

"Just a minute, young lady," said Mr. Quimby.

"Yes, what about your progress report?" asked Mrs. Quimby.

"Oh . . . that old thing," said Ramona.

"Yes, that old thing." Mr. Quimby looked amused, which annoyed Ramona. "Bring it here," he said.

Ramona faced her father. "I don't want to."

Mr. Quimby was silent. The whole family was silent, waiting. Even Picky-picky, who had been washing his face, paused, one paw in the air, and waited. Ramona turned and walked slowly to her room and slowly returned with the envelope. Scowling, she thrust it at her father who tore it open.

"Does Beezus have to hear?" she asked.

"Beezus, you may be excused," said Mrs. Quimby. "Run along and do your homework."

Ramona knew that Beezus was in no hurry to run along and do her homework. Beezus was going to listen, that's what Beezus was going to do. Ramona scowled more ferociously as her father pulled out the sheet of yellow paper.

"If you don't look out, your face might freeze that way," said Mr. Quimby, which did not help. He studied the yellow paper and frowned. He handed it to Mrs. Quimby, who read it and frowned.

"Well," said Ramona, unable to stand the suspense, "what does it say?" She would have grabbed it and tried to read it herself, but she knew it was written in cursive.

Mrs. Quimby read, "'Ramona's letter formation is excellent, and she is developing good word-attacking skills.'"

Ramona relaxed. This did not sound so bad, even though she had never thought of reading as attacking words. She rather liked the idea.

Mrs. Quimby read on. "'She is learning her numbers readily.'"

That mitten counting, thought Ramona with scorn.

"'However, Ramona sometimes shows more interest in the seatwork of others than in her own. She needs to learn to keep her hands to herself. She also needs to work on self-control in the classroom.'"

"I do not!" Ramona was angry at the unfairness of her teacher's report. What did Mrs. Griggs think she had been working on? She hardly ever raised her hand anymore, and she never spoke out the way she used to. And she wasn't really interested in Davy's seatwork. She was trying to help him because he was having such a hard time.

"Now, Ramona." Mrs. Quimby's voice was gentle. "You must try to grow up."

Ramona raised her voice. "What do you think I'm doing?"

"You don't have to be so noisy about it," said Mr. Quimby.

Of course, Beezus had to come butting in to see what all the fuss was about. "What did Mrs. Griggs say?" she wanted to know, and it was easy to see she knew that what Mr. Cardoza had said was better.

"You mind your own business," said Ramona.

"Ramona, don't talk that way." Mr. Quimby's voice was mild.

"I will *too* talk that way," said Ramona. "I'll talk any way I want!"

"Ramona!" Mr. Quimby's voice held a warning.

Ramona was defiant. "Well, I will!" Nothing could possibly get any worse. She might as well say anything she pleased.

"Now see here, young lady—" began Mr. Quimby.

Ramona had had enough. She had been miserable the whole first grade, and she no longer cared what happened. She wanted to do something bad. She wanted to do something terrible that would shock her whole family, something that would make them sit up and take notice. "I'm going to say a bad word!" she shouted with a stamp of her foot.

That silenced her family. Picky-picky stopped washing and left the room. Mr. Quimby looked surprised and—how could he be so disloyal?—a little amused. This made Ramona even angrier. Beezus looked interested and curious. After a moment Mrs. Quimby said quietly, "Go ahead, Ramona, and say the bad word if it will make you feel any better."

Ramona clenched her fists and took a deep breath. "Guts!" she yelled. "*Guts! Guts! Guts!*" There. That should show them.

Unfortunately, Ramona's family was not shocked and horrified as Ramona had expected. They laughed. All three of them laughed. They tried to hide it, but they laughed.

"It isn't funny!" shouted Ramona. "Don't you dare laugh at me!" Bursting into tears, she threw herself face down on the couch. She kicked and she pounded the cushions with her fists. Everyone was against her. Nobody liked her. Even the cat did not like her. The room was silent, and Ramona had the satisfaction of knowing she had stopped their laughing. She heard responsible old Beezus go to her room to do her responsible old homework. Her parents continued to sit in silence, but Ramona was past caring what anyone did. She cried harder than she ever had cried in her life. She cried until she was limp and exhausted.

Then Ramona felt her mother's hand on her back. "Ramona," she said gently, "what are we going to do with you?"

With red eyes, a swollen face, and a streaming nose, Ramona sat up and glared at her mother. "Love me!" Her voice was fierce with hurt. Shocked at her own words, she buried her face in the pillow. She had no tears left.

"Dear heart," said Mrs. Quimby. "We *do* love you."

Ramona sat up and faced her mother, who looked tired, as if she had been through many scenes with Ramona and knew many more lay ahead. "You do

not. You love Beezus." There. She had said it right out loud. For years she had wanted to tell her parents how she felt.

Mr. Quimby wiped Ramona's nose on a Kleenex, which he then handed to her. She clenched it in her fist and glowered at her parents.

"Of course we love Beezus," said Mrs. Quimby. "We love you both."

"You love her more," said Ramona. "A whole lot more." She felt better for having said the words, getting them off her chest, as grown-ups would say.

"Love isn't like a cup of sugar that gets used up," said Mrs. Quimby. "There is enough to go around. Loving Beezus doesn't mean we don't have enough love left for you."

"You don't laugh at Beezus all the time," said Ramona.

"They used to," said Beezus, who was unable to stay away from this family discussion. "They always laughed at the funny things I did, and it used to make me mad."

Ramona sniffed and waited for Beezus to continue.

Beezus was serious. "Like the time when I was about your age and thought frankincense and myrrh were something the three Wise Men were bringing to the baby Jesus to put on his rash like that stuff Mom used on you when you were a baby. Mom and Dad laughed, and Mom told all her friends, and they laughed too."

"Oh, dear," said Mrs. Quimby. "I had no idea I upset you that much."

"Well, you did," said Beezus, still grumpy over the memory. "And there was the time I thought toilet water was water out of the toilet. You practically had hysterics."

"Now you're exaggerating," said Mrs. Quimby.

Comforted by this unexpected support from her sister, Ramona scrubbed her face with her soggy Kleenex. "Mama, if you really do love me, why do I have to go to school?" At the same time she wondered how she could find out what frankincense and myrrh were without letting anyone know of her ignorance. She had always thought in a vague sort of way that they were something expensive like perfume done up in an extra-fancy Christmas wrapping.

"Ramona, everyone has to go to school," Mrs. Quimby answered. "Loving you has nothing to do with it."

"Then why can't I be in the other first grade, the one in Room Two?" Ramona asked. "Mrs. Griggs doesn't like me."

"Of course she likes you," contradicted Mrs. Quimby.

"No, she doesn't," said Ramona. "If she liked me, she wouldn't make me tell Susan in front of the whole class that I was sorry I scrunched her owl, and she would ask me to lead the Pledge Allegiance. And she wouldn't say bad things about me on my progress report."

"I told you Mrs. Griggs was great on apologies," Beezus reminded her family. "And she will get around to asking Ramona to lead the flag salute. She asks everybody."

"But Beezus, you got along with Mrs. Griggs when you had her," said Mrs. Quimby.

"I guess so," said Beezus. "She wasn't my favorite teacher, though."

"What was wrong with her?" asked Mrs. Quimby.

"There wasn't anything really wrong with her, I guess," answered Beezus. "She just wasn't very exciting is all. She wasn't mean or anything like that. We just seemed to go along doing our work, and that was it."

"Was she unfair?" asked Mrs. Quimby.

Beezus considered the question. "No, but I was the kind of child she liked. You know . . . neat and dependable."

"I bet you never wasted paste," said Ramona, who was not a paste waster herself. Too much paste was likely to spoil a piece of artwork.

"No," admitted Beezus. "I wasn't that type."

Ramona persisted. "*Why* can't I change to Room Two?"

Mr. Quimby took over. "Because Mrs. Griggs is teaching you to read and do arithmetic, and because the things she said about you are fair. You do need to learn self-control and to keep your hands to yourself. There are all kinds of teachers in the world just as there are all kinds of other people, and you must learn to get along with them. Maybe Mrs. Griggs doesn't understand how you feel, but you aren't always easy to understand. Did you ever think of that?"

"Please, Daddy," begged Ramona. "Please don't make me go back to Room One."

"Buck up, Ramona," said Mr. Quimby. "Show us your spunk."

Ramona felt too exhausted to show anyone her spunk, but for some reason her father's order made her feel better. If her mother had said, Poor baby, she would have felt like crying again. Mrs. Quimby led her from the room and, skipping her bath, helped her into bed. Before the light was turned out, Ramona noticed that *Wild Animals of Africa* had been returned to her bookcase.

"Stay with me, Mama," coaxed Ramona, dreading solitude, darkness, and the gorilla in the book. Mrs. Quimby turned off the light and sat down on the bed.

"Mama?"

"Yes, Ramona?"

"Isn't *guts* a bad word?"

Mrs. Quimby thought for a moment. "I wouldn't say it's exactly a bad word. It isn't the nicest word in the world, but there are much worse words. Now go to sleep."

Ramona wondered what could be worse than guts.

Questions

1. Tell two things that made Ramona unhappy.

2. List at least two things Ramona did to try to make herself feel better.

3. Why did Ramona feel better at the end of the story?

4. These words describe Ramona: **creative, defiant, conscientious, miserable.** Match a word with the sentence that gives its meaning.
    a. Ramona always worked carefully on her drawings.
    b. Ramona refused to obey her father.
    c. After supper, Ramona felt very unhappy.
    d. Ramona made up a new way to sign her name.

5. The title of this story, "Spunky Ramona," tells that Ramona is fearless and brave. What was one thing Ramona did because she was spunky?

6. Do you think that Ramona's progress report was fair? Why or why not?

Activity   Tell About a Terrible, Funny Time

"It seems funny now, but it didn't seem funny when it happened." Suppose *you* said that several years from now. Write or draw what you might be talking about.

About BEVERLY CLEARY

Though known for her humorous stories, Beverly Cleary says, "I don't try to be funny. Because of some lucky quirk . . . my stories turn out to be humorous."

Beverly Cleary has written several books about Ramona Quimby and her family. She has also written a series of books about Henry Huggins. Henry, Ramona, and their friends all live in the same imaginary neighborhood. It is much the same as the neighborhood in which Beverly Cleary grew up. The characters in her stories are similar to children she knew, and ideas for her stories often come from events in her own life.

Beverly Cleary didn't enjoy reading until she was eight. Then she went to the library often. After college, she became a librarian. Later, as an author, she wrote the books she had longed to read as a child.

More Books by Beverly Cleary

Ramona Quimby, Age 8
Runaway Ralph
Ralph S. Mouse
Dear Mr. Henshaw

My Sister Jane

A poem by Ted Hughes

And I say nothing—no, not a word
About our Jane. Haven't you heard?
She's a bird, a bird, a bird, a bird.
Oh it never would do to let folks know
My sister's nothing but a great big crow.

Each day (we daren't send her to school)
She pulls on stockings of thick blue wool
To make her pin crow legs look right,
Then fits a wig of curls on tight,
And dark spectacles—a huge pair
To cover her very crowy stare.
Oh it never would do to let folks know
My sister's nothing but a great big crow.

When visitors come she sits upright
(With her wings and her tail tucked out of sight).
They think her queer but extremely polite.
Then when the visitors have gone
She whips out her wings and with her wig on
Whirls through the house at the height of your
    head—
Duck, duck, or she'll knock you dead.
Oh it never would do to let folks know
My sister's nothing but a great big crow.

Illustrated by Mila Lazarevich

At meals whatever she sees she'll stab it—
Because she's a crow and that's a crow habit.
My mother says, "Jane! Your manners! Please!"
Then she'll sit quietly on the cheese,
Or play the piano nicely by dancing on the keys—
Oh it never would do to let folks know
My sister's nothing but a great big crow.

Folk Heroes of the United States

Back in the days when the United States was young, workers amused themselves by swapping tall tales about their favorite heroes. A *tall tale* is a story that may have a *little* bit of truth in it. Then the truth is s-t-r-e-t-c-h-e-d beyond belief to make a story that is just plain fun. Every region of the United States has its own tall tales and its own heroes. Here are some tall tales and the regions from which they came.

Illustrated by Betsy Day

THE NORTH: Tales of Paul Bunyan

Across the top of Minnesota, Wisconsin, and Michigan is a huge evergreen forest called the North Woods. Cutting down trees for lumber, or *logging,* is an important industry here. In the past, loggers cut down trees with axes and handsaws—a hard, dangerous job. Stories grew up about the great strength and daring of loggers, especially that greatest logger of them all—Paul Bunyan!

Paul Bunyan was the biggest, strongest, toughest logger who ever lived. At birth, Paul weighed 86 pounds. When he was full grown, he was taller than the tallest pine tree.

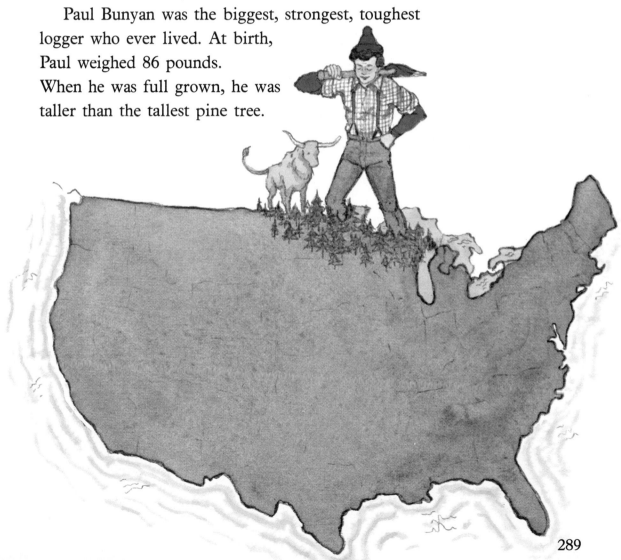

Paul began logging in Maine. He was so fast at cutting down trees that he soon ran out of woods in that state. So he hired a crew and headed west. Paul and his crew set up camp along the Onion River. Paul's crew, of course, was a *big* crew. It had many men, and the men were *big* (though not as big as Paul). Paul's camp was huge. The tables where the loggers ate were so long that the waiters wore roller skates when they served meals. Paul had to dig the Great Lakes so his men would have plenty of water to drink!

Paul didn't remain at the Onion River camp, however. After logging the North Woods, Paul turned to North Dakota. "Aha!" he thought. "A nice flat state—perfect for growing wheat!" In those days, however, North Dakota was covered with trees so tall that it took a week to see up to their tops. In no time at all, Paul Bunyan had cut down those trees and pounded their stumps right into the ground!

THE SOUTH: Tales of John Henry

While loggers in the North swapped tales about Paul Bunyan and his mighty axe, "steel-drivin' men" in the South boasted of John Henry and his mighty hammer. "Steel-drivin' men" were railroad workers who had the most dangerous job of all—blasting through mountains to make railroad tunnels. To do this job, they drove long steel rods deep into solid rock to make holes for dynamite. Those holes had to be about seven feet deep!

Some people say there really *was* a John Henry. They say he was a "steel-drivin' man" of great size and strength. John Henry worked for the Chesapeake and Ohio Railroad in West Virginia during the 1870s. Through the years the tales that were told about him grew taller and taller.

People in the South say that when John Henry was born, lightning split the air. The earth shook, and the Mississippi River ran upstream 1,000 miles. John Henry weighed 44 pounds when he was born. After his first meal, he went looking for work. He got a job with the C&O Railroad, laying track and blasting tunnels.

People say that John Henry died a hero's death. His crew had put him against a steam drill in a steel-driving race. John Henry won—but he died that night of a burst blood vessel.

THE EAST: Tales of Stormalong

In the late 1700s, New England's seaports were busy places. At about this time New England sailors began telling tales about a sailor named Alfred Bulltop Stormalong. Old Stormalong, or Stormy as he was called, was a daring and skillful sailor. It was

even said that he was born with ocean water flowing through his veins.

Like Paul Bunyan and John Henry, Old Stormalong was a huge man. Old Stormy was as tall as a whale standing on end. Only one ship was big enough for him. That was the *Courser*. The *Courser* was so big that it took a person 24 hours to make the trip from front to back on horseback. The ship's masts were so tall that they were hinged to let the sun and moon pass by.

One day, Stormalong and his crew were fishing in the Atlantic Ocean. The captain decided it was time to move on. He ordered them to pull up the anchor and set sail. The crew could not make the anchor move. Old Stormy jumped overboard to take a look. He found a giant squid holding the anchor in fifty of its slimy arms. The squid's other fifty arms grabbed the sea bottom. A huge fight took place. When the water cleared, the anchor was free. Stormalong had tied every one of the squid's hundred arms into a double knot.

THE WEST: Tales of Pecos Bill and Slue-Foot Sue

In the days of the Old West, cowhands drove cattle a long way to market. At night they would gather around the campfire and tell stories about Pecos Bill and his bride Slue-Foot Sue. Pecos Bill was raised by a coyote and taught by a grizzly bear.

Pecos Bill went on to teach ranchers a thing or two. It was Pecos Bill who invented the lasso, cattle branding, the cattle roundup, and the rodeo. He was perhaps the most remarkable man who ever rode the range.

Slue-Foot Sue, Bill's bride, was remarkable, too. It was love at first sight when Bill saw Sue riding a catfish the size of a whale down the Rio Grande. Sue and Bill raised a large family. They even adopted a litter of coyote pups. People said the pups were so smart that two of them were elected to Congress!

Questions

1. Think about the tall-tale heroes of the North, South, East, and West. How are they alike? Give at least two examples.

2. Who is your favorite tall-tale hero? Why did you choose that hero?

Activities

1. **Retell a Story**

   Choose one of your favorite American folk songs. Write the story the song tells.

2. **Make a Bulletin Board**

   Choose a tall-tale hero from the stories here or from library books. Cut pictures from magazines, or draw your own, that show the region of your hero's "birth." With your classmates make a bulletin board of the regions of the United States and their tall-tale heroes.

Four Fearsome Critters

Folklore collected by Alvin Schwartz
Illustrated by Ed Taber

It is said that there are strange creatures
all around us—
    in the woods,
        in the mountains,
            in the lakes,
                everywhere.
Ranchers, woodcutters, hunters, and other people
see these creatures again and again.
Or so they say.
Here is what they tell of them.

hide-behind

When a hunter enters the deepest woods
and does not come back,
most people say the hunter got lost.
But some say the hunter was grabbed
by a hide-behind
that hid behind a tree.

296

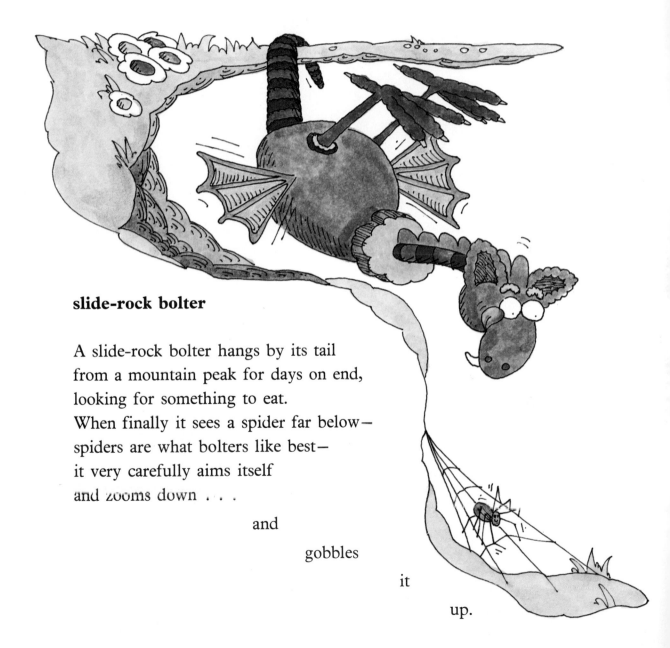

slide-rock bolter

A slide-rock bolter hangs by its tail
from a mountain peak for days on end,
looking for something to eat.
When finally it sees a spider far below—
spiders are what bolters like best—
it very carefully aims itself
and zooms down . . .

                    and

                        gobbles

                    it

                up.

kickle snifters

Kickle snifters are about the size of your thumb.
They live inside men's beards.
But this gets boring,
and they are forever peeking out.
They also are forever laughing,
because beard hair tickles.

You are most likely to see kickle snifters
at your grandfather's house,
or your great-uncle's house.
You see them when you have eaten too much supper,
and you begin to feel sleepy,
and your eyes try to close,
and things don't look the way they usually do.

whing-whang

On nights when the moon
is a giant orange in the sky,
the whing-whang leaps about the beach
and with its tail writes
whing-whang, whing-whang, whing-whang
in the sand.
But when the moon goes down
and the sun comes up,
it rubs out what it has written
and disappears.

A Note from the Author

The creatures in this bestiary live only in our
imaginations. Folklorists classify our folk animals as
"fearsome critters," although most are funny, not
fearsome. One folklorist has said that eighty-one
different kinds of "critters" have been identified. But
clearly there are more.

The next time you are in the woods or anywhere,
look closely and listen carefully. You, too, may see a
fearsome critter.

There Was an Old Man with a Beard

A limerick by Edward Lear

There was an Old Man with a beard,
Who said, "It is just as I feared!—
    Two Owls and a Hen,
    Four larks and a Wren,
Have all built their nests in my beard."

Illustrated by Marie-Louise Gay

A Young Lady of Ealing

A limerick

There was a young lady of Ealing,
Who had a peculiar feeling
    That she was a fly,
    And wanted to try
To walk upside down on the ceiling.

Illustrated by Marie-Louise Gay

Paddington Goes to the Hospital

A play by Michael Bond and Alfred Bradley
Illustrated by Tony Kenyon

Paddington, a small brown bear from Peru, is always willing to help people. Sometimes this gets him into trouble with the Browns, the kind people who have given him a home. More often, however, Paddington's problems are with the Browns' neighbor Mr. Curry. No matter what happens, if Mr. Curry is involved, Paddington is sure to get the worst of it—until now. For Mr. Curry is in the hospital pretending he hurt his leg, and Paddington finally has a chance to get even.

Characters

Mrs. Brown	Nurse	Mr. Curry
Mrs. Bird	Mr. Heinz	
Paddington	Sir Archibald	

The Browns' *sitting room.* Mrs. Brown *is making up a basket of food when* Mrs. Bird *comes in.*

Mrs. Brown: If I see another bunch of grapes, I shall scream. That's the third this week. Not to mention four pots of jam, two dozen eggs, and a jar of calves-foot jelly.

Mrs. Bird: I thought Mr. Curry was supposed to be ill. He seems to have a very healthy appetite.

Mrs. Brown: He says he hurt his leg in the launderette the other day. I don't know how long he'll be in hospital.

Mrs. Bird: If you ask me, Mr. Curry will be coming out of hospital when it suits *him* and not a minute before. He knows when he is on to a good thing. Free board and lodging.

Mrs. Brown: And everybody at his beck and call.

Mrs. Bird: He has a relapse every time the doctor says he is getting better. The ward nurse has given him some strong hints that they're short of beds, but he takes no notice. And I'm certainly not having him staying here.

(Paddington *comes in carrying a letter.*)

Paddington: There's a letter for you, Mrs. Brown. It looks like Mr. Curry's writing.

Mrs. Brown: Yes, I'm afraid you're right. (*She opens the envelope.*)

Mrs. Bird: What does he say?

Mrs. Brown (*Reading*): "Dear Mrs. Brown, My leg is still troubling me. Will you please send some more apples? I didn't like the last lot—they were too sour. Also another cherry cake. P.S. Two cherries were missing from the one you sent last week."

Paddington (*Guiltily*): Perhaps they were a bit loose?

Mrs. Bird (*With meaning*): Perhaps!

Mrs. Brown: "P.P.S. I would like them as soon as possible. Paddington could bring them round to the hospital. . . ." Do you mind taking this parcel to him, Paddington?

Paddington (*Cheerfully*): No. I don't think I've ever been to a hospital before. I wonder if it's like the Daredevil Doctor series on television?

Mrs. Bird: I shouldn't think so for one moment.

Mrs. Brown: There now. It's packed. And I've fixed the cherries *firmly* in the cake this time, so let's hope they don't fall out.

Mrs. Bird: I've packed you some sandwiches and a thermos flask of cocoa. But be careful. It's very hot.

Paddington: Thank you, Mrs. Bird. I won't be long. (*He puts on his hat as he goes out.*)

Mrs. Brown: I do hope we're doing the right thing, letting him go by himself.

Mrs. Bird: I shouldn't worry about that bear. He knows how to look after number one.

Mrs. Brown: It wasn't Paddington I was thinking of. It's the hospital. . . .

SCENE TWO

A small room in the hospital. A Nurse *sits at the desk with a telephone. She is finishing a conversation.*

Nurse: Yes, Sir Archibald. Very good, Sir Archibald.

(*She replaces the phone as* Paddington *knocks at the door.*)

Nurse: Come in.

Paddington: Good morning.

Nurse: Good morning. Can I help you?

Paddington: I've come to see Mr. Curry.

Nurse (*Looking through a list*): Mr. Curry. . . . Have you any idea what he does?

Paddington: He grumbles a lot.

Nurse: That doesn't help. I think I'd better pass you on to the person who deals with inquiries.

Paddington: Thank you very much. Is he the head man?

Nurse: The *head* man. Bless me! Why didn't you say so before? You want the doctor who looks after things up here. (*She taps her head.*)

Paddington: Up here? (*He taps his own head.*)

Nurse: He's what we call the head shrinker.

Paddington: My hat *is* a bit tight. But I don't think I want my head shrunk. Couldn't you stretch my hat instead?

Nurse: Stretch your hat?

Paddington: Yes. If it was a bit bigger, I could carry more sandwiches in it.

Nurse (*Leaning across the desk*): Sandwiches?

Paddington (*Leaning across the desk so that they are nose-to-nose*): Yes, but I would still have to find somewhere for my cocoa.

Nurse (*Alarmed*): There, there. There's nothing to worry about. (*Picks up the phone quickly and dials a number.*) Mr. Heinz, could you come quickly, please? There's a patient who needs you urgently. Thank you. (*Replaces the phone*)

Paddington: Mr. Heinz! I don't want to see Mr. Heinz. I want to see Mr. Curry. I've brought him one of Mrs. Bird's cherry cakes.

Nurse (*Soothingly*): I think you'll find Mr. Heinz much nicer. He'll soon take your worries away. (*Mr. Heinz enters.*) Oh, Mr. Heinz, I'm so glad to see you. (*She looks at Paddington.*) There's the patient. (*She hurries out.*)

Paddington: Patient? Have I got long to wait?

Mr. Heinz: Oh, no, in fact I'll start right away. Just open your coat, please.

Paddington: I'm sorry about the cherry cake.

Mr. Heinz (*Taking off his glasses and staring at Paddington*): You are sorry about the *cherry cake*?

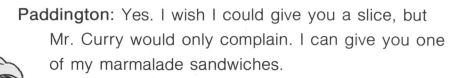

Paddington: Yes. I wish I could give you a slice, but Mr. Curry would only complain. I can give you one of my marmalade sandwiches.

Mr. Heinz (*A slight shudder*): No, thank you. Now, I'd like to play a little game. It's really to test your reactions. (*He sits down in a chair by his desk.*)

Paddington: A game to test my reactions? I didn't know I had any.

Mr. Heinz: Oh, yes. (*He puts his feet up on another chair.*) Everybody has reactions. Some have fast ones and some have slow. (Paddington *sits on his feet.*) Oooh!

Paddington: I'm sorry, Mr. Heinz.

Mr. Heinz: Now I'm going to call out some words— quite quickly—and each time I call one out, I want you to give me another word which has the opposite meaning . . . right?

Paddington (*Promptly, as he settles down in the other chair*): Wrong.

Mr. Heinz: What's the matter? Aren't you comfortable?

Paddington: Oh, yes, but you told me to say the opposite every time you gave me a word.

Mr. Heinz: That wasn't the word, bear! Wait until I give you the go ahead. Once you start I don't want to hear anything else. Ready. . . . Three . . . two . . . one . . . go!

Paddington: Stop!

Mr. Heinz: What's the matter?

Paddington: You said "go" so I said "stop."

Mr. Heinz: Oh. Very good.

Paddington: Very bad.

Mr. Heinz: Look here!

Paddington: Look there! (*A pause*) Can't you think of any more words, Mr. Heinz?

Mr. Heinz (*Drums his fingers on the desk for a moment, then decides to try again*): White.

Paddington: Black.

Mr. Heinz: Big.

Paddington: Small.

Mr. Heinz: Fast.

Paddington: Slow.

Mr. Heinz: Dark.

Paddington: Light.

311

Mr. Heinz: Fine.

Paddington: Wet.

Mr. Heinz: That's good. We've finished.

Paddington: That's bad. We've started.

Mr. Heinz: No, we haven't!

Paddington: Yes, we have!

Mr. Heinz (*Thumping the table*): No . . . no . . . no!

Paddington (*Thumps the table too, in his excitement*): Yes . . . yes . . . yes!

Mr. Heinz (*Yelling*): Will you stop!

Paddington: Will you go!

Mr. Heinz (*His head in his hands*): Why did I ever take this up? I should have my head examined.

Paddington (*Sitting up*): Perhaps it needs shrinking. I should go and talk to the nurse who was here a few minutes ago. She might be able to help you. She knows all about those things.

(*As* Paddington *gets up,* Mr. Heinz *makes a dash for the door.*)

Mr. Heinz: I shall be gone for five minutes. Five minutes! And if you're still here when I get back, I'll I'll . . . (*He hurries out, at a loss for words.*)

Paddington (*Looking round the room*): What a funny hospital. It's not at all like the one in Daredevil Doctor. Hmm. It must be time for lunch. (*He takes a sandwich out.*) I'm glad Mrs. Brown remembered to give me some cocoa. (*He fills the thermos cup and takes a mouthful.*) Ow! (*He hops round the room in agony.*) Ooh! (*He picks up a doctor's bag from the corner of the room, opens it, and examines his tongue in a mirror.*) I knew it. I've blistered my tongue . . . (*He becomes interested in the contents of the bag.*) What's this? (*He puts on a stethoscope and listens to his own heart.*) Hmm. I wonder what it's like to be a doctor.

(*He slips on a white gown and hangs the
stethoscope round his neck.*)

Paddington (*Pretending to be a television surgeon*):
Nurse! Instruments ready? All right, bring in the
patient. (*He puts on his operating mask and paces
up and down.*) Now this is serious . . .

(*The* Nurse *comes in suddenly.*)

Nurse: It certainly is serious. Sir Archibald is coming.

Paddington: Is he?

Nurse: And he's in a terrible mood. You know he doesn't like students who aren't punctual.

Paddington: Student? But I'm not . . .

Nurse: He's here now. I'd say I'm sorry straight away, if I were you.

Sir Archibald (*Storming in*): Ah, there you are.

Paddington: Good morning, Sir Archibald. I'm sorry, Sir Archibald!

Sir Archibald: Sorry? I should think so! Good afternoon's more like it! Now that you *are* here, perhaps you can give us the benefit of your advice. I'd like to have your diagnosis.

Paddington: My diagnosis! (*He begins to unload his basket.*) There's a cherry cake, some eggs, some calves-foot jelly, but I don't think Mrs. Brown packed a diagnosis.

Sir Archibald: Calves-foot jelly. Did you say *calves-foot jelly*?

Paddington: Yes. Grant Dexter says it's very good if you're ill.

Sir Archibald: Grant Dexter! And who might he be?

Paddington: You don't know Grant Dexter? He's the Daredevil Doctor. He's very good at curing people. All his patients get better.

Sir Archibald: Are you suggesting mine don't, Doctor . . . whatever your name is?

Paddington: Doctor? I'm not a doctor, Sir Archibald. (*He pulls off his mask.*) I'm a bear. I've come to visit Mr. Curry.

Sir Archibald (*On the point of exploding*): Curry? Did you say Curry?

Paddington: That's right.

Sir Archibald: Are you a friend of his?

Paddington: Well, I'm not really a friend. He lives next door and I've brought him some food.

Sir Archibald: Food! That's the last thing he needs. It will only make him stay longer. That man's entirely without scruples.

Paddington: Mr. Curry's without scruples! I thought he'd only hurt his leg!

Sir Archibald: Scruples, bear, are things that stop some people taking advantage of others.

Paddington: Oh. I don't think Mr. Curry's got any of those, Sir Archibald. Mrs. Bird's always grumbling because he takes advantage of others.

Sir Archibald: I see. (*Thoughtfully*) Are you any good at tricks, bear?

Paddington: Oh, yes, Sir Archibald. Bears are very good at tricks.

Sir Archibald: I thought you might be. Nurse, wheel Mr. Curry in here. We'll see him privately.

(*The* Nurse *goes and* Sir Archibald *turns to* Paddington.)

Sir Archibald: I think it's time we gave Mr. Curry a surprise—and I think you're the one to give it. Now, if you'll just put your mask back on, bear . . .

Paddington: Yes, Sir Archibald. (*He does.*)

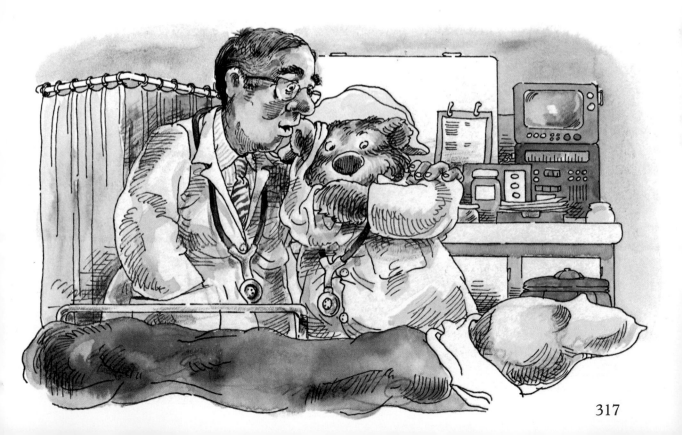

Sir Archibald: I'll give you a chance to see what it's like to be—what did you say his name was?

Paddington: Grant Dexter. The Daredevil Doctor.

Sir Archibald: Now I've an idea. (*He goes to the door and returns with a tool box.*) The workmen left these when they were doing some repairs. When I tell you to get your instruments ready, this is the box I want you to take them from.

Paddington: Right, Sir Archibald.

(Mr. Curry *arrives in a wheelchair pushed by the* Nurse.)

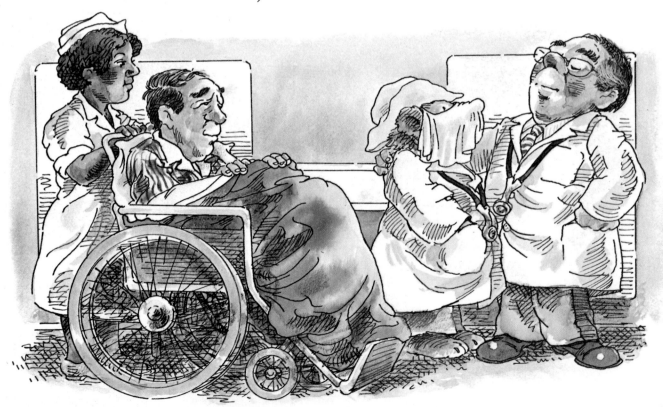

Sir Archibald: Good morning, Mr. Curry. How's the patient today?

Mr. Curry: Oooooooh! Worse, much worse.

Sir Archibald (*Cheerfully*): I thought you might be. That's why we have decided to operate.

Mr. Curry (*Sitting up quickly*): Operate? Did you say operate?

Sir Archibald: Yes, that's right. No good playing around with these things. I'd like to introduce you to . . . a colleague from overseas. He specializes in legs. Does something or other to the knee. Nobody quite knows what, but it seems to work very well in the jungle. Quite a few of his patients still manage to get about more or less. (*To Paddington*) Perhaps you'd like to listen to the patient's heart?

Paddington: Of course, Sir Archibald. (*He sticks the stethoscope under the blanket.*)

Sir Archibald: What can you hear?

Paddington: It's got a very strong beat. (*He jumps up and down to the rhythm.*) I think it's Pick of the Pops.

Mr. Curry: Pick of the Pops! You've got your stethoscope on my transistor radio!

Paddington: I'm sorry, Mr. Curry. (*In his confusion he reverses the stethoscope and puts the headpiece on* Mr. Curry. *He shouts in the other end.*) Are you there?

(Mr. Curry *jumps.*)

Mr. Curry: Of course I am! (*He turns to* Sir Archibald.) Is this . . . this *person* going to be allowed to operate on me? He's not big enough for a start.

Sir Archibald (*Calmly*): Oh, don't worry about his size. We'll give him a box to stand on.

Mr. Curry: A box to stand on!

Sir Archibald: Yes. It may make him a bit wobbly, but it'll be all right.

Mr. Curry: What!

Sir Archibald (*He turns to* Paddington *with a wink.*): Now, if you would just like to get your instruments ready.

Paddington: Certainly, Sir Archibald. (*He opens the carpenter's tool box.*) One hammer . . . (*He puts it on the desk.*)

Mr. Curry: A hammer!

Paddington: One chisel. (*He puts it next to the hammer.*)

Mr. Curry: A chisel!

Paddington: And one saw. (*He brings out a large carpenter's saw.*)

Mr. Curry: A saw!

Sir Archibald: How about something to put him to sleep with, nurse?

(*The* Nurse *hands* Paddington *an enormous mallet.*)

321

Mr. Curry: I'm off. (*He leaps out of the chair.*)

Sir Archibald: Ah, Mr. Curry, I'm glad you're feeling better. You can leave the hospital today.

Mr. Curry: Leave? I don't know what you're talking about.

Sir Archibald: You aren't limping any more, Mr. Curry. In fact, I would say you are completely cured.

Mr. Curry (*Realizes he's been beaten*): Bah! (*He storms out.*)

Sir Archibald (*After his laughter has subsided*): It seems we have another free bed in the ward after all, nurse. (*He removes* Paddington's *mask and shakes his paw warmly.*) Congratulations, bear. I've never in all my life seen a patient recover so quickly. Perhaps you would like to keep your stethoscope as a souvenir?

Paddington: Thank you very much, Sir Archibald. (*He picks up his basket.*) Would you like some of this cake? I don't suppose Mr. Curry will be needing it now.

Sir Archibald: Mmm. It does seem rather a pity to waste it. (*He looks over his shoulder to make sure the nurse can't hear and then lowers his voice.*) Do you like the cherries?

Paddington (*Lowers his voice too*): I think they're the best part. Except Mrs. Bird's put them on extra tightly this time.

Sir Archibald (*Reaches for the tool box*): I don't doubt we'll find something to lever them off with. (*He hands Paddington a suitable tool.*) After you . . .

Paddington: No, after you, Sir Archibald. (*Together, they dig into the basket.*)

(*Curtain*)

Questions

1. Why does Mrs. Brown worry about the hospital when Paddington goes there?

2. Why don't people act surprised when Paddington—a bear—walks up to them and starts talking?

3. Paddington makes friends easily. Who becomes his friend in this play? Why is it easy to become friends with Paddington?

4. Suppose you asked Paddington what he learned from his visit to the hospital. Which of these would be his best reply?
   a. "Never do what people tell you to do."
   b. "Things usually turn out all right."
   c. "If you work hard, you will be rewarded."

5. Paddington had trouble understanding some of the words people used. One of the words was *scruples.* Tell what the doctor meant by *scruples.* Then tell what Paddington thought he meant.

Activity   Draw Mixed-Up Pictures

Suppose that Paddington got mixed up when he drew pictures of these sentences. Show what he might draw.

The baseball player hit a *fly* into the backfield.
On our hike we came to a *fork* in the road.

About MICHAEL BOND

Michael Bond, creator of Paddington the bear, is an English writer. He lives with his wife and his daughter in a small town near London, England.

At first Mr. Bond wrote stories, articles, and plays for adults. Then one Christmas Eve he bought a small toy bear. ''I saw it left on a shelf of a London store, felt sorry for it, and named it Paddington,'' he said. As a result, he wrote his first children's book, *A Bear Called Paddington.*

Michael Bond has created other animal characters, too—a mouse called Thursday, and a guinea pig called Olga da Polga. ''I like writing about animals,'' Mr. Bond says. ''They sometimes seem more real to me than people. They can also get away with things people never could.''

More Books by Michael Bond

Paddington Takes to TV
Paddington Takes the Test
Paddington On Screen
The Complete Adventures of Olga da Polga

Learn About

On Stage!

The theater lights dim. The curtain goes up. You are about to see a play. As the actors move and speak, you find out what is happening. With the costumes and scenery, you picture the time and place.

A play is meant to be performed. That is the main difference between a play and a story. When it is written, a play *looks* different, too. It has

a cast of characters

Characters	Mrs. Brown Mrs. Bird	Paddington Nurse

stage directions

(Paddington *comes in carrying a letter.*)

dialogue

Paddington: There's a letter for you, Mrs. Brown. It looks like Mr. Curry's writing.

Mrs. Brown: Yes, I'm afraid you're right.

How does a story look different from a play?

1 Does it have characters?

2 Does it have stage directions?

3 Does it have dialogue?

You will find this bear's answers below.

1. A story *does* have characters, but they are not listed at the beginning in a cast of characters.

2. A story *does not* have stage directions, but it *does* tell what the characters do and how they feel. This information is not in parentheses.

3. A story *does* have dialogue, but the dialogue is usually in quotation marks.

REMEMBER!

The <u>cast of characters</u> lists the names of the characters in the play.

The <u>stage directions</u> tell what the characters do and how they speak.

The <u>dialogue</u> is what the characters say.

Read the fable of "The North Wind and the Sun." Be ready to change some of this fable into a play.

The North Wind and the Sun

One day the North Wind boasted to the Sun, "I am much stronger than you." The Sun smiled and replied, "Don't be so sure. *I* may be stronger than *you*." Just then a traveler wrapped in a cloak came walking down the road. "Let's have a contest," said the Sun. "Whoever can make that traveler take off her cloak is the stronger. You may try first."

The North Wind blew as hard as he could upon the traveler. "Who-o-o-o," he howled. The traveler only wrapped the cloak more tightly than ever around her

328

shoulders, and said, "I'm glad I wore my cloak. That north wind is *cold!*"

Then the Sun said, "Now it's my turn." She shone so brightly that the traveler began to feel warm. The traveler smiled and said, "Thank you, Sun," and she took off her cloak as she sat down to rest. "Kindness works better than force," explained the Sun to the North Wind.

On a piece of paper, write the cast of characters for the play of "The North Wind and the Sun." Then read the beginning of the play below and write the next line of dialogue for the Sun. Change the rest of the fable into a play if you wish.

Characters

North Wind *(Boasting)*: I am much stronger than you.

Sun *(Smiling)*: Don't be so sure. I may be stronger than you.

(A traveler wrapped in a cloak comes walking down the road.)

Sun:

Digging into the Past

From the story *Miss Pickerell Goes on a Dig*
by Ellen MacGregor and Dora Pantell
Illustrated by Lydia Halverson

Miss Lavinia Pickerell is heading an archaeological dig on a hillside near her home town of Square Toe City. It all started when Miss Pickerell's nephew Euphus was digging for rocks on the hillside and found an odd-shaped piece of very old glass. Now Miss Pickerell is looking for more evidence of the inhabitants who might have lived in the area hundreds of years ago. Miss Pickerell is racing against time, however. In just two days, the hillside will be leveled by the county to make way for a new road.

Miss Pickerell is aided in her dig by world-famous archaeologist Professor Tuttle and her friends Mr. Humwhistel, Mr. Rugby, and Mr. Esticott. On the second day of the dig, Miss Pickerell arrives at the site to find that Mr. Humwhistel has organized the town's Boy and Girl Scouts to help. Miss Pickerell follows Mr. Esticott down into the dig, little realizing what awaits her at the bottom.

Down to the Indians

Miss Pickerell saw Mr. Humwhistel first. He was directing three teams of workers. The first consisted of Mr. Rugby, Mr. Esticott, and the bigger Boy Scouts. They were busy digging. The second team, made up of all the smaller boys, was removing the earth from the finds. The third team was all girls. They were sifting the earth to make sure the second team had not missed anything.

"We're up to the Indians," Mr. Rugby said, emerging from the pit to announce the news.

"Down to the Indians, you mean," argued Mr. Esticott, who followed.

"Has anyone shown Miss Pickerell our discoveries?" Professor Tuttle asked.

"Euphus is standing guard over them," Mr. Humwhistel said. "He's been our official record keeper this morning."

Euphus showed Miss Pickerell some cups of buffalo horn, several copper bowls, ladles, and spoons, two cradle boards, a pile of arrowheads, another pile of blunt-tipped arrows, and what looked like a doll. Professor Tuttle blew some of the dirt off the doll by puffing on it softly, and showed Miss Pickerell that it had movable arms and legs.

"And these blunt-tipped arrows," he said, "were also toys. The Indian boys played with them. The blunt tips were to keep the boys from getting hurt."

"Forevermore!" Miss Pickerell gasped.

"Yes, indeed," Professor Tuttle said. "Our first finds, the purple glass, the snuffbox, the rusty hinge, the toothpick—all of those were from the colonial period. We're digging into the Indian times, now. Mr. Esticott, why don't you take Miss Pickerell into the test pit and show her where we made our discoveries? In the meantime, I'll sort out some of these finds for possible dating."

Mr. Esticott turned to Miss Pickerell. "You'll have to climb down a ladder to get inside now," he told her. "We've dug pretty deep."

"I'm not afraid of ladders," Miss Pickerell replied, unabashed.

She followed Mr. Esticott into the pit. It had been dug so deep, it looked like a tunnel now. Mr. Esticott led her farther and farther inside.

"It's like a house with different rooms in it," Mr. Esticott said. "This is the part where we found the doll and the cradle board and the blunt-tipped arrows."

"Mercy!" Miss Pickerell breathed.

Mr. Esticott walked on a little farther.

"And this is the place where we unearthed the bowls and the spoons and the ladles," he told her.

"Maybe it was a kitchen," Miss Pickerell said. "Or even a dining room. That is, if they had dining rooms in those days."

"And here," Mr. Esticott said, moving on quickly and motioning for her to join him, "here is where . . ."

The sound of stones falling and the sudden, choking smell of heavy dust, rapidly accumulating, came before Mr. Esticott had a chance to finish.

Miss Pickerell staggered forward. "What . . . what . . ." she asked, trying hard to talk through the dust that was sweeping around her.

"The shoring." Mr. Esticott's voice spoke from sudden darkness beside her. "I think it has caved in."

Miss Pickerell groped blindly. Right in front of her was what seemed to be a short wall, extending up only to her chin. It felt solid. She got down on her hands and knees next to it, and reached out a hand toward Mr. Esticott, pulling him down with her.

Suddenly all was quiet. Miss Pickerell could hear the sound of her own heart beating, and Mr. Esticott's quick, heavy breathing.

"Mr. Esticott!" she whispered. "Are you all right?"

"Yes," he replied, "except for this dust which has gotten up into my nose. I can't . . ."

"Do you have a flashlight?" Miss Pickerell interrupted.

"In my back pocket," Mr. Esticott said. "I'll get it."

The flashlight was small. When Mr. Esticott held it out, Miss Pickerell could just barely see what had happened. The wooden boards used as shoring on the right side of the pit had completely collapsed. With them had fallen stones and hard-packed clumps of earth. The ladder, which had been pushed by the impact into an uncertain horizontal position, was covered with rocks and boards. The opening out of the pit was solidly blocked.

In the flashlight's beam, Miss Pickerell caught a glimpse of Mr. Esticott's face. His eyes were full of fear.

"We're trapped," he said shakily. "Sealed in!"

"Stop talking that way," Miss Pickerell said, hoping she sounded firm enough. "There must be a way out."

"Where?" Mr. Esticott asked.

"I don't know yet," Miss Pickerell said. "But I plan to find out. Let me have that flashlight, please."

Mr. Esticott handed over the flashlight reluctantly. "I don't think you ought to poke around too much, Miss Pickerell," he cautioned. "It might be dangerous. You could be upsetting something that would start another avalanche."

Miss Pickerell thought about this.

"You may be right," she said, sighing.

"They know outside the pit that the shoring has caved in," Mr. Esticott went on, talking more confidently now. "They're bound to come and rescue us."

"Yes," Miss Pickerell said. She tried hard to be patient and wait. It was very difficult. Minutes passed. There was no sign of movement from outside. And the air inside was getting more suffocating by the second.

"I can't bear it," Miss Pickerell said finally. "I can't bear just sitting here and doing nothing. There must be *something* we can do to help ourselves."

"What?" Mr. Esticott asked, sounding desperate.

"Look for another way out," Miss Pickerell said, resolutely holding the flashlight out in front of her.

Both Miss Pickerell and Mr. Esticott saw the opening at the same instant. It was at the right, not too far from where the lower part of the wall ended. The crash of timber and stones had rolled away some of the earth there, revealing a hole just large enough to crawl through.

"Where do you suppose it leads?" Mr. Esticott asked breathlessly.

"We'll soon know," Miss Pickerell said.

Clutching the flashlight in one hand and Mr. Esticott's arm with the other, she began moving in the direction of the opening. It was hard to move quickly. The ground was rough and rocky and every once in a while she or Mr. Esticott came close to falling.

When they reached the hole, Miss Pickerell crawled through first. Mr. Esticott followed immediately.

What they saw made them both gasp. They were in what seemed to be a small room, shaped like an upside-down cup. And lying so near to the entrance that they almost stumbled over it, was a pile of what looked very much like weapons. Miss Pickerell turned the flashlight full on them.

"Spearheads!" Mr. Esticott exclaimed, pointing to those first.

"Arrowheads!" Miss Pickerell said, noticing these next. "Stone-tipped arrowheads."

"I've seen pictures of them in the new dictionary my cousin sent me last year," Mr. Esticott said. "In the A section."

"They're also likely to be in the F section," Miss Pickerell added. "Under FLINT. Both spearpoints and arrowheads were often made of hard flint stone. Professor Tuttle will be most interested in what we've found."

"Yes, *when* we're able to get out and tell him about it," Mr. Esticott replied.

"We'll get out soon," Miss Pickerell said, trying to feel optimistic. "We might even find an exit leading out from this room. Let's walk all around it."

Once again, holding the flashlight in front of her, she began to creep carefully forward. Mr. Esticott followed, almost in her footsteps. When she had gone far enough to be able to touch a wall of the vaultlike chamber, she stopped and deliberately dropped her bright white handkerchief. "So that we'll know where we started from," she said.

They continued to grope their way around the curve of the room. Miss Pickerell kept swinging the flashlight upward and downward in a series of slow arcs. Mr. Esticott fumbled all along the clay-packed walls for an opening. There was none.

"Let's try the ground," Mr. Esticott suggested when they were back at the spot marked by the handkerchief. "Perhaps there's a tunnel leading out from underneath."

Miss Pickerell did not answer. She was staring at something on the wall. "Here's a spot we must have missed," she said.

Mr. Esticott moved over to where she stood and stared too.

Built into the wall quite near the ground was what seemed to be a crude fireplace. And in and around this hearth were set a number of interestingly shaped stones, each bearing a pattern of regular ridges, and with a slightly hollowed-out center. The rocks were black with soot.

"Why, it looks like a fireplace—doesn't it?" exclaimed Mr. Esticott.

"It most certainly does, Mr. Esticott," Miss Pickerell replied. "But there's something about those rocks! Something strange. I'm taking one of them back with me!"

She leaned down and pulled until she had loosened one of the rocks. She examined it thoughtfully. Then she put it in her apron pocket. "I know what these rocks remind me of!" she said at last. "I know, but I don't understand it at all."

Miss Pickerell and Mr. Esticott stood now in almost total blackness. The flashlight was flickering badly.

"We'd better put it out," Miss Pickerell suggested. "Unless you have an extra battery with you."

"I haven't," Mr. Esticott sighed. "What do we do now?"

"First we'll go back and wait," Miss Pickerell said. "We'd better get back to where we started from, before your flashlight goes dead. It's certainly time the rescuers were getting down to us!"

A Sign from the Rescuers

When Miss Pickerell and Mr. Esticott had crawled back through the hole and were once more seated on the uneven ground near the low wall, Miss Pickerell took one last look around. "Let's get our bearings," she said firmly. "We're between the wall and the left-hand side of the pit. The rescuers will most probably come from the left side because that's the part where the shoring is still fairly intact. What do you think, Mr. Esticott?"

"I think so, too," he said.

"We'll listen for sounds from that direction," Miss Pickerell said, accompanying her words with a brisk snap of the "off" switch. "We'll turn the flashlight on every fifteen minutes or so to look for signs of movement."

Mr. Esticott had nothing to say.

Miss Pickerell tried to think of something to talk about that might make them feel better. "Just imagine, Mr. Esticott," she said, "hundreds and hundreds of years ago a family lived in that strange-shaped room, and a mother cooked dinner in that very fireplace."

"Is there any way we can tell exactly when that was?" Mr. Esticott asked.

Miss Pickerell reached into her pocket and pulled out the rock. She turned the flashlight on it briefly.

"The answer is in the carbon soot on this rock, Mr. Esticott," she said. "The soot is all that's left of a piece of wood that was burned in that fireplace. If we can tell how old the soot is, we'll know when people used the fireplace!"

"But how can we tell how old the soot is?" Mr. Esticott asked bewildered.

"Wait! Sh!" Miss Pickerell hissed sharply.

A tiny scratching noise seemed to be coming from somewhere up above. Miss Pickerell turned on the flashlight immediately. But she saw nothing. And the sound was not repeated.

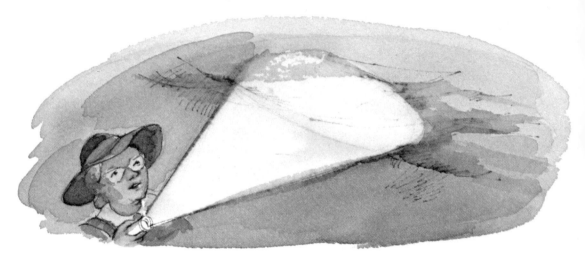

Mr. Esticott sighed. "What were you saying about dating soot?" he asked.

"I was going to tell you about the carbon-14 test," Miss Pickerell answered. "I learned about it once when I was helping someone look for uranium. It's a scientific way of dating things that were once alive."

"I don't see how that has anything to do with soot," Mr. Esticott said, sounding doubtful.

"It's really very simple," Miss Pickerell told him. "The soot on this rock was formed when wood was burned in that fireplace. And the wood came from a living tree. Of course, every living thing contains radioactive carbon-14, because carbon-14 is in the air. For example, plants take it in."

Miss Pickerell stopped suddenly. Again, it seemed to her that she heard small sounds above her. Again, there was nothing when she strained her ears to listen and when she turned the flashlight on to look. She sighed heavily.

"After a plant dies," she resumed, "the carbon-14 disintegrates at a *known* rate, a certain amount every year. If we can get a scientist to measure how much carbon-14 is left in this soot, we'll have a very good idea of its age."

"Oh!" Mr. Esticott said.

Miss Pickerell said nothing more. She felt tired after her long speech. It was becoming harder and harder to breathe in the close atmosphere. She was also very thirsty. She searched in her knitting bag for the peppermint candy drops she usually carried there.

She found two. Mr. Esticott gladly accepted one when she offered it to him.

She was just taking the wrapper off her own piece when she thought she heard noises again. This time, they sounded louder and seemed definitely to come from the left side of the pit. Miss Pickerell turned the flashlight on.

"Maybe they're tapping," she said. "I'm going to tap back."

"Why not shout?" Mr. Esticott asked and began immediately, "Hello! We're here!"

Miss Pickerell joined him. "Hello! Right here!"

No one answered.

"I'll try tapping against the shoring," Miss Pickerell said, picking up a rock from the ground. "I'll tap with this."

Miss Pickerell tapped systematically. Once, twice, three times—four times. Almost immediately, a trickle of earth began to sift down, and quickly broadened into a stream that poured and then surged toward her and Mr. Esticott.

"Oh!" Miss Pickerell gasped, not certain whether to jump back or to crouch down. "They must have heard the tapping. They know where we are now."

"I see something coming through!" Mr. Esticott cried out.

A dark, round object poked out of the earth above their heads. Slowly, the object thrust out farther and farther.

Miss Pickerell kept the dimmed flashlight fixed in that direction and peered anxiously. "Forevermore!" she blurted out in astonishment.

"What is it?" Mr. Esticott asked. "What is it?"

"It's a drainpipe," said Miss Pickerell, feeling very awed and trying hard to keep her voice steady. "The rescuers are pushing it through to make contact with us."

When the pipe stopped moving, Miss Pickerell approached it. She stood on tiptoe, her eye just reaching the level of the hollow end. She took time only to wipe off the right lens of her eyeglasses, then squinted cautiously up the length of the pipe. "I see daylight!" she shouted.

"Hooray!" yelled Mr. Esticott. "May I look, too?"

Miss Pickerell stepped away.

Mr. Esticott, cupping his hands around the end of the pipe and craning his neck as far as it would go, stared hard. "I see a little circle of daylight at the other end!" he announced. "And I think I see someone moving around up there!"

"We'll have to let them know that they have reached us," said Miss Pickerell. "We must attend to that at once."

Miss Pickerell knew immediately what she had to do. She pursed her lips up as if she were about to whistle, pressed them hard against the hollow end of the drainpipe, and, making her voice as loud as she could, called out, "YOO HOO! YOO HOO!"

The muffled answer came back instantly, "Can you hear us?"

"Yes!" Miss Pickerell shouted.

"Are you all right?" the voice, which Miss Pickerell was beginning to distinguish as Professor Tuttle's, asked.

"We're both fine," Miss Pickerell answered.

"Good," the answer came. "We're digging down to you. We're coming straight through about a yard to the left of this pipe. Stay as far away from there as possible. It may be dangerous. Do you understand?"

"Yes," Miss Pickerell said, impressed by the urgency in Professor Tuttle's voice.

"One last thing," the professor called. "We have to shore up the top of this pit as we keep digging. It may take us a while. Don't be frightened."

"I won't," Miss Pickerell said. "Thank you, Professor."

She sighed with relief and turned to Mr. Esticott. "I guess our troubles are over now," she said.

At that precise moment, the flashlight went dead. Miss Pickerell could not see even an inch in front of her.

"This is the last straw," Mr. Esticott burst out.

"That may be," Miss Pickerell agreed, "but I don't intend to sit here in the dark until we're rescued." She reached for the pipe again and shouted up to the diggers, "Light, we need light!"

Mr. Esticott cleared his throat. "Do you think that will help?" he asked.

"I wouldn't have done it otherwise," Miss Pickerell replied in very definite tones.

"What did you say?" Mr. Esticott asked.

Miss Pickerell was not surprised that he hadn't heard her. Something was loudly clanking its way down the drainpipe. It came to a halt at the very end of the pipe. It was a flashlight and it was lit.

"Why, it's Euphus' new silver flash!" Miss Pickerell exclaimed. "I bought it for him myself on his last birthday. He must have gotten my message."

"Look," Mr. Esticott said, showing her how the flashlight was tied on to a piece of wool. It was the green knitting wool that she had given to Mr. Humwhistel when he was attaching labels to the finds.

"Of course," Miss Pickerell replied. "That's the way Euphus lowered the flash through the pipe. If he'd just thrown it down, it would have fallen right out at the end and broken to bits."

"You have a very smart nephew," Mr. Esticott said admiringly.

"All seven of my nephews and nieces are smart," Miss Pickerell replied proudly. "Each in a different way."

Now that they had some light, Miss Pickerell and Mr. Esticott felt considerably more cheerful. They felt even better when the first whiffs of fresh air began to drift down into the trench. Miss Pickerell stopped to draw in long, deep breaths. Mr. Esticott did the same.

"It shouldn't be long now," he said happily.

"I don't imagine it should," Miss Pickerell agreed.

They had nothing to do now but wait. Miss Pickerell thought about Professor Tuttle's old, old rock from far, far away, and about the strange cup-shaped room. And suddenly something fell into place in her mind. "Mr. Esticott," she said, "I've been thinking. Houses are like children. They resemble their parents."

"I beg your pardon?" Mr. Esticott said, looking quite bewildered.

Miss Pickerell tried hard to explain. To her, it all seemed so clear. "What I'm trying to tell you, Mr. Esticott," she said, "is that this rock in my pocket closely resembles a rock that Professor Tuttle showed me when I met him the other day. But his rock came from another continent, and was centuries old." She stopped suddenly, as the idea came to her. "Could it be," she said a few second later, "that the descendants of the people who fashioned Professor Tuttle's rock once lived in Square Toe County?"

Mr. Esticott stared, open-mouthed.

"Yes," Miss Pickerell continued, hardly able to contain her excitement. "That's why we see the same workmanship. Square Toe County may have a past we never even dreamed existed. We may learn who . . ."

But Mr. Esticott was no longer listening to her. He was looking up at the top of the pit. A noisy downflow of earth had suddenly opened up a large hole, revealing first a shovel, then a hand, and, at last, Mr. Rugby's round, shining face, peering down at them and smiling broadly.

Questions

1. In this story, who got into deep, serious trouble? What was that trouble?

2. What three things did Miss Pickerell do to make the trouble seem less serious?

3. What was Miss Pickerell's greatest discovery? Why was the discovery important?

4. Complete these sentences by using three of these words from the story: **ladle, chamber, hearth, shoring.**
   a. Boards to keep dirt from caving in are called _____.
   b. A closed-up room is a _____.
   c. The floor of a fireplace is a _____.

Activity   Write a News Report

Sam Scoop, news reporter, wrote three headlines about Miss Pickerell's adventure. Readers said that Sam's headlines were puzzling and untrue. Fix the headlines. Make them truthful and important. Then write the first paragraph to put under one of the headlines. Include the following parts in your paragraph;

1. WHO was there;
2. WHAT happened;
3. WHEN it happened;
4. WHERE it happened;
5. HOW or WHY it happened.

Old Joe Clarke

A traditional folk song

Round and round, Old Joe Clarke,
Round and round, I say,
Round and round, Old Joe Clarke,
I don't have long to stay.

Old Joe Clarke he had a house,
Sixteen stories high,
Every story in that house
Was full of chicken pie.

I went down to Old Joe Clarke's
And found him eating supper;
I stubbed my toe on the table leg
And stuck my nose in the butter.

I went down to Old Joe Clarke's
But Old Joe wasn't in;
I sat right down on the red-hot stove
And got right up again.

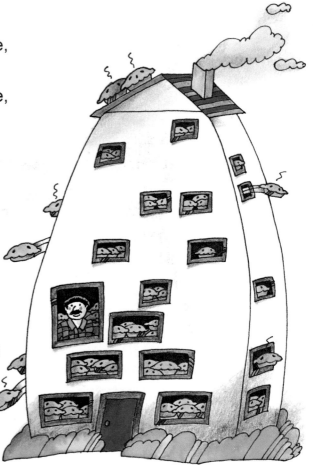

Illustrated by Marie-Louise Gay

BOOKSHELF

The Big Cheese by Eve Bunting. Macmillan, 1977. This is a funny story about two very different sisters whose lives are suddenly changed by a big wheel of cheese.

Miss Pickerell Goes to Mars by Ellen MacGregor. McGraw-Hill, 1951. No matter where she goes, Miss Pickerell does surprising things.

A Person from Britain Whose Head Was in the Shape of a Mitten & Other Limericks by N. M. Bodecker. Atheneum, 1980. Some of these ridiculous nonsense verses and limericks are sure to make you laugh.

Wingman by Manus Pinkwater. Dodd, Mead, 1975. Donald Chen read comic books all day until he met a Super Hero he called Wingman.

Getting Something on Maggie Marmelstein by Marjorie Weinman Sharmat. Harper & Row, 1971. Thad wants to get something on Maggie. If he doesn't, she is going to ruin his reputation at school.

Where the Sidewalk Ends by Shel Silverstein. Harper & Row, 1974. All kinds of characters, feelings, and events fill these poems that are especially fun, and funny, to read aloud.

6 To Live with Animals

The Carp in the Bathtub

A story by Barbara Cohen

Illustrated by Bert Dodson

When I was a little girl, I lived in an apartment house in New York City with Mama and Papa and my little brother Harry.

It was not very fancy, but Papa said we were lucky. We had our own bathroom. Mrs. Ginzburg, who lived downstairs, was also lucky—she had one too. Everyone else had to share the bathrooms in the hall.

Mama was a wonderful cook. It was well known that she made the finest chicken soup in Flatbush. Also very good *tsimmis*, noodle *kugel*, *mondel* bread, and stuffed cabbage.

357

But best of all was Mama's *gefilte* fish. Twice a year she made *gefilte* fish—in the fall for Rosh Hashanah, the Jewish New Year, and in the spring for Pesach, the festival of Passover. Aunt Malke and Uncle Moishe, cousin Zipporah, and Papa's friend Mr. Teitelbaum always came to our house for the Seder on the first night of Passover. They said that Mama's *gefilte* fish was not merely the best in Flatbush, nor the best in Brooklyn, but actually the best *gefilte* fish in all of New York City.

Harry and I loved the Seder because we got to stay up until midnight. It took that long to say all the prayers, read the Passover story out of a book called the Haggadah, sing all the songs, and eat all the food. But I will tell you a secret. I was nine years old at the time I am telling you about, and I had never put a single piece of my mother's *gefilte* fish into my mouth.

Mama made her *gefilte* fish out of carp. For a day or two before Passover, carp was hard to find in the stores. All the ladies in the neighborhood had been buying it for their own *gefilte* fish. Mama liked to buy *her* carp at least a week before Passover to make sure she got the nicest, fattest, shiniest one. But Mama knew that a dead fish sitting in the icebox for a week would not be very good when the time came to make it into *gefilte* fish.

So Mama bought her fish live and carried it home in a pail of water. All the way home it flopped and flipped because it was too big for the bucket. It would have died if Mama had left it in there.

As soon as she got home she would call, "Leah, run the water in the tub."

And I would put the rubber stopper in the drain and run some cold water into the bathtub. Then Mama would dump the carp out of the pail and into the tub.

The carp loved it there. He was always a big fish, but the tub was about four times as long as he was, and there was plenty of room for him to swim around.

Harry and I loved the carp. As long as he was there we didn't have to take baths.

But the day always came when Mama marched into the bathroom carrying a big metal strainer and removed the stopper from the tub. The carp always seemed to know what was coming. He swam away from her as fast as he could, splashing the water all over her apron with his strong, flat tail. But he didn't have a chance. Before all the water was even out of the tub, Mama had caught him in her strainer. The way he was flopping around, he would have been on the floor before Mama got out the bathroom door, so she dumped him right into her bucket and carried him to the kitchen.

We knew what she did with him when she got there, although we would never look.

Mama once told us that her Mama had not thrown away the skin of the carp. She had removed it so carefully from the carp that after the fish was cooked, she could put it back in the skin and bring it to the table. That's why the fish is called *gefilte*, Mama said, which means "stuffed." At least, Harry and I were spared that!

You can see why we managed never to eat *gefilte* fish on Rosh Hashanah or Passover. Could *you* eat a friend?

The year I was nine was the worst of all. Most people think that all fish are pretty much the same, but this is definitely not true. Some carp are much more lovable than others, and that Passover we had an unusually playful and intelligent carp in our bathtub.

This carp was larger than the others too. We were having extra company that year. Mrs. Ginzburg from downstairs and her daughter Elvira were coming up. Mr. Ginzburg had died six months before, and Mrs. Ginzburg just didn't have the heart to fuss and prepare for Passover.

This particular carp was also shinier than the others. His eyes were brighter and he seemed much livelier and friendlier. It got so that whenever Harry or I went into the bathroom, he'd swim right over to the end of the tub as if he knew we were going to feed him. There was something about his mouth that made him seem to be smiling at us after he had eaten a bread crust or the lettuce we had given him.

In those days people like us, who lived in apartments in Flatbush, did not have pets. Harry and I would have loved owning a dog, a cat, or a bird, but Mama and Papa had never thought of such a thing, and it never occurred to us to ask. I'll tell you one thing, though. After that carp had been in our bathtub for nearly a week, we knew he was not just any old carp. He was our pet. In memory of Mr. Ginzburg, we called him Joe.

Two days before Passover, when I came home from school, Mama said, "You look after Harry, Leah. I have to go shopping, and I'll never get anything done if I have him trailing after me."

As soon as Mama was gone I looked at Harry, and Harry looked at me.

"We have to save Joe," I told him.

"We'll never have another chance," Harry agreed. "But what'll we do?"

"Mrs. Ginzburg has a bathtub," I reminded him.

Harry nodded. He saw what I meant right away.

I went to the kitchen, got the bucket, and carried it to the bathroom. Harry had already let all the water out of the tub. He helped lift Joe into the bucket. It was not easy for us because Joe must have weighed fifteen pounds, but we finally managed. We could add only a little water to the pail because it was already almost too heavy for us.

With both of us holding onto the handle and banging the bucket against every step, we lugged it downstairs to Mrs. Ginzburg's door. Then we rang her bell.

"Why, Leah, Harry!" Mrs. Ginzburg said in surprise.
"I'm very glad to see you. Won't you come in? Why
are you carrying that bucket?" Mrs. Ginzburg was a
very nice lady. She was always kind to us, even when
she couldn't understand what we were doing.

We carried our bucket into Mrs. Ginzburg's front
room. "May I ask what you have there?" she said
politely.

"It's Joe," said Harry.

"Joe!" Mrs. Ginzburg closed her eyes and put her
hand over her heart.

"We named him for Mr. Ginzburg," I explained
quickly. "He smiles like Mr. Ginzburg."

"Oh . . . " Mrs. Ginzburg tried to smile too. Just then Joe twitched, his tail flashed over the top of the bucket, and a few drops of water dripped onto the oriental rug. Mrs. Ginzburg glanced into the pail. "My goodness," she said. "He looks like a fish to me."

"He is a fish," I said. "He's the best fish in the world, and Mama can't kill him for Passover. She just can't. Please let him stay in your bathtub. Please. Just for a little while. Until I can figure out where to keep him for good."

"But Leah," Mrs. Ginzburg said, "I can't do that. Your Mama is my dear friend."

"If you don't let us put Joe in your bathtub soon," Harry pleaded, "he'll be dead. He's almost dead now."

Mrs. Ginzburg and I peered into the bucket. Harry was right. Joe didn't look too good. His scales weren't shiny bright any more, and he had stopped thrashing around. There was not enough water in the bucket for him.

"All right," said Mrs. Ginzburg. "But just for now." She ran some water into her tub, and we dumped our carp in. He no sooner felt all that clear cold water around him than he perked right up and started swimming. I took a few morsels of chopped meat I had stored away in my dress pocket and gave them to him. He smiled at me, just like always.

"This fish can't stay here," Mrs. Ginzburg warned. "I'm afraid I can't help hide him from your mother and father."

"What shall we do?" Harry asked me, blinking his eyes hard to keep back the tears.

"We'll go find Papa," I told him. "Papa doesn't cook, so maybe he'll understand. We'll have to find him before Mama gets home."

Papa was a cutter in a garment factory in Manhattan. He came home every night on the subway. Harry and I went down to the corner and waited by the stairs that led up from the station. After a while, we saw a

big crowd of people who had just gotten off the train come up the stairs. Papa was with them. He was holding onto the rail and climbing slowly, with his head down.

"Papa, Papa," we called.

He looked up and saw us. He straightened his shoulders, smiled, and ran quickly up the few remaining steps. "You came to meet me," he said. "That's very nice."

We started home together. I was holding one of Papa's hands, and Harry was holding the other. "Papa," I asked, "do you like *gefilte* fish?"

"Why, yes," he said, "of course I like *gefilte* fish. Your mother makes the best *gefilte* fish in all of Flatbush—in all of New York City. Everyone knows that."

"But would you like to eat *gefilte* fish," Harry asked, "if the fish was a friend of yours?"

Papa stood absolutely still right in the middle of the sidewalk. "Harry," he said, "Harry, what have you done to Mama's fish?"

"Leah did it too," Harry said.

Papa turned to me. Putting his hands on my shoulders, he looked right into my eyes. Papa's brown eyes were not large, but they were very bright. Most of the time his eyes smiled at us, but when he was angry or upset, like now, they could cut us like knives. "Leah," he said, "what did you do to Mama's fish?"

"Please, Papa," I said, "don't let Mama kill our fish. His name is Joe. We love him, and we want to keep him for a pet."

"Where is he now?" Papa asked.

I looked down at my hands and began to pick my fingernail. I didn't want to tell Papa where Joe was. But he put his hand on my chin and forced my face up.

"Where's the fish now?" he asked again. His voice was gentle but those eyes were cutting me up.

"In Mrs. Ginzburg's bathtub," I mumbled.

Papa started walking again, faster now. We trailed along behind him, not holding his hands any more. He didn't say anything for awhile. But when we got to our

front stoop, he stopped to talk to us. "We are going to
Mrs. Ginzburg's apartment and we are getting that
fish," he said. "It's your mother's fish and it cost her a
lot of money. She had to save a little out of what I give
her each week just so she could buy such a big fish
and make an extra nice Passover holiday for all of us."
When we got to Mrs. Ginzburg's, Papa said to her,
"We've come to take the fish home. I'm sorry for the
trouble."

"Oh, he was no trouble," Mrs. Ginzburg said.

"Well, he would have been, as soon as you wanted to take a bath," Papa said.

We didn't say anything.

Mrs. Ginzburg let the water out of the tub. Papa didn't need a strainer to catch Joe. He just used his hands and the bucket.

It was much easier going back upstairs than it had been coming down. Papa carried the bucket. I ran the water, and without any ceremony Papa poured Joe in. He flitted through the water so gaily you'd think he was happy to be home. Foolish Joe.

"Carp are for eating," Papa said, "just like chicken.
You always eat two helpings of chicken."

"We never met the chicken," I said.

Papa shook his head. "That's not the point, Leah.
We don't kill more creatures than we need, and we
don't kill them for fun, but we eat what must be eaten.
It would break Mama's heart if she realized you children
didn't like to eat her *gefilte* fish. We won't tell her
about any of this. Mrs. Ginzburg won't tell her either."

So nobody told Mama about how we had stolen her
carp. Luckily, I was at school when she made Joe into
gefilte fish. When I got home, I asked Harry how he
could have stood watching her catch Joe with her
strainer and carry him off into the kitchen.

"I didn't watch," Harry said. "When I saw her go for that strainer, I went right down to Mrs. Ginzburg's. But even there I could smell fish cooking."

Although Mama opened all the windows that afternoon, and no one else seemed to notice anything, Harry and I thought we smelled fish cooking for days.

We cried ourselves to sleep that night, and the next night too. Then we made ourselves stop crying. After that, we felt as if we were years older than Mama and Papa.

One night about a week after Passover, we were sitting in the kitchen helping Mama shell peas when Papa came home. As he walked through the door, we noticed that he was carrying something orange and black and white and furry in his arms. It was a beautiful big tri-color cat.

"They had too many cats hanging around the loft," Papa said. "This one seemed so friendly and pretty that I brought her home."

Mama seemed surprised, but she let the cat stay. She was a clean cat. We called her Joe. Mama couldn't understand that.

I'm old now—a grandmother, as a matter of fact. My daughters buy *gefilte* fish in jars at the supermarket. They think their Uncle Harry and I don't eat it because it isn't as good as the kind our mother made. We don't tell them that we never ate Mama's either.

Questions

1. What did Leah and Harry like about the carp?

2. How did Papa know that Leah and Harry had tried to protect Joe?

3. Should Papa have helped the children protect the carp? Why or why not?

4. After Leah and Harry cried about the carp, Leah said, "We felt as if we were years older than Mama and Papa." What did she mean?

5. This story is about a carp, but it ends with a cat! Why is the cat in the story?

6. If you got into trouble, do you think that Leah and Harry would try to help you? Tell why or why not.

7. The story told you that *gefilte* means
   a. fish   b. stuffed   c. holiday

Activity   Make a Character Chart

Finish this chart to show what each character wanted and what each one did to get it.

Character	What Character Wanted	What Character Did
Leah & Harry		
Mama		
Papa		
Mrs. Ginzburg		

Buying a Puppy

A poem by Leslie Norris

"Bring an old towel," said Pa,
"And a scrap of meat from the pantry.
We're going out in the car, you and I,
Into the country."

I did as he said, although
I couldn't see why he wanted
A scrap of meat and an old towel.
Into the sun we pointed

Our Ford, over the green hills.
Pa sang. Larks bubbled in the sky.
I took with me all my cards—
It was my seventh birthday.

We turned down a happy lane,
Half sunlight, half shadow,
And saw at the end a white house
In a yellow meadow.

Mrs. Garner lived there. She was tall.
She gave me a glass of milk
And showed me her black spaniel.
"Her name is Silk,"

Mrs. Garner said. "She's got
Three puppies, two black, one golden.
Come and see them." Oh,
To have one, one of my own!

"You can choose one," said Pa.
I looked at him. He wasn't joking.
I could scarcely say thank you,
I was almost choking.

It was the golden one. He slept
On my knee in the old towel
All the way home. He was tiny,
But didn't whimper or howl,

Not once. That was a year ago,
And now I'm eight.
When I get home from school
He'll be waiting behind the gate,

Listening, listening hard,
Head raised, eyes warm and kind;
He came to me as a gift
And grew into a friend.

Illustrated by Bert Dodson

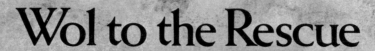

Wol to the Rescue

From the story *Owls in the Family* by Farley Mowat
Illustrated by Jenny Rutherford

Wol, who was found when he was very young, is an owl who doesn't know he is an owl. Wol prefers walking to flying, enjoys riding on the handlebars of a bicycle, and loves playing tricks on the dog. Weeps, a smaller owl, was rescued from some boys who were tormenting him, and raised with Wol as his companion. Both are very tame pets and love to go along on outings.

Toward the middle of July Bruce and I got permission from our parents to spend a night in the cave. We took Wol and Weeps with us, and of course we had both dogs, Rex and Mutt.

In the afternoon we went for a hike over the prairie, looking for birds. Mutt, who was running ahead of us, flushed a prairie chicken off her nest. There were ten eggs in the nest and they were just hatching out.

We sat down beside the nest and watched. In an hour's time seven of the little chickens had hatched before our eyes. It was pretty exciting to see, and Wol seemed just as curious about it as we were. Then all of a sudden three of the newly hatched little birds slipped out of the nest and scuttled straight for Wol. Before he could move they were underneath him, crowding against his big feet, and *peep-peeping* happily. I guess they thought he was their mother, because they hadn't seen their real mother yet.

Wol was so surprised he didn't know what to do. He kept lifting up one foot and then the other to shake off the little ones. When the other four babies joined the first three, Wol began to get nervous. But finally he seemed to resign himself to being a mother, and he fluffed his feathers out and lowered himself very gently to the ground.

Bruce and I nearly died laughing. The sight of the baby prairie chickens popping their heads out through Wol's feathers, and that great big beak of his snapping anxiously in the air right over their heads, was the silliest thing I've ever seen. I guess Wol knew it was silly, too, but he couldn't figure how to get out of the mess he was in. He kept looking at me as if he were saying, "For Heaven's sake, DO something!"

I don't know how long he would have stayed there, but we began to worry that the real mother might not find her chicks, so I finally lifted him up and put him on my shoulder, and we went back to the cave for supper.

We'd had a good laugh at Wol, but he had the laugh on us before the day was done.

After we had eaten we decided to go down to the riverbank and wait for the sun to set. A pair of coyotes lived on the opposite bank of the river, and every evening just at sunset one of them would climb a little hill and sit there howling. It was a scary sound, but we liked it because it made us feel that this was the olden times, and the prairie belonged to us, to the buffaloes and the Indians, and to the prairie wolves.

Wol was sitting in the Hanging Tree, and Rex and Mutt had gone off somewhere on a hunting trip of their own. It was growing dusk when we heard a lot of crashing in the trees behind us. We turned around just as two big kids came into sight. They were two of the toughest kids in Saskatoon. If they hadn't come on us so suddenly, we would have been running before they ever saw us. But now it was too late to run—they would have caught us before we could go ten feet. The only thing we could do was sit where we were and hope they would leave us alone.

What a hope *that* was! They came right over and one of them reached down and grabbed Bruce and started to twist his arm behind his back.

"Listen, you little rats," he said, "we heard you got a cave someplace down here. You're too young to own a cave, so we're taking over. Show us where it is, or I'll twist your arm right off!"

The other big kid made a grab for me, but I slipped past him and was just starting to run when he stuck his foot out and tripped me. Then he sat on me.

"Say, Joe," he said to his pal, "I got an idea. Either these kids tell us where the cave is, or we tie 'em to Ole Hanging Tree and leave 'em there all night with the ghost."

Just then the coyote across the river gave a howl. All four of us jumped a little, what with the talk of ghosts—but Joe said: "That ain't nothing. Just a coyote howling. You going to tell us, kid? Or do we tie you to the tree?"

Bruce and I knew they were only trying to scare us, but we were scared all right. I was just opening my mouth to tell them where the cave was when Wol took a hand in things.

He had been sitting on the big limb of the Hanging Tree and, since it was almost dark by then, he looked like a white blob up there. I don't think he'd been paying much attention to what was happening on the ground below him, but when that coyote howled he must have thought it was some kind of a challenge. He opened his beak and gave the Owl Hunting Scream.

Did you ever hear a horned owl scream? Usually they do it at night to scare any mice or rabbits that happen to be hiding near into jumping or running. Then the owl swoops down and grabs them. If you've ever heard an owl scream you'll know it's just about the most scary sound in all the world.

When Wol cut loose it made even my skin creep, and I knew what it was; but the two big kids didn't know.

Their heads jerked up, and they saw the ghostly white shape that was Wol up there in the Hanging Tree. And then they were off and running. They went right through the poplar woods like a couple of charging buffaloes, and we could still hear them breaking bush when they were half a mile away. My guess is they ran all the way to Saskatoon.

When they were out of hearing Bruce stood up and began rubbing his arm. Then he looked at Wol.

"Boy!" he said "You sure scared those two rough-necks silly! But did you have to scare *me* right out of my skin too?"

"Hoo-HOO-hoo-hoo-hoo-HOO!" Wol chuckled as he floated down out of the tree and lit upon my shoulder.

Questions

1. How do you think Wol got his name?

2. The chicks thought that Wol was a
   a. prairie chicken   b. horned owl   c. ghost

3. The two big kids thought that Wol was a
   a. prairie chicken b. horned owl   c. ghost

4. The story showed that Wol could be *funny* or *frightening.* How else do you think he could act? Tell how he would show his behavior.

5. If you were Wol, would you trust the two boys? Tell why or why not.

6. If you became the owner of an unusual pet, how would you help the pet learn to trust you?

7. Find the words the author used instead of the underlined words.
   a. It made my skin <u>tighten</u>. (page 381)
   b. Mutt <u>scared</u> a prairie chicken off her nest. (page 377)
   c. The tough kids went through the poplar woods <u>fast</u>. (page 382)

Activity   Write a News Story

Write a news story for the *Saskatoon News* to report on Wol's heroic rescue of the two boys. Tell who was there, what happened, and why Wol is a hero. Give a headline, or title, to your story.

CONNECTIONS

How Animals Protect Themselves

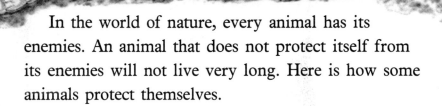

In the world of nature, every animal has its enemies. An animal that does not protect itself from its enemies will not live very long. Here is how some animals protect themselves.

Armor, Quills, and Spines

Nature has given some animals a thick coat of armor for protection. The *armadillo* is not a fighter. It does not need to be. Small plates of bone cover its body. When danger is near, the armadillo rolls itself into an armor-plated ball. Even the sharp teeth of a bobcat cannot bite through the armadillo's armor.

The *turtle* is built like an armored truck. When the turtle is scared, it pulls its head, tail, and legs into its hard shell. The common box turtle even has a shell that it closes tightly after its head, tail, and legs are safe inside.

Illustrated by Jeremy Guitar

Once a fox or weasel attacks a *porcupine,* the attacker will never try it again! When scared, the porcupine lifts its 30,000 or so quills. Each quill ends in a barb, like a fishhook. The porcupine strikes at its attacker with its quill-covered tail. It drives many quills into its attacker's face and paws. The quills keep working their way into the flesh of the enemy. If the quills pierce an important body part, the animal may die.

This *sea urchin* depends on long spines for protection. The spines of some sea urchins are poisonous.

Animals in Disguise

The *zebra* and *giraffe* have striking markings. Yet their coloring and markings make them almost invisible to their enemies. The zebra's stripes match the striped pattern of sunlight and shadows in the tall grasses where it feeds. The orange and brown marks on the giraffe's coat resemble patches of sunshine and shadows, like those in the leaves they eat.

In the Arctic, many animals have white coats that make it hard to see them against their snowy setting.

Some arctic foxes and hares change color with the seasons. In the summer their coats look like the gray-brown earth. In the fall the brown hairs are replaced by white ones.

The *chameleon* is also known for changing color to look like its background. The giant chameleon can change from bright yellow to blue to green in about a minute!

Animals That Flee

Many animals defend themselves by simply being fast on their feet. When danger is near, they run. As they run, they zigzag back and forth. This zigzagging helps to confuse their enemies. The table on the next page gives the top speeds of some animals that run from danger.

Animal	Top Speed
Pronghorn antelope	60 mph
Horse	47.5 mph
Jack rabbit	45 mph
White-tailed deer	40 mph
Giraffe	32 mph

Other Animal Weapons

The *skunk* has a strange weapon, but it is a most powerful one! If an enemy comes near, the skunk beats its front feet on the ground. If the attacker comes even closer, then the skunk turns around and fires its famous smell. The enemy quickly learns a lesson it will not forget!

Even a coyote is afraid to attack the *badger*. With its sharp teeth and long claws, the badger is a fierce fighter. The honey badger of Africa fears no animal. It will attack even large snakes.

Some animals' teeth can be deadly weapons. Wolves' teeth are sharp and pointed. They fit together so closely, they can cut like the blade of a knife.

Nature has given some animals horns or antlers to use as weapons. These animals use their horns or antlers to keep enemies from getting close. Some also use their horns or antlers to push or throw enemies out of the way.

In the animal kingdom, each animal has its enemies. Each animal also has ways to keep itself safe. In the battle for survival, each animal uses whatever weapons it has for staying alive.

Questions

1. What are the main kinds of defenses animals have against their enemies?

2. Study this picture of a hedgehog. How do you think a hedgehog defends itself against its enemies? What part of the selection might help you?

Activities

1. **Make a List**

    List animals that nature protects in each of these ways:
    a. with a shell
    b. with coloring that matches its background
    c. with long legs and a body built for speed
    d. with sharp teeth or claws

2. **Keep a Nature Journal**

    Keep a nature journal about what you have seen in the natural world around you. Try to keep your journal for a week or longer. Study birds, insects, and small animals. See if you can find out and note how they protect themselves from danger.

The Black Fox

From the story *The Midnight Fox* by Betsy Byars
Illustrated by Ron Himler

When Tom's parents leave on a two-month trip to Europe, he reluctantly goes to stay on his Aunt Millie's farm. Used to the city, Tom would rather stay there to work on his models and to be with his friend Petie Burkis.

The first three days on the farm were the longest, slowest days of my life. It seemed to me in those days that nothing was moving at all, not air, not time. Even the bees, the biggest fattest bees that I had ever seen, just seemed to hang in the air. The problem, or one of them, was that I was not an enormously adaptable person and I did not fit into new situations well.

I did a lot of just standing around those first days. I would be standing in the kitchen and Aunt Millie would turn around, stirring something, and bump into me and say, "Oh, my goodness! You gave me a scare. I didn't even hear you come in. When *did* you come in?"

"Just a minute ago."

"Well, I didn't hear you. You were so *quiet*."

Or Uncle Fred would come out of the barn wiping his hands on a rag and there I'd be, just standing, and he'd say, "Well, boy, how's it going?"

"Fine, Uncle Fred."

"Good! Good! Don't get in any mischief now."

"I won't."

I spent a lot of time at the pond and walking down the road and back. I spent about an hour one afternoon hitting the end of an old rope swing that was hanging from a tree in the front yard. I made my two models, and then I took some spare plastic strips and rigged up a harness, so that the horse was pulling the car, and Aunt Millie got very excited over this bit of real nothing and said it was the cleverest thing she had ever seen.

I wrote a long letter to Petie. I went down to the stream and made boats of twigs and leaves and watched them float out of sight. I looked through about a hundred farm magazines. I weeded Aunt Millie's flowers while she stood over me saying, "Not that, not *that*, that's a zinnia. Get the chickweed—see? Right here." And she would snatch it up for me. I had none of the difficult chores that I had expected, because the farm was so well run that everything was already planned without me. In all my life I have never spent longer, more miserable days, and I had to keep saying, "I'm fine, just fine," because people were asking me how I was all the time.

The one highlight of my day was to go down to the mailbox for the mail. This was the only thing I did all day that was of any use. Then, too, the honking of the mail truck would give me the feeling that there was a letter of great importance waiting for me in the box. I could hardly hurry down the road fast enough. Anyone watching me from behind would probably have seen only a cloud of dust, my feet would pound so fast. So far, the only mail I had received was a post card from my mom with a picture of the Statue of Liberty on it telling me how excited and happy she was.

This Thursday morning when I went to the mailbox there was a letter to me from Petie Burkis and I was never so glad to see anything in my life. I ripped it open and completely destroyed the envelope I was in such a hurry. And I thought that when I was a hundred years old, sitting in a chair with a rug over my knees, and my mail was brought in on a silver tray, I would snatch it up and rip it open just like this. I could hardly get it unfolded—Petie folds his letters up small—I was so excited.

Dear Tom,

There is nothing much happening here. I went to the playground Saturday after you left, and you know that steep bank by the swings? Well, I fell all the way down that. Here's the story—

BOY FALLS DOWN BANK WHILE GIRL
ONLOOKERS CHEER

Today Petie Burkis fell down the bank at Harley Playground. It is reported that some ill-mannered girls at the park for a picnic cheered and laughed at the sight of the young, demolished boy. The brave youngster left the park unaided.

Not much else happened. Do you get Chiller Theater? There was a real good movie on Saturday night about mushroom men.

Write me a letter,
Petie Burkis

I went in and gave the rest of the mail to Aunt Millie, who said, "Well, let's see what the government's sending us today," and then I got my box of stationery and went outside.

There was a very nice place over the hill by the creek. There were trees so big I couldn't get my arms around them, and soft grass and rocks to sit on. They were planning to let the cows into this field later on, and then it wouldn't be as nice, but now it was the best place on the farm. . . .

Anyway, I sat down and wrote Petie a letter.

Dear Petie,

I do not know whether we get Chiller Theater or not. Since there is no TV set here, it is very difficult to know what we could get if we had one.

My farm chores are feeding the pigs, feeding the chickens, weeding the flowers, getting the mail, things like that. I have a lot of time to myself and I am planning a movie about a planet that collides with Earth, and this planet and Earth become fused together, and the people of Earth are terrified of the planet, because it is very weird-looking and they have heard these terrible moanlike cries coming from the depths of it. That's all so far.

Write me a letter,
Tom

I had just finished writing this letter and was waiting for a minute to see if I could think of anything to add when I looked up and saw the black fox.

I did not believe it for a minute. It was like my eyes were playing a trick or something, because I was just sort of staring across this field, thinking about my letter, and then in the distance, where the grass was very green, I saw a fox leaping over the crest of the field. The grass moved and the fox sprang toward the movement, and then, seeing that it was just the wind that had caused the grass to move, she ran straight for the grove of trees where I was sitting.

It was so great that I wanted it to start over again, like you can turn movie film back and see yourself repeat some fine thing you have done, and I wanted to see the fox leaping over the grass again. In all my life I have never been so excited.

I did not move at all, but I could hear the paper in my hand shaking, and my heart seemed to have moved up in my body and got stuck in my throat.

The fox came straight toward the grove of trees. She wasn't afraid, and I knew she had not seen me against the tree. I stayed absolutely still even though I felt like jumping up and screaming, "Aunt Millie! Uncle Fred! Come see this. It's a fox, a *fox*!"

Her steps as she crossed the field were lighter and quicker than a cat's. As she came closer I could see that her black fur was tipped with white. It was as if it were midnight and the moon were shining on her fur, frosting it. The wind parted her fur as it changed directions. Suddenly she stopped. She was ten feet away now, and with the changing of the wind she had got my scent. She looked right at me.

I did not move for a moment and neither did she. Her head was cocked to one side, her tail curled up, her front left foot was raised. In all my life I never saw anything like that fox standing there with her pale golden eyes on me and this great black fur being blown by the wind.

Suddenly her nose quivered. It was such a slight movement I almost didn't see it, and then her mouth opened and I could see the pink tip of her tongue. She turned. She was still not afraid, but with a bound that was lighter than the wind—it was as if she was being blown away over the field—she was gone.

Still I didn't move. I couldn't. I couldn't believe that I had really seen the fox.

I had seen foxes before in zoos, but I was always in such a great hurry to get on to the good stuff that I was saying stupid things like, "I want to see the go-rillllllas," and not once had I ever really looked at a fox. Still, I could never remember seeing a black fox, not even in a zoo.

Also, there was a great deal of difference between seeing an animal in the zoo in front of painted fake rocks and trees and seeing one natural and free in the woods. It was like seeing a kite on the floor and then, later, seeing one up in the sky where it was supposed to be, pulling at the wind.

I started to pick up my pencil and write as quickly as I could, "P.S. Today I saw a black fox." But I didn't. This was the most exciting thing that had happened to me, and "P.S. Today I saw a black fox" made it nothing. "So what else is happening?" Petie Burkis would probably write back. I folded my letter, put it in an envelope, and sat there.

I thought about this old newspaper that my dad had had in his desk drawer for years. It was orange and the headline was just one word, very big, the letters about twelve inches high. WAR! And I mean it was awesome to see that word like that, because you knew it was a word that was going to change your whole life, the whole world even. And every time I would see that newspaper, even though I wasn't even born when it was printed, I couldn't say anything for a minute or two.

Well, this was the way I felt right then about the black fox. I thought about a newspaper with just one word for a headline, very big, very black letters, twelve inches high. FOX! And even that did not show how awesome it had really been to me. . . .

The days and weeks passed quickly, long warm days in which I walked through the woods looking for the black fox.

The next time I saw her was in the late afternoon at the ravine.

This was my favorite place in the forest. The sides of the ravine were heavy dark boulders with mosses and ferns growing between the rocks, and at the bottom were trunks of old dead trees. The tree trunks were like statues in some old jungle temple, idols that had fallen and broken and would soon be lost in the creeping foliage. There was only an occasional patch of sunlight.

At the top of the ravine was a flat ledge that stuck out over the rocks, and I was lying there on my stomach this particular afternoon. The rock was warm because the sun had been on it since noon, and I was half asleep when suddenly I saw something move below me. It was the black fox. There was a certain lightness, a quickness that I could not miss.

She came over the rocks as easily as a cat. Her tail was very high and full, like a sail that was bearing her forward. Her fur was black as coal, and when she was in the shadows all I could see was the white tip of her tail.

As I watched, she moved with great ease over one of the fallen trees, ran up the other side of the ravine, and disappeared into the underbrush.

I stayed exactly where I was. My head was resting on my arms, and everything was so still I could hear the ticking of my watch. I wanted to sit up. I am sort of a bony person and after I have been lying on something hard for a long time, I get very uncomfortable. This afternoon, however, I did not move; I had the feeling that the fox was going to come back through the ravine and I did not want to miss seeing her.

While I was waiting I watched an ant run across the ledge with an insect wing. He was running so fast with the wing that he would make a little breeze and the wing would fly out of his grasp. Then he would go back and get the wing and start running again.

Then I watched some birds on the other side of the ravine circling over the rocks, catching insects as they skimmed the air. It was a beautiful sight, and I thought as I watched them, *That* is what man had in mind when he first said, "I want to fly." And I thought about some old genius working up in a remote mountain valley actually making a little flying machine that he could strap on his back like a knapsack, and this old man would come down to a big air base and he would go out on the flight line and announce to everyone, "Folks, I have invented a flying machine." There would be a silence and then everyone would start laughing as if they would never stop, and finally the Captain would pause long enough to explain to the old man that flying machines had *already* been invented, that right over there—that big silver thing with the huge wings, *that* was a flying machine, and over there, those enormous bullet-shaped things, *those* were flying machines. "Well," the old man would say, shaking his head sadly, "I won't waste no more of your time. I'll just head on home," and he would press a button on his knapsack, and silently, easy as a bird, he would lift off the ground, and skimming the air, fly toward the hills. For a moment everyone would be too stunned to move, and then the General would cry, "Come back, come back," and everyone at the air base would run beneath the flying old man crying, "Wait, wait, come back, come back!" because that was the way every one of those men really wanted to fly, free and easy

and silent as a bird. But the old man, who was a little hard of hearing, would not hear their cries and would fly off into the distance and never be seen again.

Right after I stopped thinking about this, the black fox came back. She came down the rocks the same way she had gone up, her white-tipped tail as light as a plume, and I remembered a black knight I saw once in the movies who was so tall and fine and brave you could see his black plume racing ahead of all the other knights when there was a battle.

She had something in her mouth that looked like a frog—it probably was, for the creek was low now and you could always find a frog if you wanted one. She trotted on, apparently concerned only with getting the frog home, and yet I had the feeling that she was missing nothing. She passed across the ravine in a zigzag line and started up the other side.

I did not move, and yet all at once she looked up at me. She froze for a moment, her bright eyes looking at me with curiosity rather than fear, and she cocked her head to one side, listening.

I stayed perfectly still—I was getting good at this—and we looked at each other. Then she turned away and bounded up the side of the ravine, turning at the top and disappearing into the underbrush. I felt that somewhere in the shelter of the trees she had paused to see if I was going to follow. Perhaps she wanted me to follow so she could lead me back into the forest, but I stayed where I was. After a while, I got up and went back to the farm.

The next time I saw the fox, it was a marvelous accident. These don't happen very often in real life, but they do happen, and that's what this was. Like the time Petie and I were walking down the alley behind his house and there, on top of this lady's garbage, we saw a mayonnaise jar full of marbles—not just cat's-eye marbles but all different kinds, kinds I had never seen before. Petie and I turned them all out on the grass and first Petie chose one and then I chose one until they were all gone. And both of us right now, today, have every single one of those marbles.

This was an even better accident. For the past two weeks I had been practically tearing the woods apart looking for the den of the black fox. I had poked under rocks and logs and stuck sticks in rotted trees, and it was a wonder that some animal had not come storming out and just bitten my hand off.

I had found a hornet's nest like a huge gray shield in a tree. I had found a bird's nest, low in a bush, with five pale-blue eggs and no mother to hatch them. I had found seven places where chipmunks lived. I had found a brown owl who never moved from one certain limb of one certain tree. I had heard a tree, split by lightning years ago, suddenly topple and crash to the ground, and I ran and got there in time to see a disgruntled possum run down the broken tree and into the woods. But I did not find the place where the black fox lived.

Now, on this day, I did not go into the woods at all. I had gone up the creek where there was an old chimney, all that was left of somebody's cabin. I had asked Aunt Millie about it, but all she could remember was that some people named Bowden had worked on the farm a long time ago and had lived here. I poked around the old chimney for a while because I was hoping I would find something that had belonged to the Bowdens, and then I gave that up and walked around the bend.

I sat on a rock, perfectly still, for a long time and looked down into the creek. There were crayfish in the water—I could see them, sometimes partly hidden beneath a covering of sand, or I could see the tips of their claws at the edge of a rock. There were fish in the water so small I could almost see through them. They stayed right together, these fish, and they moved together too.

After a while I looked across the creek and I saw a hollow where there was a small clearing. There was an outcropping of rocks behind the clearing and an old log slanted against the rocks. Soft grass sloped down to the creek bank.

I don't know how long I sat there—I usually forgot about my watch when I was in the woods—but it was a long time. I was just sitting, not expecting anything or waiting for anything. And the black fox came through the bushes.

She set a small bird she was carrying on the ground and gave a small yapping bark, and at once, out of a hole beneath the rocks came a baby fox.

He did not look like his mother at all. He was tiny and woolly and he had a stubby nose. He tumbled out of the hole and fell on the bird as if he had not eaten in a month. I have never seen a fiercer fight in my life than the one that baby fox gave that dead bird. He shook it, pulled it, dragged it this way and that, all the while growling and looking about to see if anyone or anything was after his prize.

The black fox sat watching with an expression of great satisfaction. Mothers in a park sometimes watch their young children with this same fond, pleased expression. Her eyes were golden and very bright as she watched the tiny fox fall over the bird, rise, and shake it.

In his frenzy he dropped the bird, picked up an older dried bird wing in its place, and ran around the clearing. Then, realizing his mistake, he returned and began to shake the bird with even greater fierceness. After a bit he made another mistake, dropping the bird by his mother's tail, and then trying to run off with that.

In the midst of all this, there was a noise. It was on the other side of the clearing, but the black fox froze. She made a faint sound, and at once the baby fox, still carrying his bird, disappeared into the den.

The black fox moved back into the underbrush and waited. I could not see her but I knew she was waiting to lead the danger, if there was any, away from her baby. After a while I heard her bark from the woods, and I got up quietly and moved back down the creek. I did not want the black fox to see me and know that I had discovered her den. My cousin Hazeline had told me that foxes will pick up their young like cats and take them away if they think someone has discovered their den. . . .

I decided I would never come back here to bother her. I knew I would be tempted, because already I wanted to see that baby fox play with his bird some more, but I would not do it. If I was to see the black fox again, it would be in the woods, or in the pasture, or in the ravine, but I was not going to come to the den ever again. I did not know that an awful thing was going to happen which would cause me to break this resolution. . . .

Questions

1. The author uses three headlines in this story. The last one is FOX! What are the other two? Why does the author use these headlines?

2. At the start of the story, Tom is lonesome and bored. How does the black fox help him?

3. At the end, Tom says that "an awful thing was going to happen." What do you think the "awful thing" will be? How might the "awful thing" cause Tom to break his promise not to see the black fox again?

4. Tom said, "I was not an enormously adaptable person." Which sentence tells what *not adaptable* means?
   a. "I have never spent longer, more miserable days."
   b. "I did not fit into new situations well."
   c. "I stayed absolutely still even though I felt like jumping up. . . ."

Activity   Write an Exciting Letter

Although Tom wanted to write his friend Petie a letter about the black fox, he knew that writing "Today I saw a black fox" would not be enough. Write an exciting letter for Tom. Try to share with Petie what you (Tom) have seen.

411

frog

A poem by Valerie Worth

The spotted frog
Sits quite still
On a wet stone;

He is green
With a luster
Of water on his skin;

His back is mossy
With spots, and green
Like moss on a stone;

His gold-circled eyes
Stare hard
Like bright metal rings;

When he leaps
He is like a stone
Thrown into the pond;

Water rings spread
After him, bright circles
Of green, circles of gold.

Illustrated by Christa Kieffer

Similes and Metaphors by Myra Cohn Livingston

Poets have exciting ways to help us see things differently and more clearly. For example, when one thing reminds them of another, poets may describe how these two things are alike by comparing them. These imaginative comparisons are called *similes* (SIM•uh•lees) and *metaphors* (MET•uh•fawrz). Poets use them to help us see something in a new way.

A simile is usually introduced by the words *like* or *as*. In her poem "frog," Valerie Worth uses three similes.

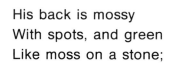

His back is mossy
With spots, and green
Like moss on a stone;

His gold-circled eyes
Stare hard
Like bright metal rings;

When he leaps
He is like a stone
Thrown into the pond.

In the first simile, the poet compares the green of the frog's back to moss on a stone and says that the moss and the frog's back are similar. In the next simile, the frog's eyes remind the poet of bright, metal rings. When the frog leaps, the poet says he is like a stone thrown into the pond.

Similes can be created about everything we know. In her poem "Some People," Rachel Field has two similes about thoughts.

> Your thoughts begin to shrivel up
> Like leaves all brown and dried!

Have your thoughts ever seemed like dried-up leaves? Perhaps, at times, they are

> . . . as thick as fireflies
> All shiny in your mind.

Poets also use metaphors to compare two different things. A poet usually introduces a metaphor with the word *is.* In his poem "Dreams," Langston Hughes uses metaphor to give us a vivid picture of what would happen if dreams should die. He says more than "life would be bad" or "things would be terrible." Instead, he paints a picture for us to see.

Life is a broken-winged bird
That cannot fly.

. . . .
Life is a barren field
Frozen with snow.

By using a metaphor, Langston Hughes gives us a new way of looking at life. So does poet Eve Merriam, who tells us how she feels about the day in her poem "Metaphor." How does the poet give us a new way of looking at the day in these first three lines from her poem?

Morning is
a new sheet of paper
for you to write on.

Now look at some things around you. Look at the shapes of clouds, people you know, buildings, windows, trees, rocks—even your own thoughts and dreams—and make your own similes and metaphors. You'll discover an exciting way of looking at and thinking about the world!

BOOKSHELF

An Insect's Body by Joanna Cole. William Morrow, 1984. Have you ever wondered what a cricket really looks like? This book takes a close look at the common house cricket.

Hawk, I'm Your Brother by Byrd Baylor. Charles Scribner's Sons, 1976. Rudy Soto plans to steal a baby hawk from a nest, hoping the hawk will help him learn to fly.

Ground Squirrels by Colleen S. Bare. Dodd, Mead, 1980. The California ground squirrel and others have many different habits that this book will help you understand.

Nature's Champions: the Biggest, the Fastest, the Best by Alvin and Virginia Silverstein. Random House, 1980. For nature lovers, this book describes more than 25 plants and animals that are unusual in some way.

Misty of Chincoteague by Marguerite Henry. Rand McNally, 1947. Would you want a wild island-pony for your very own? Maureen and Paul hope that Misty will be theirs.

A Swinger of Birches: Poems of Robert Frost for Young People by Robert Frost. Stemmer House, 1982. Discover and feel the beauty of nature in poetry form.

Drawing from Nature by Jim Arnosky. Lothrop, Lee & Shepard, 1982. For anyone who wants to learn how to draw water, land, plants, and animals, this book will interest you. In it, you will see how to make the natural world come alive on your paper.

Cross Fox by Jane Scott. Atheneum, 1980. When neighbors organize a hunt to kill the fox Jamie has been watching in the Pennsylvania countryside, he realizes he must do something to save its life.

A Frog's Body by Joanna Cole. William Morrow, 1980. Closeup pictures of a frog's body help to explain this interesting creature.

Orphans from the Sea by Jack Denton Scott. G. P. Putnam's, 1982. Sometimes birds need our help. This book tells about the people who work to rescue and heal orphaned or injured seabirds and other wild creatures.

Poisonous Snakes by George S. Fichter. Franklin Watts, 1982. Snakes have characteristics and behaviors all their own. Enter the world of these mysterious reptiles and learn about the different kinds of poisonous snakes.

RED RIVER

RIO GRANDE

FT. WORTH

DALLAS

⭐ AUSTIN

HOUSTON

SAN ANTONIO

7 Tales of Texas

CONNECTIONS

Indians of Early Texas

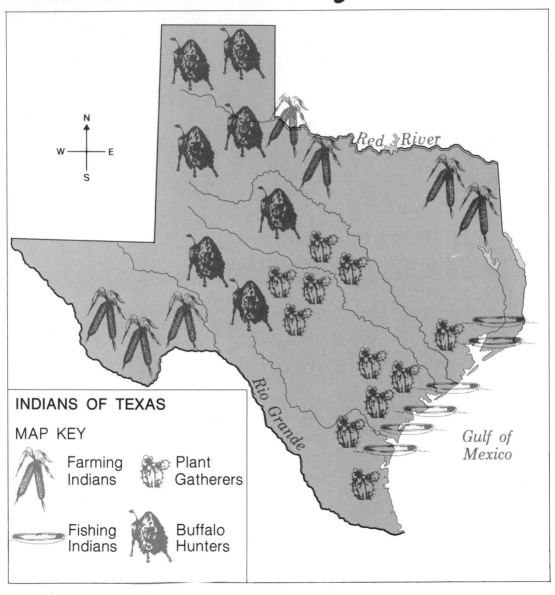

INDIANS OF TEXAS

MAP KEY

Farming Indians

Plant Gatherers

Fishing Indians

Buffalo Hunters

Red River

Rio Grande

Gulf of Mexico

The first Texans came from Asia. Experts believe they drifted through Alaska down to Texas about 12,000 years ago. Settlers from Europe later called these people Indians.

Ten Indian nations once lived in Texas. Each nation had its own rules, customs, and language. The ten nations can be divided into four groups. Some lived mainly by farming. Some lived mainly by fishing. Some gathered plants. Some hunted buffalo. The map shows where the different nations lived.

The **farming Indians** grew corn, beans, squash, and pumpkins. They hardly ever moved their villages, since they had to stay near their fields.

The **fishing Indians** ate oysters, turtles, fish, and roots. When they used up their food in one place, they moved to another. They traveled in canoes made from logs.

The **plant gatherers** lived on plants they found growing wild. They ate nuts, berries, wild beans, and prickly pear cactus. They too moved their villages when they had used up their food.

The **buffalo hunters** got nearly everything they needed from buffalo. They ate the meat. They made their tents and clothes out of buffalo hides. They even found uses for the bones and hooves. They lived on the move, following the buffalo.

Few Indians now live in Texas, but the Indians left their mark. The name *Texas* comes from a Caddo Indian word meaning "friend."

Comanche

Wichita

The Legend of
the Bluebonnet

**A Comanche legend retold and illustrated
by Tomie dePaola**

"Great Spirits, the land is dying. Your People are dying, too," the long line of dancers sang.

"Tell us what we have done to anger you. End this drought. Save your People. Tell us what we must do so you will send the rain that will bring back life."

For three days, the dancers danced to the sound of the drums, and for three days, the People called Comanche watched and waited. And even though the hard winter was over, no healing rains came.

Drought and famine are hardest on the very young and the very old. Among the few children left was a small girl named She-Who-Is-Alone. She sat by herself watching the dancers. In her lap was a doll made from buckskin—a warrior doll. The eyes, nose and mouth were painted on with the juice of berries. It wore beaded leggings and a belt of polished bone. On its head were brilliant blue feathers from the bird who cries "Jay-jay-jay." She loved her doll very much.

"Soon," She-Who-Is-Alone said to her doll, "the shaman will go off alone to the top of the hill to listen for the words of the Great Spirits. Then, we will know what to do so that once more the rains will come and the Earth will be green and alive. The buffalo will be plentiful and the People will be rich again."

As she talked, she thought of the mother who
made the doll, of the father who brought the blue
feathers. She thought of the grandfather and the
grandmother she had never known. They were all
like shadows. It seemed long ago that they had died
from the famine. The People had named her and
cared for her. The warrior doll was the only thing
she had left from those distant days.

"The sun is setting," the runner called as he ran through the camp. "The shaman is returning."

The People gathered in a circle and the shaman spoke.

"I have heard the words of the Great Spirits," he said. "The People have become selfish. For years, they have taken from the Earth without giving anything back. The Great Spirits say the People must

sacrifice. We must make a burnt offering of the most valued possession among us. The ashes of this offering shall then be scattered to the four points of the Earth, the Home of the Winds. When this sacrifice is made, drought and famine will cease. Life will be restored to the Earth and to the People!"

The People sang a song of thanks to the Great Spirits for telling them what they must do.

"I'm sure it is not my new bow that the Great Spirits want," a warrior said.

"Or my special blanket," a woman added, as everyone went to their tipis to talk and think over what the Great Spirits had asked.

Everyone, that is, except She-Who-Is-Alone. She held her doll tightly to her heart.

"You," she said, looking at the doll. "You are my most valued possession. It is you the Great Spirits want." And she knew what she must do.

As the council fires died out and the tipi flaps began to close, the small girl returned to the tipi, where she slept, to wait.

The night outside was still except for the distant sound of the night bird with the red wings. Soon everyone in the tipi was asleep, except She-Who-Is-Alone. Under the ashes of the tipi fire one stick still glowed. She took it and quietly crept out into the night. She ran to the place on the hill where the Great Spirits had spoken to the shaman. Stars filled the sky, but there was no moon.

"O Great Spirits," She-Who-Is-Alone said, "here is my warrior doll. It is the only thing I have from my family who died in this famine. It is my most valued possession. Please accept it."

Then, gathering twigs, she started a fire with the glowing firestick. The small girl watched as the twigs began to catch and burn. She thought of her grandmother and grandfather, her mother and father and all the People—their suffering, their hunger. And

before she could change her mind, she thrust the doll
into the fire.

She watched until the flames died down and the
ashes had grown cold. Then, scooping up a handful,
She-Who-Is-Alone scattered the ashes to the Home
of the Winds, the North and the East, the South and

the West. And there she fell asleep until the first light of the morning sun woke her.

She looked out over the hill, and stretching out from all sides, where the ashes had fallen, the ground was covered with flowers—beautiful flowers, as blue as the feathers in the hair of the doll, as blue as the feathers of the bird who cries "Jay-jay-jay."

When the People came out of their tipis, they

could scarcely believe their eyes. They gathered on the hill with She-Who-Is-Alone to look at the miraculous sight. There was no doubt about it, the flowers were a sign of forgiveness from the Great Spirits.

And as the People sang and danced their thanks to the Great Spirits, a warm rain began to fall and the land began to live again. From that day on, the

431

little girl was known by another name—"One-Who-Dearly-Loved-Her-People."

And every spring, the Great Spirits remember the sacrifice of a little girl and fill the hills and valleys of the land, now called Texas, with the beautiful blue flowers.

Even to this very day.

Questions

1. In the story, She-Who-Is-Alone says to her doll, "You are my most valued possession." Why was the doll so important to She-Who-Is-Alone? Give three reasons for your answer.

2. Why was rain so important to the People?

3. Which word best describes She-Who-Is-Alone? Give at least one reason for your answer.
   a. lonely   c. unselfish   e. bold
   b. kind   d. shy   f. unhappy

4. Match each word with its meaning.
   drought   a. enough for everyone
   famine   b. a long time without rain
   plentiful   c. a long time without food
   a sacrifice   d. something belonging to someone
   possession   e. the giving up of something loved

Activity Write a Story

   Choose one of the Texas wildflowers from the list below. Make up and write a story about it. First think of the characters who will be in your story. They could be people or animals from Texas history. Then think of a problem faced by one or more of the characters. The way the problem is solved should lead to the existence of the flower.

goldenrod   Mexican hat   Indian blanket
        buttercup   Indian paintbrush

Texas Wildlife

Texas has grasslands, forests, and mountains. It has swamps and hot, dry plains. Animals and plants of many different kinds live in these very different places.

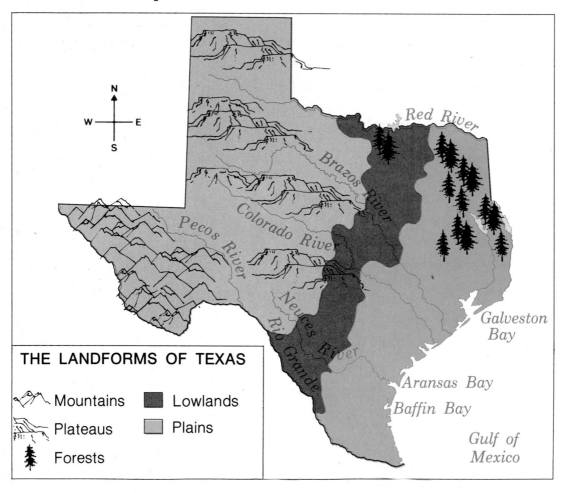

THE LANDFORMS OF TEXAS

- Mountains
- Plateaus
- Forests
- Lowlands
- Plains

Illustrated by Keith Freeman

bluebonnets

Texas Plants

In spring, some fields in central Texas look as if they are covered with a blue carpet. The color comes from millions of wildflowers called **bluebonnets**—the state flower.

Another Texas plant, the **mesquite** (mes·KEET), is not so pretty. It is a thorny bush that can live on very little water. Mesquite grows well in much of hot, dry western Texas. In dry areas, the mesquite is a small bush. The more rain it gets, the taller it grows. In wetter parts of Texas, a mesquite can grow to be a 60-foot-tall tree!

barrel cactus

mesquite

prickly pear cactus

teddy bear cactus

Cactus plants also grow well in western Texas. There are many different kinds of cactuses. The prickly pear cactus has provided food for the Indians.

Texas Animals

Dry western Texas is also a home for many kinds of snakes. **Diamondback rattlesnakes** can grow as long as nine feet. These snakes shed their skin several times a year. Each time, a little of the old skin is left on the snake's tail. These pieces of old skin make up the snake's rattle. When a rattler shakes its tail, the sound is a warning to its enemy.

The **roadrunner** is a Texas bird that sometimes eats small rattlers. This bird dances near the rattler. The snake strikes again and again, missing each time. When the poison in the rattlesnake's fangs is gone, the roadrunner moves in for a meal.

The bird was named roadrunner because it jogs along for miles. Roadrunners can fly, but they are fast runners. They can run at speeds up to 20 miles an hour.

roadrunner   rattlesnake

436

white-tailed deer

Deer live in almost every part of Texas. The **white-tailed deer** are the most common. The white tails of these animals go up like flags at any sign of danger. This warns other deer to be careful.

Texas also has many **coyotes** (ky·OH·teez). Most of them live on the west Texas plains. Coyotes eat almost anything. They eat birds, fish, insects, mice, and berries—and that is just for a start.

One small Texas animal a coyote cannot easily turn into a meal is the **armadillo.** Armadillos are covered with "armor"—very tough, thick skin. By day they sleep underground. At night they look for insects to eat.

armadillo

coyote

javelinas

The **javelina** (jav·uh·LEE·nuh) is another Texas
animal. Javelinas are wild pigs with razor-sharp
tusks. They eat roots and cactus plants.

bison

A few thousand **bison** still live in Texas. (Most
people call them buffalo, but that is not their correct
name.) Long ago millions of bison roamed the Great
Plains. Today there are fewer than thirty thousand.
Most of the bison in Texas live on ranches.

golden eagle

Bighorn sheep

mountain lion

antelope

bear

Protecting Texas Wildlife

Many parts of Texas have been set aside as state or national parks. These parks give plants and wildlife safe places to live and grow. The biggest park is called **Big Bend National Park.** The mountains of Big Bend are the home of the golden eagle and the mountain lion. Bighorn sheep, bears, and antelopes live there, too.

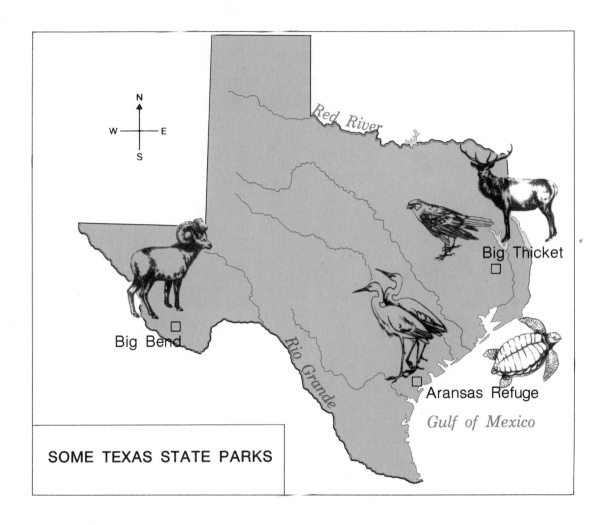

SOME TEXAS STATE PARKS

The **Big Thicket** is a special area in east Texas on the Louisiana border. In its 3½ million acres of swamps and dense forests, you may find more than 1,000 kinds of plants and 300 kinds of birds. Tiny orchids and insect-eating pitcher plants bloom in the swamps. In the forests, wolves and red-tailed hawks hunt for food.

Rare whooping cranes nest in the **Aransas National Wildlife Refuge.** Fewer than 100 "whoopers" are left in the world. Many other rare animals can also be found at Aransas. They include five kinds of sea turtles and the brown pelican.

Texas has many wildlife *preserves* (prih·ZURVZ), places where wildlife is protected by law. In these preserves, people may not hunt the animals or destroy the plants. Such places help the wildlife of Texas survive into the future.

whooping crane

brown pelican

sea turtle

Questions

1. How are mesquite and cactus alike? How are they different?

2. How do the white-tailed deer, the armadillo, and the roadrunner protect themselves from enemies?

3. What are three Texas animals that either are rare or are in danger of dying out?

4. What is a wildlife preserve? What are some animals or plants you will find in a wildlife preserve?

5. Which word correctly completes each of the sentences below?
   a. The (rattlesnake, bison, roadrunner) is a dangerous reptile.
   b. The coyote eats almost everything except (birds, armadillos, fish).

Activity   Plan and Write a Report

Choose a Texas animal or plant that interests you. Find out the following facts about it: the place where it is found, what it looks like, a few interesting facts about it, if it is a rare or common creature. Then write or give a report on the plant or animal you have chosen. Try to find or draw pictures to illustrate your report.

THE SPANIARDS IN TEXAS

Indians were the only people in Texas until the 1500s. The first visitors were hardy explorers from Spain such as Alonzo de Piñeda (ah·LON·soh deh pee·NYAY·da). In 1519, Piñeda stopped at the mouth of the Rio Grande. There, he planted the flag of Spain on the land that was Texas and Mexico. For the next 300 years, Spaniards controlled and settled the land that they called New Spain.

Cabeza de Vaca (kah·BAY·sah deh bah·kah) was another Spanish explorer. In 1528, his ship washed up on Galveston Island. He spent seven years with the American Indians there. Then he walked to Mexico City, a journey that took him through much of southern Texas.

Early Spanish explorers had heard tales that somewhere in Texas were cities made of gold. Spain sent an army captain, Francisco de Coronado (fran·SIS·koh deh koh·roh·NAH·doh), to find the cities. Coronado failed, but many Spaniards still flocked to Texas looking for gold. They never found what they were looking for.

Spanish priests came, too. The priests built *missions*—churches surrounded by small villages. They hoped Indians would settle in the villages and become Christians.

In 1685, the first settlers from France came to Texas. Soon many French people were trying to settle Texas. Spain sent troops to drive the French from Texas. The French later settled in Louisiana, and Texas stayed under Spanish control.

In 1821, Spanish colonists in New Spain broke away from Spain. They set up the new nation of Mexico. Texas was part of this new nation. It was ruled by the government in Mexico City.

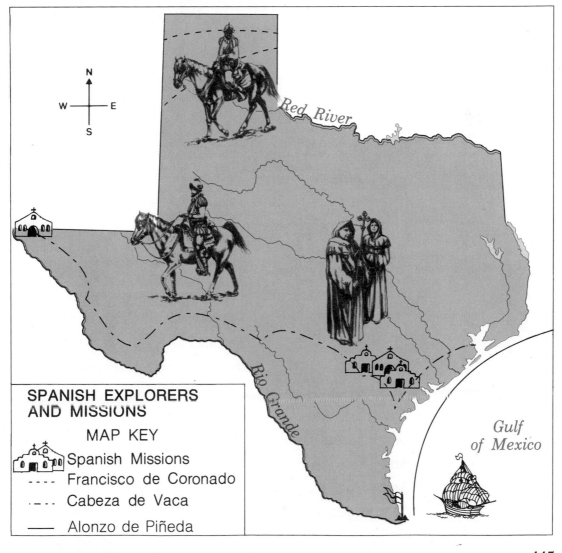

SPANISH EXPLORERS
AND MISSIONS

MAP KEY

Spanish Missions

- - - - Francisco de Coronado

- · - · Cabeza de Vaca

——— Alonzo de Piñeda

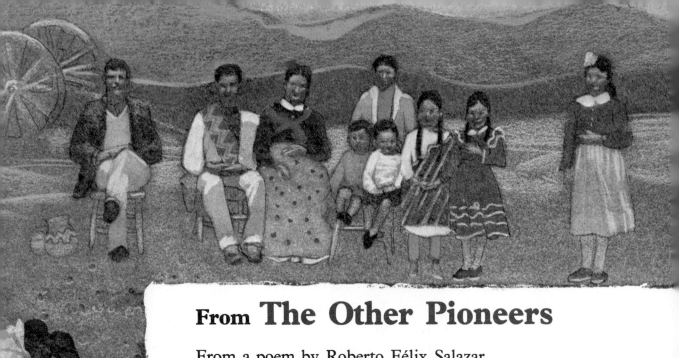

From **The Other Pioneers**

From a poem by Roberto Félix Salazar

People from the United States were not the first Texas pioneers. Long before their time, colonists from Spain and Mexico had been pushing into Texas. Many of them settled in Texas and helped it grow. They, too, were Texas pioneers.

Now I must write
Of those of mine who rode these plains
Long years before the Saxon and the Irish came.
Of those who plowed the land and built the towns
And gave the towns soft-woven Spanish names.
Of those who moved across the Rio Grande
Toward the hiss of Texas snake and Indian yell.
Of men who from the earth made thick-walled homes
And from the earth raised churches to their God.
And of the wives who bore them sons
And smiled with knowing joy.

446   Illustrated by Floyd Cooper

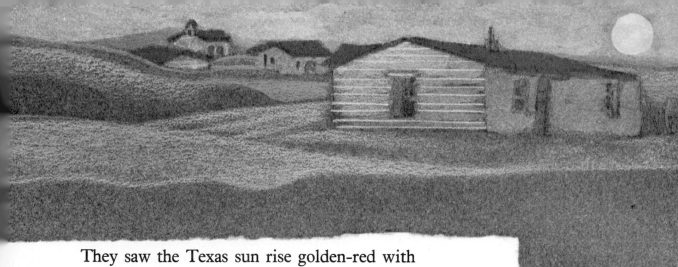

They saw the Texas sun rise golden-red with
    promised wealth
And saw the Texas sun sink golden yet, with
    wealth unspent.
"Here," they said. "Here to live and here to love."
"Here is the land for our sons and the sons of our
    sons."
And they sang the songs of ancient Spain
And they made new songs to fit new needs.
They cleared the brush and planted the corn
And saw green stalks turn black from lack of rain.

And the years moved on.
Those who were first placed in graves
Beside the broad mesquite and the tall nopal.
Gentle mothers left their graces and their arts
And stalwart fathers pride and manly strength.
Salinas, de la Garza, Sánchez, García,
Uribe, González, Martínez, de León:
Such were the names of the fathers.
Salinas, de la Garza, Sánchez, García,
Uribe, González, Martínez, de León:
Such are the names of the sons.

Texas Family Tree

JUAN SEGUIN

Juan Seguin organized Hispanic Texans to fight against Santa Anna in the battles to be free from Mexican rule. He was among the few Texans to fight at both the Alamo and San Jacinto. After the war he was elected to the Texas government, and later became mayor of San Antonio.

Some Texans were jealous of Seguin, however, and spread rumors that he was a traitor. They forced him to flee for his life to Mexico. There the Mexican government put him in jail until

he agreed to join the Mexican army. Meanwhile, the new Texas government sold Seguin's lands.

Seguin died in 1890, a man without a country. Years later the stories about him were proved false. His body was returned to the Texas town of Seguin, named in his honor. He was reburied as a Texas hero.

DOÑA MARIA CALVILLO

Doña Maria Calvillo (dohn·nyah mah·REE·ah kahl·BEE·yoh) was an expert at riding horses and roping cattle. She owned a large ranch in early Texas. On her ranch, she had cattle, sheep, and goats.

About 20 families lived on her land. Some of the families worked as ranch hands. Others worked as carpenters, blacksmiths, and tailors. Doña Maria also built a sugar mill and a *granary,* or

Illustrated by Robert Masheris

building for storing grain, on her land.

She was friendly with the Indians in her area, and in the winter gave them food. Born in 1765, Doña Maria Calvillo lived nearly 100 years.

LORENZO DE ZAVALA

Lorenzo de Zavala (loh·REN·soh deh sah·BAH·lah) was among the signers of the Texas Declaration of Independence. Before coming to Texas he had served as governor of a Mexican *province*, or state, and as the Mexican Ambassador to France.

De Zavala designed the first flag of the Texas republic. It was blue with one gold star in the middle. Around the star was the word TEXAS. De Zavala also served as the first vice-president of the new Republic of Texas.

FATHER FRANCISCO HIDALGO

Father Francisco Hidalgo (frahn·SIS·koh ee·DAHL·goh) was among the first Spanish priests to work among the Texas Indians. At the time, the Spanish government had little interest in setting up missions in Texas. Father Hidalgo asked for help from the French settlers in Louisiana. Some French people came to the Rio Grande Valley in answer to his call. When Spain saw that the French were beginning to settle in Texas, the Spanish government decided to work harder to settle in Texas. In 1716, the Spanish government helped Father Hidalgo reopen the first mission in Texas.

FATHER MIGUEL HIDALGO

Father Miguel Hidalgo (mee·GEHL ee·DAHL·goh) started the Mexican Revolution. In the early 1800s, he noticed how badly Spanish rulers treated the people of Mexico. So he tried to organize Indians and Spaniards who had been born in America to fight against Spain. Father Hidalgo's army won many battles but was finally overcome. Father Hidalgo was then taken and shot. Other leaders, however, continued the revolution Father Hidalgo had started.

WILLIAM GOYENS

William Goyens (wil·yuhm goh·ehnz), the son of a freed slave, moved to Texas in 1820. He

earned a fortune as a blacksmith making wagons and guns, two of the most important items needed by Texas pioneers. Goyens spoke several Indian languages. After Texas freed itself from Mexico, he became an Indian agent for the new government. He helped the government work with the Indians living in Texas.

PADRE NICOLAS BALLI

One of the first Spaniards to settle in Texas was the sea-going priest Padre Nicolas Balli (pah·dreh nee·coh·LAHS bah·yee). According to one story, King Charles of Spain offered Padre Balli all the Texas land he could drag a cowhide around in three days. Padre Balli sent food and fresh horses on ahead. Then, dragging a cowhide, he rode swiftly, changing horses from time to time. In this way he claimed several million acres of Texas. Padre Island, near Brownsville, is named after Padre Balli because he started a ranch there.

The Alamo: Texans Fight for Freedom

In 1836, a man named Antonio López de Santa Anna (ahn·TOH·nee·oh LOH·pehs deh sahn·tuh ahn·nuh) was the dictator of Mexico when Mexico ruled what is now called Texas. Santa Anna took away certain rights that had been promised to Texas. This made Texans very angry. Several times, they attacked and captured Mexican soldiers in Texas. In one attack, they captured the city of San Antonio, which was under Mexican rule.

Santa Anna decided to punish the Texans. He gathered a large army in Mexico and headed north. His path into Texas lay through San Antonio. There, a small band of Texans decided to block his way.

The Texans turned an old mission called the **Alamo** into a fort. Santa Anna and his army of 5,000 soldiers circled the fort. Inside the fort were less than 190 fighting men and about 15 women and children. The Texans held the fort for 13 days. During that time, Texas leaders met at a town named Washington-on-the-Brazos. They declared Texas a free country.

On March 6, Santa Anna's forces broke into the Alamo. They killed all the men inside. In doing so they may have lost the war. Santa Anna's cruelty made other Texans fight even harder against him. Other Texans remembered the brave men killed by Santa Anna. "Remember the Alamo!" became the Texas battle cry. Six weeks later, Texans attacked Santa Anna's army at San Jacinto (sahn hah·SEEN·toh). Shouting "Remember the Alamo!", they defeated the Mexican army in 18 minutes.

The fight for Texas independence would not have been possible without the help of very brave men and women. Many gave their lives. Some lived, but always remembered the battle. Whatever their role, all these men and women had a common bond—to be free from Mexico. Here are some of those brave men and women.

Stephen Austin   In 1821, Stephen Austin led the first settlers from the United States to Texas. He got permission to do so from the Mexican government. After Austin's group came to Texas, so did many other people from the United States. By 1830, they outnumbered Spaniards in Texas ten to one. Later, when Texas fought to free itself from Mexico, Austin got help from the United States.

Sam Houston   Sam Houston was a lawyer. He moved to Texas from Tennessee. In 1836, Texas leaders said Texas was a free country. They raised an army to defend themselves against Mexico. The Texas leaders put Sam Houston in charge of the army. Later that year, Houston's army beat the Mexican forces at San Jacinto. Texas became a free country. Sam Houston was made its first president.

William Travis   William Travis was one of the leaders in the war for Texan independence. He led the army of Texans at the Alamo. The Mexican army attacked the Alamo after Texas declared its freedom. Travis and his men fought the huge Mexican army in a battle that lasted 13 days. When Travis and all his men were killed, the Mexicans overran the fort.

Susanna Dickenson   Susanna Dickenson was one of the few women at the Alamo, and an eyewitness to the battle. Mrs. Dickenson's husband was one of the soldiers who had decided to stay and fight at the Alamo. Mrs. Dickenson and her small child decided to stay, too. During the 13-day battle, Mrs. Dickenson helped to care for the wounded soldiers. When Santa Anna and his army finally took over the Alamo, he let Mrs. Dickenson and her child leave.

The battle at the Alamo was real. None of the Americans who fought was left alive. But Texans remembered the Alamo and told its story over and over again.

Colonel Travis Draws the Line

From the novel *The Boy in the Alamo* by Margaret Cousins
Illustrated by Bradley Clark

One retelling of the famous battle is seen through the eyes of twelve-year-old Billy Campbell. Billy had followed his older brother Buck to the Alamo. Buck had come to help the small group of Americans and Texans fight the Mexican Army. Here, in Billy's words, is what might have happened at the Alamo when Colonel Travis called for volunteers.

The next night we were surprised by pistol shots from one of our sentries. This was followed by a great pounding on the main gate, and into the fort trotted thirty-two men on horseback. They were led by Lieutenant George C. Kimball and guided by Lieutenant Smith. They were volunteers from the town of Gonzales, where Dr. Sutherland and Lieutenant Smith had taken the news of the siege. The recruits had inched their way through the Mexican lines around the Alamo without the loss of a man. (But our own sentry, who didn't recognize them as Texan soldiers, had shot one volunteer in the foot!)

Everybody cheered as they trotted in. We roasted the last beef in the plaza and ate supper. One of the

Mexican volunteers got out his guitar and played "La
Paloma" and "La Golandrina." Colonel Travis
welcomed Lieutenant Kimball and his men. They
knew better than we did how much in danger all our
lives were. The recruits manned our positions and
relieved men who had been there for five days.

The next morning, March 2nd, at eleven o'clock
in the morning, our lookout announced the approach
of a solitary horseman, with a Mexican cavalry patrol

right behind, peppering him with bullets. The main
gate was swung open, and Colonel James Bonham
galloped in. As we slammed the gates shut, the
Mexicans fell back and disappeared.

As soon as Colonel Bonham got his breath back
he made his report to Colonel Travis. He had ridden
many weary miles in five days and had made two

sneaks through the enemy's lines.

"There will be no help from Goliad," he said. "Fannin has refused."

Colonel Travis shook his head.

"He says he cannot risk the whole Texas Army," Colonel Bonham said.

"The Texas Convention meets today at Washington-on-the-Brazos," Colonel Bonham continued. "If we can hold on—"

"We must hold on," said Colonel Travis. "But it may take weeks!"

"I was warned that it was suicide to come back into the fort," Bonham said.

"That may be true," Travis said. "You should have listened—"

"Ah, Buck," Colonel Bonham said. "How could I leave you in this hole? We will stand or fall together!"

They had gone to school together and had been friends for many years.

Colonel Travis' face was a study. It lighted up with new determination.

"How can we lose with such men as you on our side?" he asked. "Thank you, Jim. That was a good ride."

Colonel Bonham was the last man who came into the Alamo.

On that day, in Washington-on-the-Brazos, the Independence of Texas was declared and a new republic founded. But we had no way of knowing that. We knew only that the Mexican Army was closing in on us.

The next day we had heavy bombardment from all sides and the lookouts reported that the Mexicans were setting up their guns nearer and nearer our walls. Colonel Travis went from one station to the next encouraging the men. His face was gray.

That night he summoned the whole garrison to the chapel, except for the sentries. Even me.

"Men of the Alamo," he said, "I have studied Colonel Bonham's reports, and I have counted our supplies and ammunition. I have studied our positions. I feel that I must tell you that I think there is no chance that help will arrive in time to save us. General Santa Anna will launch himself on us within days—maybe hours. When the final assault comes— and it may come at any hour now—it will mean death to all of us here. Our fate is sealed. For myself, I will stay to the end and die fighting."

Colonel Travis paused. He withdrew his sword from its scabbard, and with it he drew a long line on the dirt floor of the chapel. Then he stepped across it.

"For those who wish to save themselves, there is still time. You may go if you wish. You will not be prevented. But those of you who wish to die fighting for the cause of liberty, step across to my side of this line!"

Quiet fell over the garrison as we stared at Colonel Travis. Then two or three men in the rear jumped over the line, and others began to shuffle across. Colonel Crockett and the Tennessee Volunteers crossed in a body. I crossed with them, hardly understanding what it all meant.

Colonel Bowie had been brought to the meeting on a stretcher. He was as weak as a kitten, and his face was as pale as his shirt, but the fever seemed to have gone down that day. He threshed restlessly around on his cot and then fell back. He lay there a second and then turned his face toward Travis.

"Boys," he said in a whisper, "I can't make it by myself, but I'd be much obliged if some of you would give me a hand."

Buck and I leaped to the foot of his cot, and two more Volunteers grabbed the other end, and we lifted Colonel Bowie over the line.

As soon as this was done there was a rush of feet, and everybody crossed over except one man.

He was a paid soldier, named Louis Rose, nicknamed Moses, who fought for a salary. He was a Frenchman who had fought in Napoleon's Army. He was not a Texian.

"I fight to live, not to die," he shouted in broken English and walked out of the chapel. Nobody moved. He ran into the plaza, shinnied up over the wall and dropped down to the other side, where he made his escape. Nobody stopped him. Nobody missed him. The Alamo was not a place to fight for money.

We carried Colonel Bowie back to his room, in the front of the chapel. "The die is cast," he said. "Victory or death."

Buck and I walked back to the earthworks together. "If we don't get a chance to talk any more," Buck said. "I want to tell you this. You are a man—not a boy."

"Oh, Buck," I said, and I felt like crying. "I only wanted to be like you."

"You're a better man than I am," Buck said. "For a minute there, I wanted to cut and run."

"Me, too," I said. "But we didn't!"

"No, we didn't," Buck said. "I guess that's the way Papa felt about the Comanche. You can't always be sensible. Some things are more important."

I wanted to tell my brother how much I thought of him, but I didn't know how.

"It was not Sarah Ellen Payne I was in love with," Buck said. "It was Texas."

That night Colonel Travis wrote his last letter. It was addressed to the Convention in Washington-on-the-Brazos. I don't think he had much hope that it would bring help, but he had to try. I made two copies of it for him.

"I look to the colonies alone for aid," he wrote. "Unless it arrives soon, I will have to fight the enemy on his own terms. I will, however, do the best I can . . . and although we may be sacrificed . . . the victory will cost the enemy so dear that it will be worse for him than defeat. I hope your honorable body will hasten reinforcements. . . . Our supply of ammunition is limited. . . . God and Texas. Victory or death."

When the writing was finished, Colonel Travis summoned Lieutenant Smith and gave him the paper.

Under the cover of darkness Lieutenant Smith rode his horse out of the main gate for the last time. He was the last soldier to leave the Alamo alive.

Questions

1. Who was the last Texas soldier to *enter* the Alamo before the battle? Who was the last to *leave*?

2. The day that Colonel Bonham entered the Alamo, an important event in Texas history took place. What was it?

3. If somebody said, "The battle of the Alamo was a great defeat for Texas," would you agree? Why or why not?

4. Replace the underlined words with words from the story that have the same meaning.
   a. The <u>new soldiers</u> had inched their way into the fort. (page 455)
   b. A <u>single</u> horseman was approaching. (page 455)

Activity   Write a Cast of Characters

If you were planning to make the story "Colonel Travis Draws the Line" into a play, you would need to make a list of all the characters. Write a *cast of characters* for the play. Divide the characters into two groups. The *main characters* will play the most important parts. The *supporting characters* will play the less important roles. For each main character, write a short description of what the person looks like, and what he is wearing.

CONNECTIONS

Texas Cowboys

Oh, I am a Texas cowboy, just off the Texas plains,
My trade is cinching saddles and pulling the bridle reins.
It's I can throw the lasso with the greatest of ease
And mount my bronco pony and ride him where I please.
—from "The Texas Cowboy," an old cowboy song

The Cowboys in History

The Texas cowboys have become well-known characters in American life. We know them well, from their tall hats to their high-heeled boots. We know that they love their horses, rope cattle, and ride the range, where they can be free. We know a lot about the Texas cowboys because we have sung songs, read stories, and told tales about them for more than a hundred years.

Yet Texas cowboys are not just characters from stories and songs. They were men who really lived long ago in Texas. The real cowboys were ranch workers. They were men who *drove*, or herded, and cared for longhorn cattle on the Texas plains. From about 1865 until about 1890, the Texas cowboys were an important part of the Old West. They are still a big part of its history.

464

That history begins around 1865. The Civil War had just ended. Texas soldiers were coming home from the war. The soldiers needed jobs, and Texas ranchers were hiring. The ranchers wanted men to help them handle the wild longhorn cattle that roamed throughout Texas. Many soldiers took those ranch-hand jobs. They became the first cowboys.

Cowboy Clothes

"I see by your outfit that you are a cowboy."
These are words from an old cowboy song. The
words happen to be true. Cowboys had to work out-
doors in every kind of weather. They worked in dust
storms and snow storms, in rain and blistering heat.
For this outdoor work, cowboys needed certain kinds
of clothes. Their working outfits set the cowboys
apart from all other working men.

Because cowboy work was rough, they wore shirts
and pants made of tough cloth. Over their pants,

they wore leather coverings called *chaps*. The tough leather protected them as they rode through brush and thorns. High-topped boots protected their ankles from thorns and snakes. The high heels on the boots kept their feet in their saddle stirrups.

Every piece of clothing had a special use. The bandanas around the cowboys' necks could be pulled over their mouths when the air was dusty. Their big cowboy hats protected them from both sun and rain. Cowboy hats could also be used as pillows and water pails.

Cowboys used pistols, but mainly for noise. Pistols were useful in a cattle *stampede,* when the cattle became frightened and ran in all directions. A pistol shot could turn aside a charging longhorn and save the cowboy's life.

Cowboys owned very little, but most cowboys owned their own saddle and a rope for catching cattle. Some cowboys also owned a horse, but most horses belonged to the rancher. No cowboy could do his work without a good horse to ride.

The Roundups

The cowboys' work with the cattle was seasonal. The wild longhorn cattle needed little tending during much of the year. Few ranches had fences in those days, so the cattle wandered freely over the Texas range.

Then twice a year, in the spring and fall, the cowboys had to *round up,* or gather, the cattle.

Roundups lasted for several weeks. It was then that
the cowboys rode miles and miles every day. They
rode over trackless land, looking for cattle.

Each roundup had a different purpose. In the
spring, cowboys rounded up cattle in order to brand
them. A *brand* was a mark burned into a cow's hide.
Each rancher had a different brand. A cow's brand
identified its owner.

Most of the cattle branded each spring were
calves, born just that year. A calf, or *dogie*, belonged
to the same ranch that owned its mother. Sometimes,

cowboys also found *mavericks*—grown cows that no one had ever branded. Mavericks belonged to anyone who could catch and brand them. After the spring branding, all the cattle were released to graze for the summer and get fat.

In the fall, cowboys from each ranch rounded up the cattle again. This time they looked for branded cattle that were ready for market. They rounded up these cattle in order to drive them to the nearest railroad. From there, trains would carry the cattle to meat markets in the northern cities.

The Cattle Drives

Railroad towns were hundreds of miles from Texas ranches. Moving cattle to a railroad, therefore, took two or three months. On these cattle drives, 20 to 30 cowboys had to control thousands of wild cattle in a herd stretching two or three miles long. The cattle raised choking dust clouds, and their hooves rumbled on the prairie like the sound of distant thunder. The cowboys rode along the edges of the herd, keeping it together and moving.

Besides the cowboys, three other men were necessary to the cattle drive. The *trail boss* was the man in

charge of the drive. He gave orders and settled disputes, or disagreements. On the trail, his word was law. The *wrangler* was the person who took care of the extra horses. Fifteen or twenty extra horses were always brought along on a cattle drive. Wranglers were usually young men just learning to be cowboys.

The *cook* drove a wagon that carried food and all other needed supplies. Many times, the cowboys would keep their belongings in the cook's wagon, too.

During these cattle drives, the cowboys spent long, hard days on horseback. Every day they crossed miles of land and saw no other people. They heard little but the cattle's thundering hooves on the plains.

At night, the drive stopped and silence fell. Yet even quiet times were times to fear, for silence made the cattle restless. A herd of restless cattle could *stampede,* or set off on a wild charge. Any sudden sound—a rattlesnake rustling, thunder clapping, even a twig snapping—could start a stampede. A few cowboys had to stay awake each night and sing to the cows to keep them calm. The next morning, the drive would begin again.

The Cowboys in Story

Books and movies can make the cowboy age seem very long, but it only lasted about 30 years. By 1890, railroad tracks ran to many parts of Texas. Ranchers no longer needed to make long cattle drives to railroads hundreds of miles away. Many ranchers had built fences around their land, so they no longer needed to brand their cattle. As the cowboys' jobs disappeared, so did the cowboys.

By then, however, cowboys had caught the imagination of many Americans. People admired cowboys for the hardships they endured, the dangers they faced, and the rootless freedom of their lives. Stories were written and movies were made about cowboy heroes. These heroes were men of few words. They were men who never went looking for trouble but never ran from it. They lived by a code of honor. Real cowboys had passed into history, but the storybook cowboy had just been born.

Well come along, boys, and listen to my tale,
I'll tell you of my troubles on the old Chisholm trail.

Come a ti yi yippy, yippy yay, yippy yay,
Come a ti yi yippy yippy yay.

—from "The Old Chisholm Trail"

Questions

1. Suppose you were a trail boss hiring workers for a cattle drive. What three jobs would you need to fill? What are some questions you might ask the men who applied?

2. How did railroads and fences each help bring the cowboy age to an end?

3. Would you have enjoyed working as a cowboy? Why or why not? Which parts would you have enjoyed the most? the least?

4. In each row of words below, which word does not fit with the others? Explain why it is out of place.
    a. spurs   stampede   chaps   bandana   boots
    b. maverick   saddle   dogie   brand   cattle
    c. plains   range   land   railroad   ranch

Activity   Draw a Map

Draw a map of an imaginary ranch. Show streams, gullies, hills, and other land forms on the ranch. Show what you would build on the land if you were the ranch owner. Mark at least five places on the map where you would look for cattle if you were a cowboy on a roundup. Make a key explaining what your map shows.

The Old Chisholm Trail

An old cowboy song

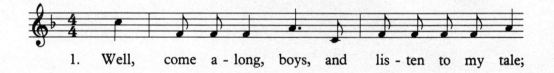

1. Well, come a-long, boys, and lis-ten to my tale;

I'll tell you of my trou-bles on the old Chis-holm Trail.

Chorus

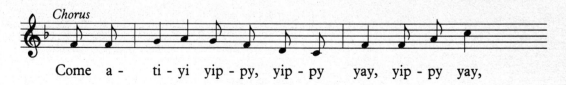

Come a-ti-yi yip-py, yip-py yay, yip-py yay,

Come a-ti-yi yip-py yip-py yay.

Illustrated by Robert Masheris

2. With a ten-dollar horse and a forty-dollar saddle,
   I started in herding these Texas cattle.
   (*Chorus*)

3. I started up the trail October twenty-third;
   I started up the trail with the Lone Star herd.
   (*Chorus*)

4. I jumped in the saddle and grabbed hold of the horn,
   The best cowpuncher that ever was born.
   (*Chorus*)

5. My foot in the stirrup, my seat in the saddle,
   The best cowpuncher that ever rode a-straddle.
   (*Chorus*)

6. I'm on my horse, and I'm going on the run,
   The quickest-shooting cowboy that ever pulled a gun.
   (*Chorus*)

From SPINDLETOP

A story by Sibyl Hancock
Illustrated by Lyle Miller

In 1901, an event happened that changed Texas history. Oil was discovered on Spindletop hill near the town of Beaumont. Until then, people thought that oil could be found only on the eastern coast of the United States.

Jimmy and his family lived in Beaumont. Jimmy's father worked at Spindletop. This is Jimmy's story of what happened on Spindletop hill on January 10, 1901.

"I'll see you later, Mama," Jimmy said. "Papa and I are going now."

Mama hurried from the kitchen. She wiped flour from her hands onto her apron. She bent to pick baby Robert up off the floor.

"Both of you be careful today," Mama said.

"We will," Papa said. "Who knows? Maybe today we will strike oil."

Jimmy had heard Papa say those same words every day for more than three months. That was how long they had been in the little Texas town of Beaumont.

Today was January 10, 1901. It was Mama's birthday. When the day's work was done, Papa and he would go into town. They would pick up a locket they had ordered for Mama.

"What are you thinking about?" Papa asked. "You're so quiet."

Jimmy climbed into the wagon beside Papa. "I was thinking of Mama's locket," Jimmy said.

Papa nodded and flapped the reins. The horses started off toward a small hill named Spindletop. There wasn't enough money this year to buy Mama a new stove for her kitchen. Papa had taken all their savings and bought land near Spindletop. Papa and four other men were drilling for oil on the Spindletop land owned by Captain A. F. Lucas. Papa felt sure oil would be found there soon.

"Ouch!" Jimmy cried. He swatted a fat mosquito on his neck. "Whoever heard of mosquitoes in January!" Jimmy said.

Papa laughed. "You can find just about anything in Texas," he said.

As the wagon rounded a bend in the road, the top of Spindletop hill came into view. Jimmy could see the tall derrick that stood over the well.

"I wonder what it's like to strike oil?" Jimmy asked.

"Maybe we'll find out," Papa said. Papa stopped the wagon at the top of the hill. "I picked up the new drill bit," Papa called to the men at the derrick. "Good," Curt called back. "We will really need it."

Jimmy liked Curt. He liked the other men, too, but Curt was special. Curt wasn't as tall as Papa, but he was very strong. Curt had a wide grin, and he liked to tease Jimmy.

Jimmy followed Papa up the steps to the derrick floor. Curt reached over and rumpled Jimmy's hair with his big hand.

"Let's go to work," Papa said.

Jimmy handed Papa tools. The sharp new drill bit was put onto the end of the pipe that had been drilling far into the ground.

"So far we can't break through that last layer of rock," Curt said.

Jimmy stared at the drill pipe. His heart sank. If they couldn't drill through the rock, then they would never find any oil.

Papa started the machinery, and the clattering, grinding noise began.

"The drill is 700 feet down into the ground," Papa said.

Suddenly mud began boiling up past the drill. Then the drill pipe began rising. It went higher and higher and started going through the top of the derrick.

"Run!" Papa yelled.

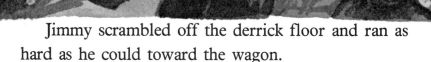

Jimmy scrambled off the derrick floor and ran as hard as he could toward the wagon.

"Look!" Curt shouted.

The drill pipe was still coming out of the well. It began to break into pieces and fall to the ground. The last piece of pipe was followed by rocks and a deafening roar of gas.

"What was that all about?" Curt exclaimed.

"Let's go see," Papa said. "Bring your shovel, Jimmy."

The floor of the derrick was covered with mud. And there was no sign of oil.

"What a mess," Jimmy said.

"Watch out!" Papa shouted.

A great chunk of mud flew out of the well with an explosion like a cannon. A cloud of blue gas followed. Jimmy threw down his shovel and ran. The other men were close behind him.

Once again the noise stopped. Slowly the men walked toward the well. Jimmy climbed back onto the derrick floor. He was a little scared, but he wasn't going to let it show.

Papa stood over the well and looked down the hole. They could hear a bubbling sound deep in the earth. Then foamy oil began to pour out of the hole.

"Oil!" Jimmy cried. "It's oil!"

It was as if the well had a heart beating beneath the ground. The oil pushed upward, then settled back. And it kept pushing up a little higher with each great heartbeat.

All at once the oil spurted through the top of the derrick and kept climbing until it reached twice the height of the derrick.

"Ya-hoo!" Curt shouted.

Everyone slapped each other on the back. Oil! They had struck oil. Jimmy blinked as the black oil soaked his clothes and sprayed into his face. Never in all his life had he seen anything like this.

"How are we going to keep the oil from spraying?" Jimmy asked.

Curt had stopped smiling. He looked worried. "It's going to be hard," he said.

It wasn't long before Captain Lucas came bouncing over the rough road in his wagon.

"It . . . it is oil!" he shouted. Captain Lucas was so excited he could hardly speak. He shook Papa's hand. "Wonderful job," he said.

Papa grinned. Then he sent a man into town to get the parts they would need to try and cap the well to stop the spurting oil.

In an hour's time people from Beaumont began to come to Spindletop. They came in buggies and on horseback and on foot.

Papa had asked extra men from town to hold the crowd back.

"Don't let anyone smoke," Papa told them.

But it wasn't long before Jimmy saw a young man on a horse light a pipe and drop the match to the oily ground. Flames leaped up.

"Fire!" Jimmy yelled. "Fire!"

Papa and Curt and some of the other men came running. They pulled off their coats and pounded the flames. When their coats burned, they used their shirts. Jimmy took off his coat and beat the flames.

The people who had gathered fled back to Beaumont. Oil spray had drifted in the breeze. Sulphur gas was in the air. People had to hold their noses because of the bad smell. Houses painted white were soon streaked with orange and black stains.

At last the men put the fire out. Jimmy had burned his thumb a little, but he was glad he had helped.

"Now you must go home," Papa told him. "Wash up and eat. Then bring us food and some clean clothes. Bring some slicker suits, too."

"But what about capping the well?" Jimmy asked.

Just then a huge rock flew from the well into the air with a great roar of gas.

"We can't cap the well until it stops throwing out rocks," Papa said. "We'll have to wait."

The men took turns staying at the well. Jimmy always took his turn with Papa. They watched as the oil kept shooting 160 feet into the air. Jimmy's face was always covered with oil. Everything smelled and tasted and felt like oil, even when he went home to rest.

One day passed. Then two. Then five. And finally ten days had passed.

Jimmy helped the men throw up dirt walls far around the well. The walls held back the oil that was pouring over the ground. First the oil fell in pools. And the pools turned into lakes of oil.

"Today we'll cap the well," Papa said. "There haven't been any more rocks thrown from the well since yesterday." Papa put on some special glasses to protect his eyes. "I'll cap the well," he said.

"No," Curt said. "I'm the only man who doesn't have a wife and family. I'll cap the well."

Papa thought for a moment. "All right," he said, "but I'll stand close by you."

Curt put on some special glasses like Papa's. Jimmy felt a cold knot of fear inside him. Jimmy knew that Curt was in danger as he began to fit pipes over the well. And Papa was standing so close to the well that he was in danger, too. The well could explode very easily.

Clouds of gas drifted past Curt's face. He stepped back to get fresh air. Then he was over the well again. Jimmy moved closer. He had to help if he could.

Curt worked at fitting pipes together for hours. Papa worked hard, too. He handed lumber and even some railroad track railing to Curt.

What Curt was putting together would one day be called a *christmas tree* by oil workers. That was because of the way it looked with all of its branches of pipes. The christmas tree helped cut down the great force that was blowing the oil high in the sky.

"Ready!" Curt yelled at last.

Papa helped lower a big valve over the pipe. The great hissing roar stopped, and there was silence. The well was capped.

The men who helped look for oil took many risks. They used new methods and equipment that were unknown and untried. Every day, the men at Spindletop worked in danger of losing their lives. But they felt it was worth it. The "black gold" known as oil could turn Texas from a farming state to an important industrial and manufacturing state.

Questions

1. The story shows that finding oil can be dangerous. What were two of the dangerous problems that Papa and Curt faced when they
   struck oil? How did they solve each problem?

2. What might have happened to Jimmy's family if
   oil had *not* been found? Why do you think so?

3. Which four things would you need to start
   an oil drilling business? Why would you need
   them?

   a. drill   d. locket
   b. derrick   e. valve
   c. christmas tree   f. wagon

Activity   Write a Friendly Letter

Imagine that you are living in Beaumont in
1902. One year ago, oil was discovered at
Spindletop. Write a letter to a friend in another
city, describing how the oil strike has changed
your life. Think of ways in which the discovery
of oil might have affected your family. Try to
imagine how it might have changed your town.
Remember that before oil was discovered
Beaumont was a small, quiet city. Your letter
should tell how you feel about the changes.

About SIBYL HANCOCK

Sibyl Hancock, a native Texan, began a writing career during her last years in college. At first, she wrote about experiences she had as a child. "I used to write stories about my pets, my family, and even about comic book characters." As she grew older, she would take parts of books she read and rewrite them according to how she wanted the characters to act. All this time, however, she had no idea that she wanted to become an author. Writing just seemed to come naturally for her.

Sibyl Hancock attributes her success to a number of things. "Living in Texas, I am lucky to be able to draw upon a heritage of cowboys riding the range, of booming oil wells, and of the experiences in riding out hurricanes." This, along with all the reading she did growing up, and the influence she had from her parents, gave her a good background for her writing.

More Books by Sibyl Hancock

Mario's Mystery Machine
Esteban & the Ghost

Texas Today

Texas is a big state with many faces. In some ways it is leading the nation into the future. At the same time, the past is very much alive in Texas today.

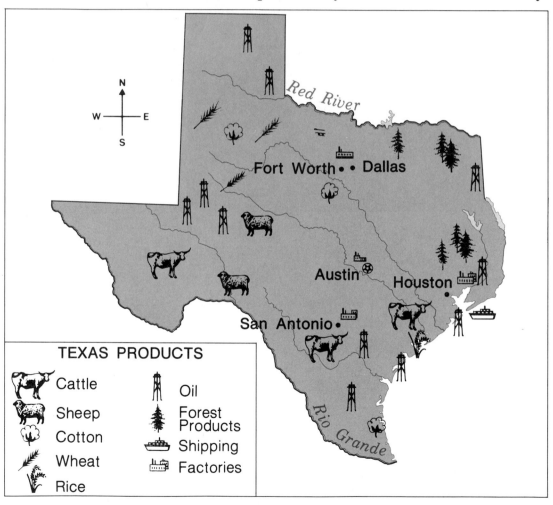

TEXAS PRODUCTS

- Cattle
- Sheep
- Cotton
- Wheat
- Rice
- Oil
- Forest Products
- Shipping
- Factories

Ranching

Texas raises more cattle than any other state—about 15 million head of cattle a year. Cowboys, therefore, are not just part of Texas history. Many Texans still work as cowboys.

Today, however, cowboys not only ride horses. They also drive around the range in pickup trucks. Sometimes they use helicopters to find their cattle. The cattle they find are no longer half-wild long-horns, but short-horned breeds such as Herefords.

Many Texas ranches have no cattle at all. They are sheep and goat ranches. These animals are now just as important to Texas as cattle. Texas produces the most wool of any state in the United States.

Farming

Texas is also a leading farm state. It has more than 185,000 farms, more farmed space than any other state. The first settlers from the United States started cotton farms in Texas. Cotton is still a leading crop. It is grown in many parts of the state. Rice is grown in the southern lowlands. Wheat is grown on the central and western plains.

To water all these farms Texans have built dams across rivers. They have made or enlarged more than 1,000 lakes in their state. The Dennison Dam across the Red River, for example, has made Lake Texoma. This lake stretches across 225 square miles of Texas and into Oklahoma.

Industry

Texas today has about one-third of all the known oil in the country. Texans pump more than a billion barrels of oil out of the ground every year.

Finding oil and gas has brought huge changes to Texas. Factories have been built to *refine,* or purify, the oil. Cities have grown up around the factories. The growth of cities has led to the building of more factories.

Today, Texas factories refine oil. Many factories also produce chemicals. Texas factory workers can food, pack meat, and build airplanes, spacecraft, and computers.

1. San Antonio
2. Austin
3. Dallas
4. Houston
5. Fort Worth

Important Cities

Only 50 years ago, most Texans lived in the country. Eight out of every ten Texans now live in a city or town.

Houston is the biggest city in Texas and one of the largest cities in the United States. More than 2,000,000 people live there. People in Houston work at many different kinds of jobs. Some work in oil refineries. Some work in chemical plants. Some work in Houston's busy port. There, oil and other products are loaded onto ships.

Another important business in Houston is medicine. About 26,000 people work in the Texas Medical Center. Each year, more than 1,500,000 people come there to be helped. Scientists at the Texas Medical Center are looking for a way to cure cancer.

Dallas is the second largest city in Texas. Most of the people in Dallas work in offices instead of factories. Many work for banks and insurance companies. Dallas has several important industries, too. One of these industries is the manufacturing of computers.

The city of **Fort Worth** started as a cattle town. Today, its stock yards and meat packing plants still provide many jobs in Fort Worth. Many people also work for oil refineries and for the aircraft industry, which builds most of America's helicopters. Fort Worth is also known for its fine museums.

Dallas and Fort Worth lie within 25 miles of each other. The two cities have spread out until their edges have almost met. They are like one big city with two downtowns.

San Antonio is the oldest city in Texas. Because it was started by settlers from Spain, it still has a Spanish flavor. Many people there speak Spanish. Many of the streets have Spanish names. The Alamo, carefully rebuilt, stands in downtown San Antonio.

Austin is the state capital. The Colorado River runs through the city. The river banks are lined with parks. These parks are the work of Lady Bird Johnson, the wife of Lyndon B. Johnson, who was the 36th president of the United States.

Future of Texas

Texas is a busy, growing state. People are streaming to its cities from all parts of the United States. New jobs are opening up every day. In the last hundred years, Texas has gone through great changes. If Texas continues to grow as it is doing, the next hundred years may be a time of even greater growth.

Questions

1. Complete this sentence: Texas produces more
   _____, _____, and _____ than any other
   state.

2. How has oil changed the cities in Texas?

3. What is one important fact about each city?
   Houston   Dallas   San Antonio
   Fort Worth   Austin

4. Why are the following statements untrue? Give
   a reason for each one.
   a. Texas factories produce more Herefords
      than any other state.
   b. Many workers in Houston refine cotton.
   c. Texas farmers use machines to harvest
      chemical plants.

Activity   Write Questions for an Interview

Prepare a list of questions to ask someone who
has lived in your area for at least ten years. Your
questions should include how particular things
have changed in the last ten years: new buildings,
number of people, work.

When you interview the person, be sure that
you take notes on the answers. Then write two
paragraphs about your conversation. In the first,
describe the person you interviewed. In the second, give a summary of what the person said
about changes in your area.

BOOKSHELF

Pecos Bill Catches a Hidebehind by Watts Blassingame. Garrard, 1977. Two tall-tale heroes from Texas, Pecos Bill and Sluefoot Sue, donate another present to the zoo when they realize the hidebehind they have lassoed is very shy.

Old Yeller by Fred Gipson. Harper & Row, 1956. Fourteen-year-old Travis is left in charge of his family's Texas home back in the 1860s, and he has lots of trouble at first with a big yellow dog.

How Did We Find Out About Oil? by Isaac Asimov. Walker, 1980. This book describes how oil is formed underground, what it is made of, and how we explore it, bring it up, and prepare it for our many uses.

Red Power on the Rio Grande by Franklin Folsom. Follett, 1973. This book discusses the American Indian Revolution of 1680 when the Indians fought for their freedom from Mexico.

The Black Mustanger by Richard Wormser. William Morrow, 1971. The Riker family has been hit with hard times and moves to Texas. When Mr. Riker breaks his leg, his son Dan must provide for his family. Dan goes to work for Will Mesteño, an expert at finding and rounding up wild mustangs.

LITERARY TERMS

CHARACTERS   *The people (or animals) in a story, poem, or play.* Sometimes authors are concerned mainly with bringing their story characters to life. How the characters think, feel, act, and change are more important than the story's main action, or *plot.* For example, in "Spunky Ramona," author Beverly Cleary gives us much information about Ramona Quimby. We learn what Ramona thinks and feels and how she acts. The story is *about Ramona,* not just about the events in Ramona's life. Other stories, such as "The Case of the Missing Roller Skates," are built mainly around the plot.

CHARACTERIZATION   *The ways in which writers present and develop characters to make the characters seem real.* Here are several ways in which writers develop their characters:

1. *By describing how the character looks* ("Her delicate face glowed like a peach beginning to ripen in the summer sun. And her dark eyes sparkled in the dancing firelight.").

2. *By showing the character's words and actions* ("Pa did not whistle about his work as usual, and after a while he said, 'And what we'll do in a wild country without a good watchdog I don't know.'").

3. *By telling the character's thoughts and feelings* ("I do not want anyone to sit with me, but he is sitting with me now. I am afraid I will spill and he will see me.").

4. *By telling what others think of the character* ("Mama was a wonderful cook.").

5. *By stating something about the character* ("After all, Wilbur was a very young pig—not much more than a baby, really.").

DIALOGUE   *Conversation between or among characters.* Dialogue is used in almost all forms of literature to move the *plot,* or main action, forward and to tell the reader something about the characters. In the story "The Case of the Missing Roller Skates," author Donald J. Sobol uses dialogue to show how Encyclopedia Brown solved the case:

"We just want to be sure you weren't in Dr. Vivian Wilson's

office this morning. That's all,'' said Sally.

"Well, I wasn't. I had a sprained wrist, not a toothache. So why should I go near his office?'' demanded Billy.

These few lines of dialogue give the reader enough information to guess the solution of the case.

Dialogue is especially important in plays, where conversation is the main way to tell the story and to show each character's personality. In the play *Paddington Goes to the Hospital,* Paddington and a doctor named Sir Archibald discuss Mr. Curry, a patient at the hospital:

Sir Archibald: Are you a friend of his?
Paddington: Well, I'm not really a friend. He lives next door and I've brought him some food.
Sir Archibald: Food! That's the last thing he needs. It will only make him stay longer. That man's entirely without scruples.

Through this conversation, the reader learns that Sir Archibald is upset because he feels that Mr. Curry is taking advantage of the hospital.

See also **Play**.

FABLE   *A brief story that teaches a lesson.* Many fables state the lesson, or *moral,* at the end of the story. The characters in fables are often animals that speak and act like people. The best-known fables were written long ago in Greece by a man named Aesop. "The Lion and the Mouse" is one of Aesop's fables.

FANTASY   *A fiction story with fanciful characters and plots.* A fantasy may take place in a world much like the one you know. Yet in the "real world" presented in a fantasy story, ordinary people and animals do impossible things. In the fantasy story *Charlotte's Web,* for example, an ordinary farm contains a pig that can talk and a spider that can write.

Often, however, fantasies take place in imaginary kingdoms or worlds that are quite different from the real world. Author C. S. Lewis has created the fantasy Kingdom of

Narnia in his series of seven books called *The Chronicles of Narnia.* It is a world filled with unusual creatures and magical events.

The different kinds of fantasy offer us the chance to wonder *"What if. . . ?" What if* you could be three inches tall, or ride a magic carpet, or travel through time?

See also **Fiction.**

FICTION   *A story invented by the writer.* A work of fiction may be *based* on real events, but it always includes made-up (fictional) characters and experiences. A work of fiction may be brief, like a fable, a folk tale, or a short story, or it may be a book-length story called a **novel.**

FOLK TALE   *A fiction story made up long ago and handed down in written or spoken form.* Many folk tales have no known authors. Though folk tales come from different parts of the world, many characters, plots, and ideas in them are similar. *Fairy tales* like the story "Cinderella" are a kind of folk tale.

LIMERICK   *A humorous five line poem written in three long and two short lines and containing a certain pattern of rhythm and rhyme.* In a limerick, lines 1, 2, and 5 always have the same rhythm and ending rhyme. Lines 3 and 4 have the same rhythm and ending rhyme, too. The poet Edward Lear has written many well-known limericks, including "There Was an Old Man with a Beard" on page 300.

METAPHOR   *A way of comparing how two different things are alike.* A metaphor *suggests* a comparison by saying that one thing *is* another: "This car **is** a lemon" or "The sun **was** a bright, new penny." Writers use metaphors to help us picture things in new ways.

See also **Simile.**

NONFICTION   *A true (factual) story; any writing that describes things as they actually happened, or that presents information or opinions about something.* One type of nonfiction is the written history of a person's life. When a person writes his or her own life story, it is called an **autobiography.** When someone else writes a person's life story, it is called a **biography.** Other common forms of nonfiction include news reports, travel stories, personal journals and diaries, and articles on science or history.

PLAY   *A story that is acted out, usually on a stage, by actors.* In its written form, a play begins with a **cast of characters,** or a list of the people, or sometimes animals, in the play. A play has a *plot,* or action, just like a story. However, a play is meant to be acted out. The characters in a play tell the story through their words, or **dialogue.**

During a play the actors follow **stage directions,** which tell them *how* to act and speak. Stage directions may also describe the **setting,** where the action takes place. Stage directions are usually not read aloud when a play is acted out.

See also **Dialogue.**

PLOT   *The action in a story.* When you tell *what happens* in a story, you are talking about the plot. For instance, in the story ''The Escape,'' by E. B. White, the plot tells how Wilbur, a young pig, escapes from his pen to see the world but is lured back with a bucket of slops.

The plot is also the writer's overall *plan* of the action—how,

when, and why things happen. The writer uses this plan to arrange the action in an interesting and reasonable order. Each happening becomes a link in a chain of events that makes sense and holds the reader's attention.

The most important part of plot is **conflict,** a character's struggle with opposing forces. Sometimes a character struggles with nature (as in Laura Ingalls Wilder's story ''Crossing the Creek''). Sometimes a character struggles with another character (as in Eleanor Estes's ''The Ghost in the Attic''). At other times the conflict is within the character's own mind. In the story ''The Escape'' by E. B. White, for example, Wilbur the pig struggles to decide whether he should give up his freedom in return for food.

SETTING   *When and where a story takes place.* If you say, ''Today at school Susan won a race,'' you have given the setting (when and where) before describing the action. Authors can choose any time or place as a setting for a story. In the story ''Crossing the Creek,'' author Laura Ingalls Wilder gives us a clear picture of how the prairie looked to the Ingalls family at sunset:

No road, not even the faintest trace of wheels or of a rider's passing, could be seen anywhere. That prairie looked as if no human eye had ever seen it before. Only the tall wild grass covered the endless empty land and a great empty sky arched over it. Far away the sun's edge touched the rim of the earth.

The writer does not always give us the setting so directly. Sometimes we figure it out as the story goes along. Most stories include several different types of information about where and when the story takes place. For instance, at the beginning of the story "An Eskimo Birthday," by Tom D. Robinson, the action begins in a schoolroom during a snowstorm. As the story continues, we find out that the school is part of a modern Eskimo village in Alaska.

SIMILE *A way of comparing how two different things are alike.* Writers use similes to surprise us or to make us look at our world in a new way. Similes are different from metaphors because they use the words *like* or *as.* In the story "Sound of Sunshine, Sound of Rain," author Florence Parry Heide describes two voices using similes to compare them: "My mother's voice is **as** warm and soft **as** a pillow. My sister's voice is little and sharp and high, **like** needles flying in the air."

See also **Metaphor.**

GLOSSARY

This glossary gives the meanings of unfamiliar words used in the text of this book. The meanings given here define words only the way they are used in the book. You can find other meanings for these words in a dictionary.

The correct pronunciation of each glossary word is given in the special spelling after that word. The sounds used in these spellings are explained in the following Pronunciation Key. Each symbol, or letter, stands for a sound, a sound you can recognize in the words following it. In addition to these sounds, each glossary pronunciation includes marks to show the kind of force, or stress, with which certain syllables are pronounced. A heavy mark, **'**, shows that the syllable it follows is given the strongest, or primary, stress, as in **sis•ter** (sis'•ter). A lighter mark, **'**, shows that the syllable it follows is given a secondary, or lighter, stress, as in **tax•i•cab** (tak'•sē•kab').

Several abbreviations are used in the glossary: *v.,* verb; *n.,* noun; *adj.,* adjective; *pl.,* plural.

Pronunciation Key

a	add, map	m	move, seem	u	up, done
ā	ace, rate	n	nice, tin	û(r)	urn, term
â(r)	care, air	ng	ring, song	yo͞o	use, few
ä	palm, father	o	odd, hot	v	vain, eve
b	bat, rub	ō	open, so	w	win, away
ch	check, catch	ô	order, jaw	y	yet, yearn
d	dog, rod	oi	oil, boy	z	zest, muse
e	end, pet	ou	out, now	zh	vision, pleasure
ē	even, tree	o͞o	pool, food	ə	the schwa,
f	fit, half	o͝o	took, full		an unstressed
g	go, log	p	pit, stop		vowel representing
h	hope, hate	r	run, poor		the sound spelled
i	it, give	s	see, pass		a in above
ī	ice, write	sh	sure, rush		e in sicken
j	joy, ledge	t	talk, sit		i in possible
k	cool, take	th	thin, both		o in melon
l	look, rule	th	this, bathe		u in circus

ac·cu·mu·lat·ing (ə·ky$\overline{oo}$′·my$\overline{oo}$·lāt′·ing) *adj.* Piling up; collecting.

al·fal·fa (al·fal′·fə) *n.* A cloverlike plant used for cattle feed.

am·mu·ni·tion (am′·yə·nish′·ən) *n.* Bullets, gunpowder, cannonballs.

ap·pe·tiz·ing (ap′·ə·tī′·zing) *adj.* Appealing in appearance or smell.

arc (ärk) *n.* Something that forms an arch or a curve.

ar·ro·gance (ar′·ə·gəns) *n.* Too proud; too convinced of one's own importance.

as·sault (ə·sôlt′) *n.* A violent attack.

a·strad·dle (ə·strad′·əl) *adv.* With one leg on each side.

awe·some (ô′·səm) *adj.* Inspiring feelings of wonder and fear.

bab·ble (bab′·əl) *v.* To make meaningless sounds.

ba·leen (bə·lēn′) *n.* The easily bent material that hangs from the upper jaw of whalebone whales and that strains the tiny sea animals on which they feed.

barge (bärj) *n.* A flat-bottomed boat used for carrying cargo.

bar·ren (bar′·ən) *adj.* Without growth; empty; lacking crops or trees or other plants.

bed·lam (bed′·ləm) *n.* A place or condition of noise or confusion.

bes·ti·ar·y (bes′·chē·er′·ē) *n.* A book of fables about the habits of actual and mythical animals.

blanch (blanch) *v.* To turn pale.

blub·ber (blub′·ər) *v.* To weep loudly.

blunt (blənt) *adj.* Having a tip or point that is not sharp.

blus·ter·ing (bləs′·tər·ing) *adj.* Speaking in a noisy, boastful, or bullying manner.

bolt (bōlt) *n.* A roll of cloth.

bom·bard·ment (bom·bärd′·mənt) *n.* An attack with guns and cannonballs.

brin·dled (brin′·dəld) *adj.* Having dark-colored streaks on a light gray or brownish background.

ca·nal (kə·nal′) *n.* A waterway dug across land, and connecting already existing bodies of water.

cap·tiv·i·ty (kap·tiv′·ə·tē) *n.* The state of being held prisoner.

ca·reen·ing (kə·rēn′·ing) *adj.* Lurching; moving rapidly in an uncontrolled way.

ca·reer (kə·rir′) *n.* Work one chooses and trains for.

car·i·bou (kar′·ə·b$\overline{oo}$) *n.* A large North American deer closely related to reindeer.

cat·tle (kat′·əl) *n.* A word for cows.

cham·ber (chām′·bər) *n.* A cave or an enclosed space.

col·lapse (kə·laps′) *v.* To cave or fall in completely.

col·league (kol′·ēg) *n.* A member of the same profession.

Co·man·che (kə·man′·chē) *n.* A group of American Indians living in Wyoming and Nebraska south into New Mexico and northwestern Texas.

com·mo·tion (kə·mō′·shən) *n.* Noisy confusion or disturbance.

con·sci·en·tious (kon′·shē·en′·shəs) *adj.* Being careful to do things correctly and to be good.

con·tra·dict (kon′·trə·dikt′) *v.* To deny (a statement).

con·ven·tion (kən·ven′·chən) *n.* A group of people meeting for a single purpose, such as to organize a government and to select candidates for office.

cor·ri·dor (kôr′·ə·dər) *n.* A hallway.

cow·punch·er (kow′·pən′·chər) *n.* Cowboy.

crock·ery (krok′·rē) *n.* Pottery made of clay.

cun·ning (kun′·ing) *n.* Slyness or cleverness in getting something.

cur·sive (kûr′·siv) *n.* Handwriting in which the strokes of the letters are joined in each word.

daze (dāz) *v.* To confuse.

de·fi·ant (di·fī′·ənt) *adj.* Boldly refusing to obey.

de·mol·ished (di·mol′·isht) *adj.* Torn down completely; ruined.

der·rick (der′·ik) *n.* A tower built over the opening of an oil well, used to support drilling equipment and to lift and lower pipe.

di·ag·no·sis (dī′·əg·nō′·sis) *n.* A conclusion reached as to the nature of an illness or disease.

dig (dig) *n.* An archeological excavation or its site.

dis·in·te·grate (dis·in′·tə·grāt′) *v.* To break down into small parts.

dis·loy·al (dis·loi′·əl) *adj.* Breaking faith; not supporting another.

dis·solve (di·zolv′) *v.* To disappear.

dron·ing (drōn′·ing) *adj.* Making a continuous humming or buzzing sound with little variation.

drought (drout) *n.* A long period of time without rain.

ei·der·down (ī′·dər·doun′) *n.* Fine, soft duck feathers that are often used to fill comforters or quilts.

e·merge (i·mərg′) *v.* To come up into view.

em·ploy·ee (im·ploi′·ē) *n.* A person hired by another.

ex·treme·ly (ik·strēm′·lē) *adv.* Very.

fam·ine (fam′·ən) *n.* A great shortage of food.

fan·ta·sy (fan′·tə·sē) *n.* A fiction story with fanciful characters and plots.

fash·ion (fash′·ən) *v.* To carve, mold, or give shape to.

fast (fast) *adj.* Tightly.

fear·some (fir′·səm) *adj.* Scary.

feath·er bed (feth′·ər bed) *n.* A comforter stuffed with feathers.

fine (fīn) *adj.* Clear; sunny; used in speaking about the weather.

flint (flint) *n.* A stone that is shaped into sharp tools and arrowheads.

flush (fləsh) *v.* To drive or frighten (game birds) from cover.

folk·lore (fōk′·lôr′) *n.* The stories, traditions, and superstitions of a group of people.

folk·lor·ist (fōk′·lôr′·əst) *n.* A person who studies the traditional beliefs, stories, and customs of a people or culture.

ford (fôrd) *n.* A shallow place in a stream or a river that can be crossed on foot, on horseback, or in a vehicle.

frank·in·cense (frangk′·in·sens) *n.* A gum or resin from various Arabian and African trees, and often burned as incense for its sweet, spicy smell.

fren·zy (fren′·zē) *n.* A fit of wild or violent excitement or activity.

gap·ing (gāp′·ing) *adj.* Wide open.

gar·ri·son (gar′·ə·sən) *n.* Troops stationed at a military post or fort.

gasp (gasp) *v.* To draw in one's breath quickly in surprise.

ge·fil·te fish (gə·fil′·tə fish) *n.* Oval fish cakes or balls made from a white fish such as carp.

ge·ni·i (jē′·nē·ī′) *n. pl.* In Arabian stories, supernatural beings with magical powers who can take human or animal form.

glow·er (glou′·ər) *v.* To glare; to look or stare at angrily.

gnaw (nô) *v.* To chew.

grope (grōp) *v.* To feel about in the dark in search; to look for something in the dark.

hearth (härth) *n.* The fireside.

hud·dle (həd′·əl) *v.* To crouch; to bend close to the ground.

hys·ter·ics (his·ter′·iks) *n., pl.* Sudden uncontrolled laughter.

im·mi·grant (im′·i·grənt) *n.* A person who leaves a native country to live in another country.

im·pact (im′·pakt) *n.* A striking of one body against another.

in·tact (in·takt′) *adj.* Untouched; with no part missing.

in·vest (in·vest′) *v.* To spend money in order to earn more.

jeer·ing (jir′·ing) *adj.* Insulting; teasing in a mean way.

keg (keg) *n.* A small barrel.

ki·mo·no (kə·mō′·nə) *n.* A loose robe with short, wide sleeves and a sash, traditional to Japan.

lead (lēd) *n.* A clue.

lieu·ten·ant (lo͞o·ten′·ənt) *n.* An officer in the army ranked below a colonel.

lit (lit) *v., past of light.* Came down from the air and settled.

lug (ləg) *v.* To drag or move heavily.

lurch (lûrch) *v.* To sway or tip to one side suddenly.

lure (lo͝or) *v.* To tempt or entice, especially into danger.

lus·ter (lus′·tər) *n.* Brightness.

lynx (lingks) *n.* A wildcat with long legs and a short tail, common in northern North America; also called a *bobcat*.

maid·en (mād′·ən) *n.* A young unmarried woman.

mal·let (mal′·ət) *n.* A hammer with a large head.

ma·nure (mə·no͞or′) *n.* Waste material from barns and barnyards used to improve the soil.

mes·quite (məs·kēt′) *n.* A spiny shrub in the southwestern U.S. and Mexico that has long roots to reach underground water.

mid·dlings (mid′·lings) *n.* A mixture of coarsely ground wheat and bran used for animal feed.

mi·rac·u·lous (mə·rak′·yə·ləs) *adj.* Marvelous; similar to a miracle.

mis·er·a·ble (miz′·ər·ə·bəl) *adj.* Very unhappy.

mourn·er (môr′·nər) *n.* A person who expresses sorrow for someone who is dead.

mourn·ing (môr′·ning) *adj.* Making a low, continuous sound that seems to express sorrow or grief.

muk·luk (mək′·lək′) *n.* A soft Eskimo boot made of sealskin or reindeer skin.

mus·tang (məs′·tang′) *n.* A small wild horse that is commonly found on the southwestern plains.

myrrh (mûr) *n.* A fragrant gum resin used in incense and perfume.

nav·i·gate (nav′·ə·gāt′) *v.* To steer or guide a boat or ship.

nudge (nəj) *v.* To get someone's attention by a push of the elbow.

om·i·nous (om′·ə·nəs) *adj.* Threatening; being an evil omen.

out·crop·ping (out′·krop′·ing) *n.* The coming out, at or above the ground, of a mineral.

out·skirts (out′·skûrts′) *n., pl.* The edges of a city.

pan·try (pan′·trē) *n.* A small room off the kitchen where food or kitchen supplies are stored.

par·ka (pär′·kə) *n.* A fur or cloth jacket or coat with a hood.

Pass·over (pas′·ō·vər) *n.* A Jewish holiday celebrating the ancient Hebrews' freedom from slavery in Egypt.

pea·sant (pez′·ənt) *n.* A poor farmer.

pe·cu·liar (pi·kyo͞ol′·yər) *adj.* Strange; odd.

peer (pir) *n.* A person of one's own age group.

per·sist (pər·sist′) *v.* To go on stubbornly even though opposed.

pit·i·ful (pit′·i·fəl) *adj.* Worthy of pity or sympathy.

plume (plo͞om) *n.* A large showy feather.

pot (pot) *n.* Jar.

prai·rie (prâr′·ē) *n.* A large area of level or rolling grassy land, mostly the plains of the central U.S.

pro·ces·sion (prə·sesh′·ən) *n.* A long line of people moving in a slow, orderly manner.

punc·tu·al (pənk′·cho͞o·wəl) *adj.* Being on time; prompt.

range (rānj) *n.* Open land where cattle can roam.

rash (rash) *adj.* Acting without thought.

ra·vine (rə·vēn′) *n.* A long, deep hollow in the earth usually formed by the action of a stream.

re·ac·tion (rē·ak′·shən) *n.* The act of answering quickly with little thought.

re·cess (rē′·ses) *n.* A hidden or secret place.

re·cruit (re·kro̅o̅t′) *n.* A newly drafted member of an armed force.

re·fined (re·fīnd′) *adj.* Free from anything coarse.

re·in·force·ment (rē′·in·fôrs′·mənt) *n.* A new member sent to help troops already in action.

re·lapse (rē′·laps) *n.* A falling back into an illness after improving.

re·luc·tant·ly (ri·lək′·tənt·lē) *adv.* Unwillingly; holding back.

re·proach (ri·prōch′) *n.* Blame.

re·sem·ble (ri·zem′·bəl) *v.* To look like or be similar to.

res·o·lu·tion (rez′·ə·lo̅o̅′·shən) *n.* A promise to oneself.

roam (rōm) *v.* To wander.

rough·neck (ruf′·nek′) *n.* A rough, rude, or disorderly person.

ruff (ruf) *n.* A high, full collar, in this case, made of fur.

run·ning gear (rən′·ing gir) *n.* The working parts of a wagon that help the wagon move.

runt (rənt) *n.* The smallest pig in a litter.

sac·ri·fice (sak′·rə·fīs) *v.* To make an offering of something precious.

sal·a·ry (sal′·ə·rē) *n.* Money paid for services.

salt·y (sôl′·tē) *adj.* Having to do with the sea.

scorn (skôrn) *n.* A feeling of disgust.

scrunch (skrənch) *v.* To squeeze together into a small bundle.

scru·ple (skro̅o̅′·pəl) *n.* A misgiving or objection about something that one thinks is wrong.

scut·tle (skut′·əl) *v.* To run or move quickly, especially from danger.

Se·der (sā′·dər) *n.* The meal served on the first two nights of Passover, a Jewish holiday.

sen·try (sen′·trē) *n.* A soldier standing guard at a gate.

sha·man (shäm′·ən) *n.* A person believed to have special powers who performs sacred ceremonies for a people.

shor·ing (shōr′·ing) *n.* A group or system of supporting boards used to uphold something.

shriv·el up (shriv′·əl up) *v.* To wrinkle and dry up.

shut·tle (shut′·əl) *n.* A device used in weaving to carry a thread from side to side between the threads that run lengthwise.

sieve (siv) *n.* A utensil made of wire mesh or metal with many small holes, used for straining.

slops (slops) *n., pl.* Leftover food fed to animals.

snare (snâr) *n.* A kind of trap for small animals.

snow ma·chine (snō mə·shēn′) *n.* A machine that travels over snow; also called a *snowmobile.*

sod (sod) *n.* Ground covered with grass.

sol·i·tude (sol′·ə·tood′) *n.* The condition of being alone.

sooth·ing (sooth′·ing) *adj.* Calming.

sou·ve·nir (soo′·və·nir′) *n.* Something that is kept as a reminder of a place, a person, or an occasion.

spec·ta·cles (spek′·tə·kəlz) *n., pl.* A pair of eyeglasses.

spunk (spungk) *n. informal* Courage; spirit.

stoop (stoop) *n.* A small porch, platform, or set of steps at the entrance of a house or building.

sub·side (səb·sīd′) *v.* To become less or quiet.

suf·fo·cat·ing (səf′·ə·kāt′·ing) *adj.* Making uncomfortable by not allowing one to breathe.

su·i·cide (soo′·ə·sīd′) *n.* The act of losing one's life by one's own choice.

sur·geon (sûr′·jən) *n.* A doctor who can operate on people.

sus·pect (səs′·pekt) *n.* A person who is thought to be guilty of a wrongdoing.

taw·ny (tô′·nē) *n.* Brownish orange.

thatched (thacht) *adj.* Covered with straw, especially on the roof of a house.

thrash (thrash) *v.* To swing, roll, or move around wildly and rapidly.

thrum (thrum) *n.* The ends of thread left on a loom after the cloth has been cut off. *v.* To pluck on, as a guitar; to strum.

ti·pi, also **tepee** (tē′·pē) *n.* An American Indian tent made from animal skins and shaped like an upside-down cone.

toi·let wa·ter (toi′·lət wô′·tər) *n.* A light-scented liquid, like perfume.

tri·col·or (trī′·kəl′·ər) *adj.* Having three colors.

troll (trōl) *n.* In folk tales, a troublesome creature, either dwarf or giant, who lives in caves, in hills, or under bridges.

trudge (truj) *v.* To walk wearily or with great effort.

valve (valv) *n.* A mechanical device that opens and shuts to start or stop the flow of a liquid or gas.

vault·like (vôlt′·līk′) *adj.* Built with arches or curves.

vol·un·teer (vol′·ən·tir′) *n.* A person who freely chooses to join the armed forces.

weft (weft) *n.* In weaving, the threads carried by the shuttle from side to side across the fixed threads in a loom.

whisk (hwisk) *v.* To move quickly and lightly.

wol·ver·ine (wool′·və·rēn′) *n.* A meat-eating animal of the weasel family.

Words and Word Parts: PREFIXES

A **prefix** is a word part added to the beginning of a word. The word to which the prefix is added is the **root word.** The meaning of a root word is changed when a prefix is added. Knowing the meaning of a prefix can often help you define a word.

prefix + root = new word
un + kind = **un**kind (meaning "not kind")

The prefixes below are often added to words. Look at the meaning of each prefix. Notice how it changes the meaning of each root word.

un-

un often means "not	**un** also means "to do the opposite of"
un + able = **un**able	**un** + buckle = **un**buckle
unable means "not able	**un**buckle means "to undo the buckle"

Words from the Selection
unhappy p. 29	unlikely p. 18	unfastened p. 97
unload p. 64	unexpected p. 280	unharnessed p. 152
unpack p. 65	unlatched p. 90	unearthed p. 333

Which word above means "not likely to happen"?
What is the meaning of unearthed?

re-

re often means "back"	**re** also means "again"
re + gain = **re**gain	**re** + do = **re**do
regain means "to gain back"	**re**do means "to do again"

Words from the Selection
repay p. 198	reactions p. 310	reconsider p. 228
returned p. 22	relapse p. 304	

Which word above means "to get sick again"?

Words and Word Parts: SUFFIXES

A **suffix** is a word part added to the end of a **root word**. The meaning of a root word is changed when the suffix is added. Knowing the meaning of a suffix can often help you define the meaning of a word.

> root + **suffix** = new word
> breath + **less** = breathless (meaning "out of breath")

The suffixes below are often added to words. Look at the meaning of each suffix. Notice how it changes the meaning of each root word.

-ly	**-able, -ible**
-ly means "in the manner of" polite + **ly** = polite**ly** polite**ly** means "in a polite manner"	-**able** and -**ible** mean "can be done" or "inclined to" adapt + **able** = adapt**able** adapt**able** means "can adapt"

Words from the Selections

completely p. 52	dependable p. 281	comfortable p. 310
cautiously p. 99	urgently p. 308	suitable p. 323

-ness	**-ment**
-ness means "state" or "condition of" dark + **ness** = dark**ness** dark**ness** means "the condition of being dark"	-ment means "action" move + **ment** = move**ment** move**ment** means "the act of moving"

Words from the Selections

excitement p. 84	advertisement p. 23	lightness p. 404
payment p. 117	roughness p. 232	quickness p. 404

-ion, -tion, -sion, -ition, -ation
-ion, -tion, -sion, -ition, -ation all mean "process, act of, or state of"   celebration + **ion** = celebrat**ion**   Celebrat**ion** means "the act of celebrating"

Words from the Selections

multiplication p. 33	direction p. 54	confusion p. 320
suggestion p. 37	attention p. 66	permission p. 379

The final **e** of a root word is dropped when adding a suffix that begins with a vowel. For example, **love** + **able** = lovable.

Define each word below using the prefixes and suffixes to help you.

unfriendly   rearrangement   movable   unpleasantness   reaction